PRAISE

CHRISTOLOGICAL ANTHROPOLOGY
IN HISTORICAL PERSPECTIVE

In this book, one of today's foremost experts on theological anthropology reintroduces some neglected thinkers and launches an intriguing new research angle. Marc Cortez has some surprises in store for those who think they know the exact parameters of what counts as Christology or what it means for Jesus to embrace our humanity.

DANIEL J. TREIER,
Blanchard professor of theology,
Wheaton College Graduate School

What makes us human? And how does Jesus make a difference? Marc Cortez offers a stimulating and convincing tour of the role of Christology in theological anthropologies from Gregory of Nyssa to James Cone, via Mother Julian of Norwich and Martin Luther, amongst others. The reader is invited to explore the varied ways in which major thinkers have made Jesus the key to being human, and to ask the crucial questions that will decide between their accounts. The readings are persuasive and the expositions lucid—and the whole is a compelling tour of the ways in which belief in Christ might change our vision of our common humanity. This is a quite excellent book; I commend it unreservedly.

STEPHEN R. HOLMES,
senior lecturer in theology,
University of St Andrews

As is the case in every sphere of Christian existence, theology must learn to listen before it speaks. Following this rule requires that we listen to tradition with openness toward its gifts and alertness to its potential missteps before we endeavor to engage in the work of constructive theology. In this fine book, Marc Cortez lends his well-trained ear to the often wonderful (and occasionally weird) tradition of Christian teaching about human beings, specifically, what it has to say about how the person and work of Jesus Christ shapes our understanding of human being and action. The result is a clear, exceptionally learned, and rewarding overview of different approaches to christological anthropology in the Christian tradition. This book will prove to be a useful resource for anyone seeking to develop a theological anthropology that honors the supremacy of Jesus Christ.

SCOTT R. SWAIN,
professor of systematic theology and academic dean, Reformed Theological Seminary, Orlando, Florida

Many scholars talk about doing "theology of retrieval," but Marc Cortez actually does it. Employing several fascinating case studies, he looks wide and digs deep for insights into a theological anthropology that is properly christological. The result is a work of erudition that sets the table for Cortez's own much-anticipated offerings.

THOMAS H. MCCALL,
professor of biblical and systematic theology, Trinity Evangelical Divinity School

At different periods in Christian history, different doctrines have ascended to the center of theological debate. In the early decades of the twenty-first century, the doctrine of humanity seems to be near the epicenter. I'm grateful to Marc Cortez for this helpful, judicious survey of how different theologians have grounded their anthropology in their understanding of the person and work of Jesus Christ. *Christological Anthropology in Historical Perspective* is a welcome contribution to ongoing discussions of human nature. As in many doctrinal discussions, we need to look to the past for wisdom for the present and future. Cortez helps us to do just that in this timely book. Highly recommended.

NATHAN A. FINN,
dean of the School of Theology and Missions, professor of Christian thought and tradition, Union University

Marc Cortez has established himself as one of the more important thinkers around what it means to be human in theological perspective. His theological acumen, sense of humour, and ability to adeptly navigate large swathes of the Tradition result in a work that is as profound as it is useful. In an age when the centrality of Christ is too often replaced by a cultural sentimentality, Cortez reminds us that what it means to be human can only be defined in relation to Jesus Christ; and knowing that makes all the difference in the world. A christological anthropology will challenge, on the one hand, those who opt for a Trinitarian anthropology and on the other hand, those who seek to define what it means to be human simply with reference to some notion of humanity in general. Cortez's case study approach makes for enlightening reading from across the Tradition, providing a further resource for reflecting upon a theological anthropology.

MYK HABETS,
head of Carey Graduate School,
Carey Baptist College,
Auckland, New Zealand

As he leads readers through important historical figures, Marc Cortez makes a valuable contribution to the doctrine of the human being and to Christology. He demonstrates how key biblical themes have been taken up in the tradition and, in doing so, points readers to what it means to be human in Christ. This book will be valuable to students and professionals alike.

BETH FELKER JONES,
associate professor of theology,
Wheaton College

In what way does God's entering history in the fully and truly human Jesus serve to ground or establish a Christian anthropology? How does christological warrant for anthropological claims extend beyond ethics to offer a fuller picture of what it means to be human? With careful and insightful analysis, Marc Cortez engages key theological voices from the history of the church and unfolds a striking breadth to the ways that Christology informs anthropology. This book unearths the essential starting points to continued constructive work in Christian anthropology with unparalleled clarity and comprehension.

KEVIN DILLER,
associate professor of philosophy
and religion, Taylor University

For those who take seriously the fact that there is one truly human being for and with us by the Spirit—Jesus Christ, Son of Mary and God—this is a helpful book. It seats us with saints through the ages who have also considered the implications of Christ's humanity for our own. Cortez is a gracious host, inviting us to listen and hear, that we might hear more clearly when visiting these saints in their original "homes." This makes for the best kind of resource book—one that welcomes, engages, and ultimately serves a critical need in the life of the church.

CHERITH FEE NORDLING, associate professor,
Northern Seminary

Good theologians listen before they speak, and this volume provides a master class in learning how to listen well. Marc Cortez shows us what it looks like to hear the voices of the church's greatest theologians clearly and interpret them charitably. The diverse cast of characters and provocative topics make for absorbing reading, and we learn how to speak of Jesus Christ, human beings, and our life in relationship with God better than before. This book comes highly recommended for students and scholars alike.

KEITH L. JOHNSON, associate professor
of theology, Wheaton College

CHRISTOLOGICAL ANTHROPOLOGY

IN HISTORICAL PERSPECTIVE

CHRISTOLOGICAL ANTHROPOLOGY

IN HISTORICAL PERSPECTIVE

Ancient and Contemporary
Approaches to Theological Anthropology

MARC CORTEZ

ZONDERVAN

Christological Anthropology in Historical Perspective
Copyright © 2016 by Marc Cortez

This title is also available as a Zondervan ebook. Visit www.zondervan.com/ebooks.

Requests for information should be addressed to:
Zondervan, 3900 *Sparks Dr. SE, Grand Rapids, Michigan 49546*

Library of Congress Cataloging-in-Publication Data

Cortez, Marc (Marc Allen), 1972-
    Christological anthropology in historical perspective : ancient and contemporary
approaches to theological anthropology / Marc Cortez.
       pages cm.
    Includes bibliographical references and index.
    ISBN 978-0-310-51641-5 (softcover)
    1. Theological anthropology—Christianity—History. 2. Jesus Christ—Person and offices—
History. I. Title.
BT701.3.C673 2016
233—dc23   2015024056

Cover design: Kirk DouPonce, DogEared Design
Interior design: Denise Froehlich

Printed in the United States of America

16 17 18 19 20 21 22 23 24 /DHV/ 20 19 18 17 16 15 14 13 12 11 10 9 8 7 6 5 4 3 2 1

*To Leah and Sydney—for more love and
patience than I deserve.*

To Mary—for making this all worthwhile.

*To those who inspired this work—even if they
never read it.*

Contents

Foreword

WHEN ONE SURVEYS THE PLETHORA of theological books and articles on what it is to be human, one cannot help but be struck by what are treated as the critical controls on the task of theological anthropology. The defining sources and resources tend to be the following: (1) studies of Adam in Genesis; (2) accounts of what are perceived to be the key, universally discernible characteristics of "human nature," with an orientation toward the religious or "spiritual"; (3) analyses of the facets of human nature that are perceived to be presupposed by Christian thought, most notably, reason, moral responsibility, and "transcendence"; and (4) accounts of whatever capacity is deemed as defining the *imago dei*. What emerges is that our accounts of the "essentially human" or, more specifically, the "image of God" serve all too easily to attach a kind of authority ("papal infallibility," as Karl Barth suggested) to the worldviews we bring to bear on our interpretation of what it is to be human. The result is that some particular facet or attribute (reason, the *sensus moralis*, the capacity for the transcendent, or "spirituality") is identified as the locus of the "image" and as constituting, therefore, our true essence. The effect is to underwrite the particular cultural values and worldview within which the relevant account is conceived.

The unacknowledged elephant in the room in such approaches is the fact that Christian faith is defined by the recognition that the God responsible for the existence of the contingent order in its totality has himself *become human*. The obvious and incontrovertible implication of the doctrine of the incarnation is that, in Christ, we are presented not only with the fullness of the Godhead but also with the fullness of humanity, that is, all that humanity was intended both to be and (as Irenaeus would have it) to become. What we have in the Gospels and the Epistles, moreover, is a remarkably full and multifaceted witness of the nature, character, and ends of the one who alone is both the true "image" of the Father and the *eschatos Adam*. It is hard to see how any account that seeks to articulate the Creator's purposes for humanity could contemplate beginning anywhere else than with an analysis of the one who is the eternal, creative *dabar* (*logos*) become human! In him we see God's purposes for humanity presented *in human form*.

To put the point another way, if anthropologists from some planet in Alpha Centauri were to visit earth and discover that we believed God had become a human being, would they not find it counterintuitive to discover that, despite this fact, we did not look to this individual as the fullest expression of all that human beings were created to be? And if we were to argue that they had missed the point and that the incarnate one had simply come to repair what is better discerned by looking elsewhere (either to the earliest ancestor whom God had created or by engaging in some kind of general phenomenology of the human race), would they not find that somewhat puzzling?

Christological Anthropology in Historical Perspective is an impressive attempt to redress the imbalances and eccentricities that have characterised so much of theological anthropology. He does this by encouraging us to ask what precisely is involved in rethinking anthropology in the light of the one who defines what it is to be human and what it is to be the image of God in truth. What begins to become clear is that to conceive theological anthropology from a christological reference point is to interpret it in the light of the one who reconciles our alienated preconceptions of what it is to be human—transforming and reschematising them in and through Jesus Christ for the sake of discerning the truth of God's purposes in creating us (Romans 12:2). Not only does this volume explore and expose the diversity of the ways in which Christology has served and may serve the task of theological anthropology; it does so by means of a profoundly constructive and creative form of theological retrieval.

Its effect is to encourage us to rethink the methodologies that constrain theological anthropology and the Procrustean beds into which we seek to fit our interpretation of God's *telos* for humanity. As with all of Marc Cortez's writings, this volume's breadth and depth of scholarship, its fluency, and its conceptual clarity make it not only informative but easy to read. As such, it can only inspire those engaged in the whole field of theological anthropology to appreciate anew the profound significance of reconceiving the field in light of the one in whom our "chief end" is not only exemplified but realised.

ALAN J. TORRANCE,
UNIVERSITY OF ST ANDREWS,
SCOTLAND

Acknowledgments

THIS BOOK WOULD NOT BE what it is without the faithful assistance of so many good friends and partners. So, if you have any complaints, feel free to blame them.

My interest in the relationship between Christology and anthropology began when I was a ThM student at Western Seminary (Portland, Oregon), so I owe a tremendous debt of gratitude to Gerry Breshears and the rest of the faculty there for asking great questions, showing me how to pursue the answers, and putting up with me along the way. I carried this same interest into my doctoral program at the University of St. Andrews, and I will always be indebted to Alan Torrance for pushing me to understand more deeply what it means to say that Jesus reveals true humanity, introducing me to Karl Barth as a valuable dialogue partner, and showing me what it really means to mentor someone in his or her academic vocation. This book would not have been possible if not for the tremendous support I received at both of these institutions.

I am also grateful for the many people who commented on various parts of this project. Without them, I would still be in my office trying to figure out what I was talking about. So thanks to Beth Felker-Jones and Matt Jenson for reading through various chapters and trying to catch as many heresies as possible. Thanks to the students in my initial doctoral seminar at Wheaton College — Jack Bates, Jared Brown, Craig Hefner, Chris Smith, and Kevin Wong. They suffered through early drafts of many of these chapters, and their questions and comments helped refine the book in key ways. Even more importantly, thanks to Kevin Wong and Daniel Treier, who somehow found time to read through and comment on the entire book. Without their input, this book would have been done much faster. Yet their insights helped me understand my own project far better than I could have on my own. And finally, thanks to my editor, Katya Covrett, for her interest in this project, her grace and patience when I fell behind schedule, and, most importantly, the sage advice she offered at every stage, without which this book would not have been possible.

And thanks to my family, my friends, and the members of the youth group at First Baptist Church of Wheaton, Illinois. You showed tremendous grace when I was stressed, and without your prayers and support, I probably would still be binge-watching *The Walking Dead* instead of moving on to what comes next.

A book is a team project, and I have a great team. A big thank-you to all of you.

A Christ-Centered Lens

What Does It Mean for Anthropology to Be "Christological"?

Christian understanding of what it is to be human unfolds through shared engagement and meditation in the community of faith ... A fuller theological account of who and what we are as humans emerges from the Church's prayerful engagement with each of these realms, as we keep the person of Jesus in focus.

World Council of Churches, *Christian Perspectives on Theological Anthropology*[1]

IN 2005, THE WORLD COUNCIL of Churches produced a Faith and Order Study Document on theological anthropology. In response to modern crises like increasing violence, worldwide poverty, and the spread of HIV/AIDS, as well as the questions raised by a growing awareness of people with disabilities and the rapid development of new technologies, they felt the time had come for a cooperative document that would "articulate what the churches can say together about what it means to be a human being."[2] Consequently, the document offers an interesting reflection on what its authors thought about (1) the most important things we can say about what it means to be human in light of these modern difficulties that (2) we can all agree on. As anyone who knows theology can attest, that second criterion is a beast.

So it was with great interest that I read through the "Ten Common Affirmations" that serve as the theological backbone of the work—the

---

1. World Council of Churches, *Christian Perspectives on Theological Anthropology: A Faith and Order Study Document*, Faith and Order Paper, no. 199 (Geneva: World Council of Churches, 2005), 51.

2. Ibid., 9.

ten core truths about the human person that we need to hear in the midst of these modern challenges and on which there is sufficient consensus to qualify as "common" Christian truths. And embedded in the very first affirmation we find the claim that "Jesus Christ is the one in whom true humanity is perfectly realized."[3] According to the document, at the heart of Christian anthropology lies a christological claim. And this christological claim is of such importance that it must be a key aspect of a properly Christian response to all of these difficult modern issues.

As important as this christological claim is, however, it needs a little unpacking if it is going to have any real significance for contemporary anthropology. After all, it is entirely possible to claim that *Jesus* is fully and truly human, a central claim of orthodox Christology, without making the further claim that his humanity somehow reveals or determines something about the nature of *humanity in general*. Indeed, some theologians explicitly reject this latter conclusion, arguing that it is not possible for a single individual, limited by the particular circumstances of his lived existence, to reveal the full reality of something as complex as the human person.[4] How can a Jewish male living in first-century Palestine reveal what it means to be human for those of us whose human lives are shaped by entirely different circumstances? Or, as a thirteen-year-old girl once asked after I had just explained that Jesus understands and empathizes with all of us because he is human just like us, "How can Jesus understand me when he's never gone through puberty as a teenage girl?"[5] Without realizing it, my teenage interlocutor was asking about the relationship between Christology and anthropology entailed in the WCC statement. Is it merely claiming that Jesus is fully human, or does it have something more in mind?

The latter is clearly the case. According to the document, since Jesus is "the true image ... of our humanity,"[6] we will only understand "what we are as humans" if we "keep the person of Jesus in focus."[7] This is the

---

3. Ibid., 51.

4. For a more thorough discussion of these issues, see Marc Cortez, "The Madness in Our Method: Christology as the Necessary Starting Point for Theological Anthropology," in *The Ashgate Companion to Theological Anthropology*, ed. Joshua Ryan Farris and Charles Taliaferro (Aldershot: Ashgate, 2015), 15–26.

5. I wish this footnote could simply record the eloquently theological response I offered to this query. Instead, after four years as an undergraduate theology major, I was only able to muster a little hemming, a lot of hawing, and a feeble, "I'll get back to you on that." In some ways, this book is part of my answer, though I don't suppose she'll ever read it!

6. World Council of Churches, *Christian Perspectives on Theological Anthropology*, 33.

7. Ibid., 34.

"Christ-centered lens" through which we must look if we want to see what it really means to be human.[8] Consequently, "the Christian understanding of true humanity is rooted in reflection on the person of Jesus Christ."[9] According to the authors of this statement, the fundamental intuition of Christian anthropology that we must affirm in our modern context is not merely the important truth that *Jesus is human*, but the corresponding epistemological affirmation that *Jesus reveals true humanity*.

Whether or not this latter claim is one with which most Christian theologians would agree is a question that we will not pursue here. But the claim does find strong support among modern theologians. In recent theological anthropologies, it is not difficult to find statements about Jesus as "the mystery of man,"[10] "true humanity,"[11] the "archetype" of humanity,[12] and the revelation of "what human nature is intended to be,"[13] exemplifying what may be described as a widespread consensus among theologians that Jesus Christ lies at the heart of theological anthropology. Thus, at the beginning of his magisterial work on theological anthropology, David Kelsey claims that the way in which Christians understand anthropological issues "is shaped in some way by their beliefs about Jesus Christ and God's relation to him" and that this "is ultimately what qualifies theological answers to proposed anthropological questions as authentically Christian theological anthropology."[14]

At this point, however, an obvious question lurks. Given this widespread consensus about the importance of Christology for understanding humanity, do we really need an entire book on the subject? After all, there are still plenty of debated issues that deserve our attention. Can we not just celebrate the fact that the theologians have actually agreed on something and move on? We must give a negative response to this last question for one simple reason. It is one thing to claim *that* Jesus is the

---

8. Ibid., 36.

9. Ibid., 37.

10. John D. Zizioulas, "Human Capacity and Human Incapacity: A Theological Exploration of Personhood," in *Communion and Otherness: Further Studies in Personhood and the Church* (New York: T&T Clark, 2006), 248.

11. Charles Sherlock, *The Doctrine of Humanity* (Downers Grove, Ill.: InterVarsity, 1996), 18.

12. Panayiotis Nellas, *Deification in Christ: The Nature of the Human Person* (Crestwood, N.Y.: St. Vladimir's Seminary Press, 1987), 33.

13. Millard J. Erickson, *Christian Theology* (Grand Rapids: Baker, 1998), 532.

14. David H. Kelsey, *Eccentric Existence: A Theological Anthropology* (Louisville: Westminster John Knox, 2009), 8–9.

perfect realization of true humanity in whom we see the revelation of what it means to be human; it is something else entirely to explain *what that means* and *how it should be done.* As David Kelsey recognizes, claiming that our beliefs about human persons are "in some way" related to Jesus Christ is different from being able to stipulate how this "in some way" actually works.[15] Important questions remain about the nature of the Christology/anthropology relationship, the aspects of Jesus' person and work that are involved, the method for deriving anthropological truths from our christological vantage point, and the role of other doctrinal loci (e.g., soteriology, pneumatology, ecclesiology) in developing a christological account of humanity. Simply claiming that Jesus is important "in some way" for a Christian vision of the human person does nothing to address these other important questions. As we will see through the course of this study, once we move beyond the claim that Jesus reveals humanity and begin to explore how people have developed that claim in their theological anthropologies, considerable diversity arises.

TOWARD A DEFINITION OF CHRISTOLOGICAL ANTHROPOLOGY

Before we continue, it might help if we take a moment to define more carefully what a *christological* anthropology entails. Although I would prefer that we allow a more robust definition of christological anthropology to unfold from the various studies in this book, an initial definition may help clarify both the scope and purpose of this study.

In its most basic form, the fundamental intuition of a christological anthropology is that beliefs about the human person (anthropology) must be warranted in some way by beliefs about Jesus (christological). We will explore more deeply what this "in some way" actually means through these various studies. Even without a more precise explanation, though, the distinctive nature of a christological anthropology is that Christology warrants at least some anthropological claims in such a way that those claims are only true in virtue of the truth of their christological ground.[16] Ian McFarland expresses this fundamental intuition well

---

15. Thus Kelsey goes on to note that the phrase "in some way" is intended as a placeholder for "seams and stark breaks within and between Christian communities" (Kelsey, *Eccentric Existence*, 9).

16. My use of *warrants* in this context should not be understood as implying any strong philosophical analysis of what constitutes proper warrant and how warrant functions in human knowing. Questions of warrant and justification are among the most complex issues in modern epistemology, and we do not need to pursue those discussions here. For our purposes, it will suffice to note that a christological anthropology requires a relation-

when he argues that if Jesus is "the criterion" for Christian talk about what it means to be human, no argument about humanity "can be theologically binding unless it has a clear christological warrant."[17]

In addition to this epistemological component, this study will also explore issues related to the proper scope of a christological anthropology. Although we noted above that theologians routinely affirm the central significance of Christology for understanding anthropology, the application of that insight to particular anthropological issues is often somewhat lacking. When we turn to the actual content of many theological anthropologies, we find that the explicit development of this christological insight tends to focus on a few key issues: especially the image of God and ethics. This should come as no surprise, given that both have obvious links to Christology. After all, few theologians would deny that Jesus is central to an adequate understanding of the *imago Dei*. The New Testament declares that Jesus alone is the image of God (2 Corinthians 4:4; Colossians 1:15), and all other humans only participate in the image insofar as they are restored to the likeness of Jesus (Romans 8:29; 1 Corinthians 15:49). Similarly, ethics connects to the long-standing Christian intuition that Jesus should be the model or exemplar of Christian living. Even if we reject "What would Jesus do?" as overly simplistic, the conviction remains that Christian conduct should be guided by the example of faithful human living that we see in Jesus. In both of these areas, then, it is not difficult to find theologians who follow the basic conviction that Christology should ground at least some anthropological claims.

As important as these areas are for understanding humanity, however, they do not exhaust the whole range of anthropological issues. When we move beyond the image of God and ethics, though, the christological orientation of many anthropologies becomes decidedly less pronounced. For example, Charles Sherlock's *The Doctrine of Humanity* begins with strong affirmations of Jesus' central significance for theological anthropology, yet the majority of the work focuses on issues like economics, human dignity, culture, gender and sexuality, and family life, areas in which we see little direct appeal to Jesus Christ as the criterion for Christian thinking about the human person. Similarly, Hans Schwarz's *The*

---

ship between Christology and anthropological claims such that the truth of the latter depends in some important way on the truth of the former.

17. Ian A. McFarland, *Difference & Identity* (Cleveland, Ohio: Pilgrim, 2001), 115. His focus here is specifically on the significance of Christology for understanding personhood, but this still expresses well the fundamental claim of a christological anthropology.

Human Being: A Theological Anthropology deals extensively with issues like human constitution, evolution, freedom, and evil, all of which are developed almost entirely in isolation from explicitly christological concerns. And despite offering a robustly christological framework through much of the work, Paul Jewett's *Who We Are: Our Dignity as Human* goes on to address issues like embodiment, racism, sexuality, and the environment in general isolation from that christological framework. I could multiply examples, but this suffices to demonstrate the concern. Given that these anthropologies operate from a broader "worldview" that is itself shaped by christological concerns, it may be possible to retrieve a kind of christological emphasis, but only one that has been made so indirect as to offer little real help in understanding what it means to say that Jesus informs our vision of humanity in some unique way.

We are thus left with the question of whether Christology has something uniquely substantive to say about what it means to be human across this broader range of issues. Does Christology shed light on issues like the significance of the human body, the reality of gender and sexuality, the existence and meaning of human freedom, and the nature of race and ethnicity, as well as the painful realities of suffering and oppression that shape so many people's experiences of their own humanity? In short, does Jesus shed light on *all* aspects of human existence, or only those that have traditionally been associated with Christian spirituality? Or, to return to my teenage interlocutor from earlier, does Jesus only offer us a model of a life well lived, or does his human existence have something to say about what it means to exist as a gendered teenager with a body going through something as awkward and difficult as puberty?

Our initial definition of "christological anthropology" as I will be using that phrase in this book should thus address both the epistemological emphasis on Christology as the ground of anthropological claims and the application of this christological criterion to a broad range of anthropological issues. Thus we arrive at the following minimal definition:

> A *minimally* christological anthropology is one in which (1) Christology warrants important claims about what it means to be human and (2) the scope of those claims goes beyond issues like the image of God and ethics.

We will return to this definition in the final chapter and see if there are ways in which we can clarify and strengthen it in light of the various case studies. But it will serve for now as an initial definition and a way of helping explain how I chose the theologians for this project.

FRAMING THE DIALOGUE

In this study, then, we are exploring two basic questions. First, what does it mean to say that Christology somehow grounds anthropological claims? And second, what issues in anthropology can such christologically oriented anthropologies meaningfully address? The first queries the method of a christological anthropology, the second its scope.

Whenever we face broad methodological questions like these, we have two options. On the one hand, we could take a "top-down" approach, seeking to understand what it means to develop a christological anthropology by identifying the relevant parameters, distinguishing characteristics, and ultimate desiderata of a christological anthropology. This would be an interesting exercise in its own right, and one that I hope to develop in a future work. In this book, however, I have opted for an alternate approach, one that tries to understand the method by analyzing representative figures and the anthropologies they have produced. From there, it becomes possible to draw some conclusions about how people have developed christological approaches to anthropology. Such a "bottom-up" perspective adopts a more descriptive posture, avoiding the prescriptive stance necessary to the top-down approach. This means the various studies in this book will focus on describing and understanding these representative approaches, trying to avoid evaluative comments whenever possible. Thus, the goal of the book is not to craft an argument for any particular way of approaching anthropology from a christological perspective; instead, we will explore a variety of possible approaches in order to generate a better understanding of how Christology has been used to inform anthropology. This will be particularly important to keep in mind as we look at how each theologian used Christology to address a specific issue in anthropology. Even there our task will not be to *evaluate* their specific proposals but to *understand* the ways in which Christology informed those proposals.[18]

The challenge of any such bottom-up approach, of course, is identifying the relevant figures and determining which to include in the study. If we were to establish in advance the criteria by which a work qualified as a christological anthropology, we would first need to engage in the kind of top-down study mentioned above. So we cannot expect the kind of

---

18. As we will see in a moment, a study like this necessarily involves making decisions about which theologians to include and which aspects of their respective theologies to analyze, which means that no such project can be *purely* descriptive. That does not change the intent of the project, though, which is to identify and describe approaches to christological anthropology rather than critique or evaluate those proposals.

precise criteria that would be generated by such an approach. Instead, I selected figures based on a fairly loose set of criteria.

First, they need to meet the basic requirements of a christological anthropology outlined above. In other words, they need to have articulated anthropological conclusions that are informed in some way by their Christology, and they need to have applied those christological insights to issues other than the *imago Dei*, soteriology, and ethics.

Second, I also chose to exclude from the study theologians with the kinds of "low" Christologies in which there appears to be little to ground the uniqueness of Jesus among other humans. If the basic contention of a christological anthropology is that our view of Christ should shape our view of humanity, it seems necessary that we have some way of establishing the claim that Jesus alone fills this role. Although it might be possible for a theologian with a low Christology to address this issue—in this study, the chapter on Friedrich Schleiermacher comes the closest to exploring this possibility—I chose to restrict our dialogue partners to those with generally higher Christologies and, consequently, more resources for grounding Jesus' unique significance for anthropology.[19]

Third, I intentionally selected figures from various periods in church history to demonstrate the historical breadth of christological anthropology. Nonetheless, only half of the figures chosen for the study come from the premodern eras of the church. This was not done in order to privilege modern conversations about the human person, but it does reflect the fact that theological anthropology as a distinct area of theological inquiry is a relatively recent development in the history of theology. Thus, although I strove for historical balance in selecting our dialogue partners, I also wanted to represent the significant growth of anthropological reflection in modern theology.

Fourth, as I mentioned in the prior section, I also selected theologians who would help us discern the ways in which Christology might inform anthropology across a range of anthropological issues. Thus, for example, I selected Julian of Norwich specifically because she applies Christology to issues of human pain and suffering in a unique way. Similarly, Gregory of Nyssa's view of gender and sexuality, Martin Luther's understanding of vocation, and James Cone's christological analysis of oppression all demonstrate how Christology can inform anthropology on a broad range of issues.

---

19. I would hypothesize that a low christological starting point would be even more likely to generate the kinds of christological anthropologies that limit their focus to just a few aspects of humanity (especially ethics). But that is a question for another time.

Finally, I selected figures who offered diverse examples of how anthropological insights can be grounded in Christology. As you work through the case studies, you will notice that each offers a distinct vision of how Christology and anthropology should be related to one another. Indeed, some of the case studies differ enough in method and content that it might be easy to lose sight of the thread that holds them all together. That was intentional. Since this study does not utilize a top-down approach that determines in advance what qualifies as a legitimate christological anthropology, I thought it would be most helpful to consider theologians who exemplify a broad range of approaches to the subject.

Thus, the various studies were selected for the purpose of exploring the historical, methodological, and thematic diversity of christological anthropology. Given the necessarily selective nature of a project like this, I have no illusions that these studies somehow represent all of the ways in which we might develop christological anthropologies. Indeed, one could easily argue that some of the individuals not chosen have an equal, if not greater, commitment to developing christologically shaped anthropologies (e.g., Irenaeus, Maximus, Calvin, Owen, Kierkegaard, Balthasar). Nor have I attempted to use these studies to develop any kind of taxonomic framework within which to categorize christological anthropologies. In the final chapter, I will attempt to bring all of the studies into dialogue with each other, and there I will highlight some similarities and dissimilarities between the various case studies, seeking to generate insights for developing christological anthropologies in general. But the individual chapters are intended merely as case studies in how Christology has been used to inform our understanding of the human person.

THE CASE STUDIES

Chapter 1 launches the study with Gregory of Nyssa's christological anthropology. Gregory provides an interesting starting point for several reasons. Most obviously, his is the earliest voice in the project, offering a patristic view of the relationship between Christology and anthropology. Given the importance of patristic theology in general for shaping subsequent theological conversations, Gregory offers an invaluable perspective. Additionally, although we will see that the image of God plays a fundamental role in shaping Gregory's view of the Christology/anthropology relationship, he oriented much of his discussion around the incarnation and the consequent transformation of humanity in Jesus Christ. Since this incarnational perspective has been one of the most influential ways of developing christological insights into the nature of the human person, this chapter offers a needed look at this important approach. Finally, Gregory utilized his christological framework to discuss what it means to be created male and female and the ultimate significance of gender and sexuality for being human. Although he approached the issue in ways that many modern thinkers will find uncomfortable, he nonetheless models a way of thinking *from* Christology *to* anthropology on an important anthropological issue.

In the second chapter, we will fast forward into the medieval period and consider the theological anthropology of Julian of Norwich. Julian is famous for her visionary experiences of the crucified Christ and her extended discussions of pain and suffering both in the crucifixion and in everyday human living. Thus, Julian's theology offers an example of a christological anthropology that takes the crucifixion as its point of departure, but in such a way that the resulting christological anthropology does not focus exclusively, or even primarily, on issues related to the doctrine of salvation. Instead, Julian develops a christological vision of humanity in which the very ontology of the human person is grounded in a crucicentric vision of divine love.

Chapter 3 brings us to the Reformation and the theology of Martin Luther. Somewhat unsurprisingly, Luther focused his anthropology on the doctrine of justification by faith. Although we might expect that this would be a classic example of a christological anthropology that is exclusively focused on soteriological issues, Luther's anthropology presses further. For Luther, although right understanding of the human person begins with the human person as he stands before the cross, it does not end there. Instead, Luther develops a whole range of anthropological insights based on the idea that we are always and only justified before God through Jesus by faith. Specifically, we will see that Luther's important theology of vocation flows from his christological understanding of the human person.

The fourth chapter takes us into the early modern era and Friedrich Schleiermacher's understanding of religious experience. As I mentioned earlier, some might question the extent to which Schleiermacher fits the intentions of this project, particularly given concerns about the overall orthodoxy of his Christology. In this chapter, though, I will argue that Schleiermacher's Christology has the resources to maintain the uniqueness of Jesus necessary for the kinds of christological anthropologies that we are considering. Thus, even if we conclude that Schleiermacher does not have a "high" Christology in the classic sense of that phrase, it still is not the kind of "low" Christology that would generate problems for this study. At the same time, Schleiermacher's distinctive Christology, generated by his experiential-redemptive starting point and his understanding of the religious self-consciousness, offers a unique perspective on how to develop a christological anthropology and its significance for understanding the role of the church and the community in shaping human identity.

With the fifth chapter, we arrive at Karl Barth's theological anthropology, widely regarded as among the most rigorous examples of a "christocentric" anthropology in the history of theology. According to Barth, we must ground anthropology in Christology because Jesus is the one in whom God has eternally decided to be God-for-humanity, and consequently has determined that humanity will be his covenantal copartners in the outworking of his redemptive purposes. In other words, through this eternal decree of election, God has decided in Jesus both the kind of God that he will be (God for us in Christ) and the kind of creatures that humanity will be (God's covenantal copartners in Christ). Because of this Jesus must be the center of any theologically adequate understanding of humanity; he alone is the eternal determination of what it means to be human. With this robust statement of Jesus' central significance for anthropology, Barth develops every aspect of his theological anthropology in dialogue with his Christology. For our purposes, we will focus specifically on how Barth's Christology shapes his view of the mind/ body relationship.

The sixth chapter marks the first of two studies in how contemporary theologians have developed christological anthropologies. For John Zizioulas, the entry point into the discussion is the doctrine of the Trinity. According to Zizioulas, the Trinity alone defines what it means to be a person: a unique being living in and shaped by free communion with other persons. This might suggest to some that we should view Zizioulas's anthropology as properly Trinitarian rather than specifically christological. Yet we will see in this chapter (and others) that these should not be placed in opposition to one another; instead, for almost all of our theologians, their christological approaches to theological anthropology always involve Trinitarian concerns as well.[20] In other words, defining

---

20. For more on the relationship between christological/christocentric and Trinitarian, see Marc Cortez, "What Does It Mean to Call Karl Barth a 'Christocentric' Theologian?," *Scottish Journal of Theology* 60, no. 2 (2007): 127–43.

humanity through the lens of Jesus Christ necessarily leads to under-standing humanity in light of the Trinity. For Zizioulas, although we only understand the nature of personhood in the light of the Trinity, it is in Jesus that we see the truth of what personhood means for *human* persons. The fact that Zizioulas defines personhood largely in terms of community will also lead us into Zizioulas's ecclesiological, and hence eucharistic, vision of true humanity.

Our final study comes in chapter 7 with James Cone. Here we will explore the resources of an anthropology that focuses largely on the themes of liberation, oppression, freedom, and race. As a leading repre-sentative of black liberation theology in America, Cone's christological anthropology begins with the conviction that in Jesus we see and experi-ence the truth that God is the great Liberator who seeks to liberate people from oppression and free them for full human flourishing. At the same time, in Jesus we also see and experience the truth of our own human-ity. We are beings who have been created for freedom, and, consequently, we are beings whose very natures are shaped by the ways in which we live, or fail to live, in free solidarity with all other humans. Cone comes the closest to offering an exemplarist understanding of the Christology/anthropology relationship. Yet I will argue that Cone presses further with an actualistic understanding of human nature in which the moral/ethical and the ontological/essential come together.

After this historical journey through representative ways of devel-oping specifically christological anthropologies, chapter 8 will draw the study to a close by pulling together some of the key strands of the discus-sion, highlighting themes that recur throughout the various studies, and also noting some important differences between our dialogue partners. Although even this chapter will remain in a largely descriptive mode, not trying to adjudicate these various differences, the chapter will con-clude with some reflections on the difficulties that face any christological anthropology and the questions that should guide any such endeavors in the future.

By now it should be clear that the present volume does not seek to offer a definitive answer to the question of what a christological anthro-pology should be, the kinds of questions that it should ask, or how we should go about developing christological anthropologies today. Although I think the various case studies in this book offer considerable resources for addressing those issues and examples that can illuminate our own christological reflections on the human person, we should not look to them for any definitive statement on what a christological anthropology must be. Instead, think of them more as explorations of a basic Christian intuition. Throughout the ages, Christians have thought that Jesus somehow informs our understanding of what it means to be human. In each of these case studies, we have the opportunity to watch as a great theological mind of the church develops that intuition into a specific anthropological proposal. Let us watch together.

CHAPTER 1

Beyond Genitalia

Gregory of Nyssa's Transformative Christology and the (Re)orientation of Sexuality

———•———

The scope of our proposed enquiry is not small: it is second to none of the wonders of the world,—perhaps even greater than any of those known to us, because no other existing thing, save the human creation, has been made like to God.

Gregory of Nyssa, *On the Making of Man*, preface[1]

AT FIRST GLANCE, GREGORY OF Nyssa might seem an unusual starting point for our study in christological anthropology. Some might even question whether Gregory offers a truly christological anthropology at all. Although no one would deny that Christology sits at the heart of Gregory's theological project, and several scholars have specifically labeled Gregory as a "christocentric" theologian,[2] questions can be raised about the extent to which Gregory offered an explicitly christological approach to theological anthropology. In his famous *On the Making of Man*, one of the few treatises in the early church dedicated entirely to theological anthropology, Christology played a relatively limited role. Indeed, Gregory explicitly referred to Jesus only a handful of times in the entire

---

1. All of the references to this work will be taken from *A Select Library of the Nicene and Post-Nicene Fathers*, ed. Philip Schaff, vol. 5, Series 2 (Grand Rapids: Eerdmans, 1978). After this, I will refer to *On the Making of Man* using the chapter and section numbers contained in that work.

2. E.g., Anthony Meredith, *Gregory of Nyssa*, Early Church Fathers (London: Routledge, 1999); Brian Daley, "Divine Transcendence and Human Transformation: Gregory of Nyssa's Anti-Apollinarian Christology," in *Rethinking Gregory of Nyssa*, ed. Sarah Coakley (Oxford: Blackwell, 2003), 67–76; Hans Boersma, *Embodiment and Virtue in Gregory of Nyssa: An Anagogical Approach* (New York: Oxford University Press, 2013).

manuscript.[3] How can his theological anthropology be meaningfully informed by Christology when it makes almost no reference to Christ?

Additionally, Gregory is famous, even infamous, for construing human sexuality such that it appears not to be a fundamental aspect of what it means to be human. Instead, he seems to suggest that sexuality is an extraneous "add on" to human nature, and thus something that will not characterize humanity in its resurrected form. In the eschaton, we will transcend sexuality as we finally achieve the "true" and non-sexed humanity that God always intended.[4] But one might legitimately wonder, how can a theological anthropology that starts with Jesus Christ and takes seriously the reality of the incarnation along with the fact that Jesus was male, avoid the apparently obvious conclusion that sexuality is important for being human?

Issues like these raise legitimate questions as to whether Gregory really qualifies as having developed a christological understanding of the human person. Nonetheless, as we move through this chapter, we will see that Gregory's anthropology is thoroughly christological, albeit rooted in a vision of human transformation that began with the incarnation and will continue on into eternity. Understanding this will help us appreciate Gregory's surprising interpretation of sexuality. Contrary to what some might think, Gregory was not simply captive to Greek suspicions of physicality in general and sexuality in particular. Instead, we will see that his vision of human sexuality flows from an anthropology that is transformational, eschatological, and ultimately apophatic, all three of which flow directly from his christological starting point.

Despite initial impressions, then, Gregory of Nyssa stands as one of the earliest theologians to develop a thoroughgoing theological anthropology

---

3. *On the Making of Man*, 5.2; 6.3; 16.5; 16.7; 25.10.

4. Human sexuality is notoriously complicated and involves at least issues related to biology (e.g., sexual organs, hormones, genes, brain chemistry), culture (how sexuality is interpreted and performed in a given cultural context), identity (how one perceives one's own sexuality), and sexual activity/ethics. To avoid confusion, in this chapter I will use "sexuality" as a broad term referring to all aspects of human sexuality; "biological sexuality" will refer specifically to the biological aspects of sexuality; "sexual differentiation" will refer to the ways in which we distinguish between human persons based on these various considerations; and "gender" will refer to the ways in which we construct sexual identities through the complex interaction of biological and cultural realities. For more information on these distinctions, see David P. Barash and Judith Eve Lipton, *Gender Gap: The Biology of Male-Female Differences* (New Brunswick, N.J.: Transaction, 2002); Alice H. Eagly, Anne E. Beall, and Robert J. Sternberg, eds., *The Psychology of Gender* (New York: Guilford, 2004); Richard A. Lippa, *Gender, Nature, and Nurture*, 2nd ed. (Mahwah, N.J.: Lawrence Erlbaum Associates, 2005).

rooted in Christology. That he does so in ways that produce startling conclusions about the human person in general and human sexuality in particular, conclusions that often challenge modern assumptions about what it means to be human, makes him an interesting interlocutor for our anthropological project.

WEIRDER THAN YOU THINK: THE PROBLEM OF THE "HUMAN"

Gregory's understanding of the human person is framed by three theological loci: the *imago Dei*, the incarnation, and the resurrection. And it is not difficult to see why, since all three loci introduce challenging questions about what it means to be human. According to many theologians, the *imago Dei* claims that fallen and finite beings somehow "image" the infinite and glorious divine being. Yet the attributes and actions of the divine and the human seem so radically contrary that it becomes difficult to imagine what it could possibly mean for one to image the other. Our imaginations are stretched even further when we consider the incarnation and its claim that two such disparate natures are actually joined in one person. And finally, the resurrection presents a vision of transformed humanity, leading to questions about whether there is any real continuity with our present existence and whether we remain truly human in such a radically transformed state.

Many theologians engage these issues by wrestling with *how* such things can be possible. Gregory, on the other hand, although he was certainly willing to ask *how* questions, prefers a logic flowing in a different direction. Instead of beginning with an existing understanding of the human person and focusing on how that kind of being can possibly image God or be united with a divine nature, Gregory allows his discourse to be directed by the *that*—given *that* humans image God, given *that* the incarnation is a reality, and given *that* the resurrection will take place, *what must we believe about human nature*? Taking these theological convictions as his starting point, Gregory offers a radical reinterpretation of what it means to be human.

Mirrors of God: Finite Images of an Infinite Reality

Like many theologians, Gregory begins his anthropological reflection with what it means to be made in the image of God. As he says at the beginning of *On the Making of Man*, the human person is "second to none of the wonders of the world" because the human person is the only creature "who truly was created after God, and whose soul was fashioned in the image of Him Who created him."[5] Thus, the human person is a "mirror" of God that functions as an image so long as it "keeps its resemblance to the prototype."[6] This is what distinguishes the human person from the rest of creation and establishes the value and dignity of the human person before God.[7]

Despite this confident beginning, however, Gregory later argues that understanding the *imago* is far from easy. Indeed, it serves as one of the fundamental problems of a Christian anthropology, one that may well transcend our ability to comprehend. In Gregory's words, "How then is man, this mortal, passible, short-lived being, the image of that nature which is immortal, pure, and everlasting? The true answer to this question, indeed, perhaps only the very Truth knows."[8] Gregory's discussion of the *imago*, then, is an attempt to explain—or, more accurately, to speculate about possible explanations of—how finite and fallen human creatures can be said to "mirror" the divine being in any sense.[9]

Gregory's definition of the *imago Dei* is fascinating and multifaceted. Although he is often lumped together with those who define the *imago* as humanity's capacity for rationality, and he did describe the image in such terms on a number of occasions,[10] he presents a more complex view of the image, one that includes an equal emphasis on both love and free will.[11] And Gregory goes further, claiming that "the image is properly

---

5. *On the Making of Man*, preface.

6. Ibid., 12.9; 16.3.

7. Ibid., chapter 3.

8. Ibid., 16.4. In many ways, this question is the hinge on which *On the Making of Man* swings. In the first fifteen chapters, Gregory develops a robust understanding of the human person that incorporates both capacities and functions in a multifaceted view of the *imago Dei*. With this question, Gregory introduces the problems of finiteness and fallenness into the equation, asking how the human person can possibly be the kind of image that Gregory has just finished describing. The second half of the book then wrestles with the implications of this question.

9. Gregory notes that much of what he will offer in the second half of *On the Making of Man*, particularly in reference to human sexuality and other postlapsarian human characteristics, is said by way of "conjectures and inferences" (*On the Making of Man*, 16.4), conforming to his appeal at the beginning of the work that his "kindly readers" would make allowances given the difficulty of the materials with which he is dealing (*On the Making of Man*, preface).

10. E.g., *On the Making of Man*, 4.4. Gregory even uses the classic Aristotelian definition of the human person as "a rational animal" (ibid., 8.8).

11. For love, see *On the Making of Man*, 5.2; 18.5. Gregory frequently talks about freedom as essential, but see 16.11 for a particularly clear example. Gregory also incorporates aspects of a functional view in his understanding of the *imago*. In one place, he virtually equates the image with the idea that human persons are "royal" figures who

an image *so long as it fails in none of those attributes which we perceive in the archetype.*[12] Rather than limiting the image to a particular attribute like rationality, then, Gregory argues that humans image the divine being in *all* of its attributes, even attributes typically viewed as inimical to creaturely existence. Thus, for example, Gregory argues elsewhere that human persons image even divine simplicity.[13] Ultimately, Gregory concludes that imaging God is about participating in God's own goodness and all of its associated virtues.[14]

To make the picture even more complex, unlike many early thinkers Gregory does not limit the image to the soul alone. Although the soul is the proper seat of the image, he refuses to exclude the body entirely. Instead, the body images the soul in much the same way as the soul images God: "it too is adorned by the beauty that the mind gives, being, so to say, a mirror of the mirror."[15] God specifically designed the human body as an instrument uniquely suitable for the task of imaging God in the world.[16] This means the body itself is mediately involved in imaging the divine nature.

This seems to create an impossible tension. How can a finite, creaturely nature manifest all of the divine attributes? Or, as Gregory himself asks, "How then is man, this mortal, passible, short-lived being, the image of that nature which is immortal, pure, and everlasting?"[17] As mentioned earlier, however, the logic of Gregory's argument flows in another direction. Rather than wrestle with *whether* it is possible for a human creature to image the divine nature, Gregory began with the theological conviction *that* humans in fact do so. Thus, Gregory's real question is this: Given that humans image the divine nature, what must we conclude about human nature? And the only possible conclusion Gregory can identify is that human nature is far more glorious than we

---

rule creation as God's chosen stewards (*On the Making of Man*, 2.1). And he goes on to suggest that the glorious capacities of the human person serve to identify humans as God's stewards and empower them to carry out that task (*On the Making of Man*, 4.1). Nonetheless, Gregory's predominant emphasis when discussing the human person is how the human virtues model divine excellencies.

12. Ibid., 11.3 (emphasis added).

13. Gregory of Nyssa, *On the Soul and the Resurrection: St. Gregory of Nyssa* (Crestwood, N.Y.: St. Vladimir's Seminary Press, 1993), 79–80.

14. *On the Making of Man*, 9.1; 16.10.

15. Ibid., 16.3.

16. Ibid., 4.1. For example, Gregory argues that humanity's upright posture facilitates the exercise of our intellectual virtues and ruling function (ibid., chapter 8).

17. Ibid., 16.4.

imagine. Gregory recognizes that a finite human nature will never exemplify the divine attributes in the same way that the divine nature will,[18] but the fact that a human nature can do so *in any way* suggests that our definition of "human" is far too limited.

Indeed, Gregory argues that human nature itself ultimately transcends our ability to understand. And this should come as no surprise. We were created to image an incomprehensible God, so we should expect that incomprehensibility would be part of the image itself. Thus, "since the nature of our mind, which is the likeness of the Creator evades our knowledge, it has an accurate resemblance to the superior nature, figuring by its own unknowableness the incomprehensible Nature."[19] For Gregory, an apophatic anthropology is the only possible result. We are more than we imagine, indeed, more than we *can* imagine.

In the Ocean of the Divine: Incarnation and the Transformation of Human Nature

Like the *imago Dei*, Gregory's theology of the incarnation presses us to understand that humanity is far more than we could possibly imagine. Indeed, Gregory presents an anthropology in which the union of the divine and the human in Christ, and the corresponding transformation of human nature, is the lens through which we come to understand what comprises true humanity.

Gregory articulates much of his understanding of the incarnation in his writings against Apollinarius and his followers. In this context, his real concern is to show how the incarnation requires a *real* union of divine and human. Thus, Gregory is sharply critical of the incomplete human that he thought Apollinarius was proposing with his union of the human body with the divine mind.[20] For Gregory, such an approach

---

18. Gregory thus draws a clear distinction throughout between the image and the archetypal reality that it seeks to mirror; otherwise it would no longer be just an image (*On the Making of Man*, 16.12). And Andrew Radde-Gallwitz rightly points out that Gregory also distinguishes between human participation in divine attributes by grace and divine possession of those attributes by nature (*Basil of Caesarea, Gregory of Nyssa, and the Transformation of Divine Simplicity* [New York: Oxford University Press, 2009], 220).

19. *On the Making of Man*, 11.4.

20. See esp. George D. Dragas, "The Anti-Apollinarist Christology of St Gregory of Nyssa: A First Analysis," *Greek Orthodox Theological Review* 42, no. 3–4 (1997): 299–314; Daley, "Divine Transcendence and Human Transformation"; Christopher A. Beeley, "The Early Christological Controversy: Apollinarius, Diodore, and Gregory Nazianzen," *Vigiliae Christianae* 65, no. 4 (January 1, 2011): 376–407.

necessarily denigrates the true humanity of Christ, turning it into a mere "beast of burden" since it lacks the soul that is an essential aspect of any truly human being.[21] Like his fellow Cappadocians, Gregory insists that the incarnation must involve the Son taking on a complete human nature, including a human soul, if it is going to result in the salvation of human persons. In short, any aspect of human nature not included in the incarnation would not be healed.[22]

However, it is precisely this union of the divine and the human that raises so many critical questions. How is it possible for the two to be joined in one person? Although Gregory wrestled with this question in the face of Apollinarian objections to the coherence of the Cappadocian account of the incarnation, here as well his anthropological focus rests on what must be true of human nature given the reality of the incarnation. In other words, if the incarnation is a reality, and if our understanding of human nature is incompatible with the incarnation, then it is our understanding of human nature that must change. From this perspective, Gregory argues for a christological transformation of human nature that, while remaining creaturely, becomes something far more amenable to union with the divine.

One of the primary ways in which Gregory distinguishes the creature from the Creator is the creature's liability to change. For Gregory, "all things that are seen in the creation are the offspring of rest and motion."[23] This is the necessary result of having been "brought into being by the Divine will."[24] The simple fact that all creatures have changed from non-being to being means creaturely nature is necessarily malleable. And for Gregory, this stands in obvious contrast to the immutable divine being since "that which may happen to move or change would cease to admit of the conception of Godhead."[25] Although this causes problems

---

21. *Antirrheticus*, 23. Brian Daley cites a quote from one of Gregory of Nazianzus's letters that makes the same point: "If (Jesus) is endowed with a soul, but not with a mind, how is he human? For a human being is not an animal without intelligence. Of necessity, the outward form and tabernacle would then be human, but the soul would be that of some horse or ox or some other unintelligent being; and this will be what is saved" (Daley, "Divine Transcendence and Human Transformation," 505, n. 32).

22. All of the Cappadocians thus affirm Gregory of Nazianzus's famous maxim: "that which he has not assumed he has not healed" (Ep. 101, in *A Select Library of the Nicene and Post-Nicene Fathers*, ed. Philip Schaff, vol. 7, Series 2 [Grand Rapids: Eerdmans, 1978], 861).

23. *On the Making of Man*, 1.2.

24. Ibid.

25. Ibid., 1.4.

for understanding what it means for humans to image God, the essential malleability of humanity's creaturely nature also creates resources for dealing with the challenge of the incarnation. In the incarnation, Jesus transforms humanity into that which is suitable for participating in the divine life, reshaping and exalting it. Taking humanity to himself, the Son brings it into his "own exalted place," and by the "combination" of divinity and humanity, makes the human to be what the divine is by nature.[26] Thus, "all the corruptible may put on incorruption, and all the mortal may put on immortality, our first-fruits having been transformed to the Divine nature by its union with God."[27]

At this point, some grow concerned that such a "transformation" of human nature entails its destruction. What does it mean for humanity to "put on immortality" such that we come to participate in divine attributes like impassibility and incorruptibility? Does that not sound as though humanity ceases to be human and becomes divine instead? Such concerns grow louder when we consider Gregory's famous explanation that Christ's humanity is like a drop of vinegar in the ocean of the divine: "by mingling with the divine, the mortal nature is renewed to match the dominant element, and shares the power of the deity, as if one might say that the drop of vinegar mingled with the ocean is made into sea by the mixing, because the natural quality of this liquid no longer remains in the infinity of the dominant element."[28] At first glance, such an analogy seems to suggest that the human element has been absorbed into the divine nature in such a way that it ceases to have any meaningful existence of its own. Although Gregory refers to the human nature as being "renewed," he explains this renewal as mingling the human with the divine to such an extent that the human element "no longer remains." Thus, although the human nature may have a continued existence in some sense, it is only the kind of existence that a drop of vinegar might have when mingled with an entire ocean!

Nonetheless, as Brian Daley argues, this transformation "does not seem to involve ... an annihilation of human nature, so much as the

---

26. *Contra Eunomium*, III.3.44. References to *Contra Eunomium* are taken from *Gregory of Nyssa: Contra Eunomium III: An English Translation with Commentary and Supporting Studies: Proceedings of the 12th International Colloquium On Gregory Of Nyssa (Leuven, 14–17 September 2010)*, ed. Johan Leemans, Supplements to Vigiliae Christianae, volume 124 (Leiden: Brill, 2014).

27. *Contra Eunomium* III.13.

28. *Contra Eunomium* III.3.68.

suffusion of all its naturally changeable, 'fleshly' characteristics with the stability and luminous vigour of God."[29] And he goes on to point out that Gregory consistently used terms for union (*henōsis*) and mixture (*mixis, krasis,* etc.) that denote for him "the close unification of elements that still remain naturally or numerically *different*: a relationship (*schesis*) rather than a total absorption."[30] Thus, to use slightly different language, Gregory seems to be describing a situation in which the essence of humanity remains—in other words, the human nature does not become some other kind of nature (e.g., divine)—even though the properties exemplified by that nature become "deified" in the sense that they come to resemble divine properties so closely as to be virtually indistinguishable. Thus, the transformation of the properties of the human nature demonstrates that those properties, as *human* properties, were capable of far more than we generally imagine. When Gregory says that the human takes on the property of "immortality," for example, he seems to suggest that this is the completion of humanity's own *telos*, the completion of its nature through transformative union with the divine.[31]

Gregory thus develops what Daley refers to as a "Christology of transformation."[32] He envisions a christological "refashioning" of our humanity in which it transcends the limitations of humanity *as we currently experience it*, demonstrating that the real end of human nature is far

---

29. Daley, "Divine Transcendence and Human Transformation," 71.

30. Ibid. Scholars have debated the philosophical background Gregory's analogy and its implications for Gregory's Christology. According to Richard Sorabji, the Stoics described a mixture as involving the combination of two elements that both remain actually existent in the mixture, neither is eliminated (*Matter, Space, and Motion: Theories in Antiquity and Their Sequel* [Ithaca, N.Y.: Cornell University Press, 1988], 79ff). Aristotle, on the other hand, thought a true mixture involved the combination of elements to create something truly new, a *tertium quid*, with only the potentialities of the original elements remaining. Interestingly though, he used the analogy of a drop of wine in an ocean as an example where one of the elements is actually destroyed, thus not comprising a true mixture. And Sorabji concludes that the parallel demonstrates that this is the background of Gregory's analogy, suggesting that the humanity does *not* remain, either potentially or actually, in the incarnation. Others rightly object that this would be at odds with Gregory's overall theology of the resurrection in which Christ clearly remains human (e.g., Meredith, *Gregory of Nyssa*, 48; Morwenna Ludlow, *Gregory of Nyssa, Ancient and (Post)modern* [New York: Oxford University Press, 2007], 99–100). Indeed, as we will see, the continued, albeit transformed, humanity of Christ will be fundamental to Gregory's understanding of the salvation of humans in general.

31. For a similar assessment, see Ludlow, *Gregory of Nyssa, Ancient and (Post)modern*, 98–100.

32. Brian E. Daley, " 'The Human Form Divine': Christ's Risen Body and Ours according to Gregory of Nyssa," in *Studia Patristica Vol. 41* (Leuven: Peeters, 2006), 316.

more glorious than we imagine.[33] As Gregory explains in *On the Soul and the Resurrection*, human persons were created to serve as "receptacles" for the divine virtues; so despite the limitations of humanity as we perceive them, human nature is sufficiently malleable to be reshaped for that purpose.[34] And that reshaping has begun in Christ.

Resurrected Bodies: Reshaping Physicality for a Transcendent Reality

At this point, we may begin to wonder whether Gregory envisioned a future reality for the human person in which we are no longer embodied. After all, how could a material being, one limited by the particularities of a physical body, be transformed to the extent that he or she can participate in the properties of the divine nature? As difficult as that is to answer, Gregory clearly affirmed that the resurrected human person retains a material body of some kind. Indeed, despite a cultural context in which it was common to be rather suspicious of material realities, Gregory had a notably high view of the human body and thought it critical that humanity remains embodied throughout the eschaton.[35]

Gregory argued that the resurrection will comprise reuniting a human soul with its particular body.[36] Indeed, he devotes considerable attention to wrestling with how a soul can be united to *its own* body, arguing that the soul will be able to draw together the very elements of its physical body because of the intimate relationship between the two. As Daley explains, "the soul 'stamps' its own unique character permanently on all its body's elements and particles, and is in turn indelibly (if analogously) 'stamped' or marked by them."[37] In the resurrection, then,

---

33. *Contra Eunomium*, III/3, 69.

34. Gregory of Nyssa, *On the Soul and the Resurrection*, 87. See the useful discussion of Gregory's "receptacle" language in Verna E. F. Harrison, "Receptacle Imagery in St Gregory of Nyssa's Anthropology," in *Studia Patristica Vol. 22* (Louvain: Peeters, 1989), 23–27.

35. See esp. Thomas J. Dennis, "Gregory on the Resurrection of the Body," in *Easter Sermons of Gregory of Nyssa* (Cambridge, Mass.: Philadelphia Patristic Foundation, 1981), 55–80; J. C. M. van Winden, "In Defence of the Resurrection," in *Easter Sermons of Gregory of Nyssa* (Cambridge, Mass.: Philadelphia Patristic Foundation, 1981), 101–21; and Lawrence R. Hennessey, "Gregory of Nyssa's Doctrine of the Resurrected Body," in *Studia Patristica Vol. 22* (Louvain: Peeters, 1989), 28–34.

36. Thus, it would not be correct to say that Gregory thinks the soul's destiny "is to be altogether freed from the body" (Rowan A. Greer, *Christian Life and Christian Hope: Raids on the Inarticulate* [New York: Crossroad, 2001], 94).

37. Daley, "The Human Form Divine," 308. See esp. Gregory of Nyssa, *On the Soul and the Resurrection*, 65–73 and *On the Making of Man*, chapter 26.

"the soul ... once again easily reassembles its own matter according to its own continuing form."[38] Thus, Gregory clearly affirms not only that we exist as embodied souls in the eschaton, but that our resurrected bodies are directly and ontologically connected to our current bodies through their intimate relationship with our souls.

Despite Gregory's high view of the body, his transformative vision means that the body must be radically reshaped through our union with Christ. This should not come as any surprise given what we have already said about the christological transformation of the human person. To complete the picture specifically as it relates to the body, though, we need to add more pieces to Gregory's anthropological puzzle: the "garments of skin" and the ontological unity of humanity.

Early theologians often interpreted the "garments of skin" in Genesis 3:21 as a metaphorical reference to the "lower" aspects of human existence that God added to human nature as a consequence of the fall. Although some viewed the garments as physical embodiment itself, Gregory avoided this, maintaining that embodiment was part of humanity's original creation.[39] Instead, the garments of skin refer to the fallen condition of the human body, including things like "sexual intercourse, conception, childbirth, uncleanness, nursing, feeding, excretion, the gradual growth into adulthood, the prime of life, old age, illness, and death."[40] Although these are all aspects of fallen humanity, Gregory did not view them as sinful in themselves. Instead, when used rightly, they serve as the means through which God redirects fallen humanity back to himself.[41]

Nonetheless, the garments of skin are part of humanity's fallen condition, and consequently, are among those aspects of human nature as we currently experience it that will need to be transformed in the resurrection. Thus, we "shed" these garments of skin as we "put on" Christ.[42]

---

38. Daley, "The Human Form Divine," 174.

39. Gregory dealt with the garments of skin in various places throughout his writings, but see esp. *On Virginity*, 12; *On the Dead*, 53; and *On the Soul and the Resurrection*, chapter 10. For a good summary of Gregory's understanding of the garments of skin, see Boersma, *Embodiment and Virtue in Gregory of Nyssa*, 87–92.

40. *On the Soul and the Resurrection*, 114.

41. As Louth explains, the Greek Fathers did not typically view the material world as an impediment to spiritual growth: "the purified soul does not simply learn the vanity of all created things, but also learns to see in them a manifestation of the glory of God" (Andrew Louth, *The Origins of the Christian Mystical Tradition* [New York: Oxford University Press, 1981], 85).

42. See esp. *Commentary on the Song of Songs* 1.14.13–15.2.

As Hans Boersma summarizes: "Human beings can share in Christ as the new garment because, according to Gregory, his human nature is ours ... This human nature functions as a garment that mediates his divinity to us."[43] As we are clothed with Christ's transformed humanity, we begin to experience that same transformation ourselves, shedding the fallen aspects of human nature, and being brought ever more into conformity with the divine image. Since Gregory describes the garments of skin in ways that are inherently linked to human bodies as we currently experience them, shedding the garments seems to require a significant reshaping of the body itself.

Additionally, Gregory emphasizes the transformation necessary for human persons to realize fully our oneness in Christ. Looking at the creation of the *adam* in Genesis 1:26–27, Gregory concludes that the indefinite noun refers not to a particular individual but to all humanity.[44] All human persons were included in the initial act of creation, establishing for Gregory a fundamental unity of humanity that transcends particular differences. As he says a little later, "Now just as any particular man is limited by his bodily dimensions, and the peculiar size which is conjoined with the superficies of his body is the measure of his separate existence, so I think that the entire plenitude of humanity was included by the God of all, by His power of foreknowledge, as it were in one body."[45] For Gregory, then, things like bodily size and shape constitute the "separate existence" of the human person, but such particularities should not blind us to the deeper reality of our unity in the "one body" of humanity. Elsewhere Gregory uses the unity of humanity to ground human moral action, concluding that despite the many particularizing features of human existence (especially social inequalities), we should recognize and emphasize our common humanity as more fundamental than our differences.[46]

---

43. Boersma, *Embodiment and Virtue in Gregory of Nyssa*, 90.

44. *On the Making of Man*, 16.16. Scholars have debated the precise meaning of "humanity" in this context, whether some kind of abstract human nature, the sum total of all particular humans who will ever exist, or some combination of the two (see esp. Johannes Zachhuber, *Human Nature in Gregory of Nyssa: Philosophical Background and Theological Significance*, Supplements to Vigiliae Christianae [Leiden: Brill, 2000]). As Verna Harrison points out, all of the interpretations point to the idea that "Gregory regards humankind throughout time, space, and the eschaton as a single whole whose unity is foundational and is constitutive by the divine image.... For him, unity is prior to diversity" (Verna E. F. Harrison, "Gregory of Nyssa on Human Unity and Diversity," in *Studia Patristica Vol. 41, Orientalia; Clement, Origen, Athanasius; the Cappadocians; Chrysostom* [Leuven: Peeters, 2006], 337).

45. *On the Making of Man*, 16.17.

46. See Harrison, "Gregory of Nyssa on Human Unity and Diversity."

Gregory's eschatological vision maintains that creational emphasis on the unity of humanity. As Harrison summarizes, "Gregory states that at the final stage of the eschaton all people will be one, and they will be united in their alikeness and equality with each other."[47] Once again, then, we see that the end is like the beginning. The unity of humanity in God's creational intent finds an eschatological echo in the reuniting of humanity in Christ.

This eschatological unity, however, requires that any of those features of humanity that serve to divide us from one another must themselves be transcended in the christological transformation so that we can truly become *one* in Christ. For many, this raises the question of whether Gregory envisioned a situation in which humans lose all of their individuality and particularity, salvation becoming a kind of absorption into a unified whole in which there are no distinct persons. Remember that Gregory included bodily size and shape as among those things that separate humans from one another. Presumably such limitations would need to be overcome so we can experience true unity in Christ. Without anything to differentiate us from each other, not even the basic limitations of our material bodies, does this not entail the denial of any real personal existence in the eschaton?

Gregory, however, did not envision an eschatological state in which human persons cease to exist as individuals. As Morwenna Ludlow points out, we must at least acknowledge Gregory's emphasis on the social nature of the eschatological state: "An examination of most of Gregory's later eschatology shows the great importance of the *social* aspect of the resurrection. Although he highlighted the perfect union of heaven, he meant not a monistic union, but a harmony created from all parts and members of the created universe."[48] For Gregory, then, the issue is not whether we remain recognizable persons in the resurrection, but the basis upon which we ground that individual personhood. Rather than focusing on creaturely realities like bodily size, spatial location, external appearance, or even a substantial soul, Gregory argues that humans' differentiation will be based on their participation in and manifestation of the divine virtues. Although we are all being transformed in Christ so that we all participate in the divine virtues, we are all at different stages in that process and we each manifest those virtues in particular ways. Thus, as Daley

---

47. Ibid., 342.
48. Ludlow, *Gregory of Nyssa, Ancient and (Post)modern*, 373.

suggests, "the determining feature of these bodies will be, in the end, their virtue, the holiness and goodness that most closely resemble the holiness and goodness of God, the source and standard of virtue."[49] Gregory thus individuated humans through his understanding of the *imago Dei*. Since the *imago* is about participating in and manifesting the divine virtues, and since the *imago* is fundamental to what it means to be human for Gregory, it stands to reason that the *imago* would be fundamental to establishing and identifying human personhood in the resurrection. And this means that having a resurrected "body" means something far different than we typically imagine.[50] We remain embodied in that we seem to retain enough of a material identity to instantiate the virtues, which is the fundamental purpose of human beings made in the image of God.[51]

This christological transformation led Gregory to an apophatic view of true humanity. In the end, Gregory concludes that the transformation begun in the incarnation and continued through the resurrection means that the true humanity to be revealed in the future simply cannot be understood or even anticipated on the basis of our current experiences of being human. As Gregory concludes at the end of *On the Soul and the Resurrection*, "every reasoning which conjectures about the future restoration will be proved worthless when what we expect comes to us in experience."[52]

TRANSPOSED TO A NEW KEY: SEXUALITY IN THE ESCHATON

Gregory's transformative Christology thus opens the door to a far more expansive view of what it means to be human, one that radically transcends everything we currently understand and experience human nature to be. For Gregory, this is required by the theological framework offered by the *imago Dei*, the incarnation, and the resurrection, all of which suggest that humanity as we currently experience it is far removed

---

49. Daley, "The Human Form Divine," 315; cf. Verna E. F. Harrison, "Male and Female in Cappadocian Theology," *Journal of Theological Studies* 41, no. 2 (1990): 470.

50. As Sarah Coakley points out, though, we frequently talk about the "body" as though its meaning were obvious, missing the fact that this is a debated and difficult concept even more for modern thinkers (Sarah Coakley, "The Eschatological Body: Gender, Transformation, and God," *Modern Theology* 16, no. 1 [2000]: 62).

51. Thus, although Gregory's position suggests a radically new kind of materiality, one that has been so radically transfigured that it can transcend the limitations of time and space (Boersma, *Embodiment and Virtue in Gregory of Nyssa*, 22–23), Morwenna Ludlow correctly argues that "Gregory held that the resurrection is not some mysterious new materiality, but the perfection of the same materiality" (Ludlow, *Gregory of Nyssa, Ancient and (Post)modern*, 372).

52. *On the Soul and the Resurrection*, 113.

from the protological humanity of the Garden or the eschatological humanity of the resurrection. Gregory's transformative vision, however, especially as it relates to the transformation of the body, raises important questions about human sexuality. And many worry about an apparent dismissal of sexuality in Gregory's vision of the resurrection that seems unacceptable in light of the modern emphasis on the fundamental importance of human sexuality.

In this section, we will focus our attention on understanding the implications of Gregory's christological transformation of the human person for understanding human sexuality. And we will see that Gregory's view of sexuality follows the same basic logic as his view of the body in general: neither are completely eliminated, though both need to be transposed to a key appropriate to our eschatological purpose. In other words, they are not simply dismissed, but they are transformed in such a way that their appearance and significance are rather different from what we might expect.

Transposing Sexuality: Male, Female, and the Image of God

The radical transformation of the body raises obvious questions for the nature of human sexuality in the resurrected state. Do we remain "male and female" in the eschaton, or does Gregory place sexuality among those aspects of human nature that are set aside through our union with Christ? Although we will see in the next section that there are reasons for thinking that our sexuality has continued significance into the eschaton, this is not because we retain our biological sexuality, which is set aside through our transformative union with Christ.

Although not equally developed, Gregory offers three arguments for thinking that biological sexuality will *not* be part of our resurrected bodies. The first argument stems from Gregory's conviction that the resurrection is both a restoration and a continuation of protological humanity, and there is an important sense in which protological humanity was not sexually differentiated. In a famous passage Gregory interprets Genesis 1:27 as describing a "dual creation" of human persons:

> We must, then, examine the words carefully: for we find, if we do so, that that which was made "in the image" is one thing, and that which is now manifested in wretchedness is another. "God created man," it says; "in the image of God created He him." There is an end of the creation of that which was made "in the image": then it makes a resumption of

the account of creation, and says, "male and female created He them." I presume that every one knows that this is a departure from the Proto-type: for "in Christ Jesus," as the apostle says, "there is neither male nor female." Yet the phrase declares that man is thus divided.[53]

In other words, God first declares his intention to create beings in his image (v. 26), an intention that finds its creative fulfillment in the first half of the following verse. But the narrative continues with the addition of "male and female he created them," something not mentioned in the expression of divine intent. To Gregory, this suggests that the verse contains two logical moments in creation: (1) God's determination to create humans in his image and (2) the addition of sexual differentiation to that original creative vision.[54]

Some caveats are in order here. First, as we will see, we should not envision these as two distinct *acts* of creation, as though God originally created a non-sexed human and only later added sexual differentiation. Instead, the first moment refers to God's original intention for humanity and the second to the historical outworking of that intention. Thus, as we will see, although Gregory did not think that biological sexuality is a part of God's original creative design for human persons, every human person that has actually existed has in fact been sexually differentiated. Second, Gregory does not suggest anywhere that the body itself was added to God's

---

53. *On the Making of Man*, 16.7.

54. John Behr has challenged this traditional interpretation of Gregory's theology, argu-ing that Gregory did not envision a "dual" creation with the addition of sexual differentia-tion coming only as a logical consequence of the fall (John Behr, "The Rational Animal: A Rereading of Gregory of Nyssa's De Hominis Opificio," *Journal of Early Christian Studies* 7, no. 2 [1999]: 219–47). He draws instead on Gregory's understanding of the human person as standing between the rational/spiritual and irrational/physical worlds. Sexuality is part of humanity's physical being, which, along with the soul, makes it possible for human-ity to play a mediatorial role in the universe. Behr's proposal has received support from some scholars (e.g., Martin Laird, "Under Solomon's Tutelage: The Education of Desire in the Homilies on the Song of Songs," in *Rethinking Gregory of Nyssa*, ed. Sarah Coakley [Oxford: Blackwell, 2003], 77–95; Eric Daryl Meyer, "Gregory of Nyssa on Language, Naming God's Creatures, and the Desire of the Discursive Animal," in *Genesis and Christian Theology* [Grand Rapids: Eerdmans, 2012], 103–16), and his argument certainly cautions us about not neglecting the importance of human sexuality in the historical outworking of God's creative plan. Other scholars have made compelling arguments against the proposal and in favor of the traditional interpretation (see esp. Valerie A. Karras, "A Re-Evaluation of Marriage, Celibacy, and Irony in Gregory of Nyssa's On Virginity," *Journal of Early Chris-tian Studies* 13, no. 1 [2005]: 111–21; J. Warren Smith, "The Body of Paradise and the Body of the Resurrection: Gender and the Angelic Life in Gregory of Nyssa's 'De Hominis Opificio'," *Harvard Theological Review* 99, no. 2 [2006]: 207–28; Boersma, *Embodiment and Virtue in Gregory of Nyssa*, esp. 100–109).

creational intention.[55] Unlike some readings of Origen's anthropology,[56] Gregory does not present a creation narrative in which we exist as disembodied souls prior to receiving embodiment as a sort of punishment for a spiritual fall into sin. The only issue in question is that of sexual differentiation. And third, Gerhart Ladner is surely correct to warn against drawing too sharp a distinction between "the 'original supra-historical' image of God' (i.e., the *pleroma*) and the 'original historical image of God' (i.e., man's state in Paradise)."[57] Given the eternal nature of God's decisions and actions, sharp distinctions are always problematic. Nonetheless, Gregory himself suggests a logical distinction that warrants consideration.

It is important to notice here that Gregory does not make this argument out of any deep-seated suspicion of sexuality. Instead, he offers an explicitly christological explanation for the twofold creation. Gregory argues that human persons cannot be male/female essentially because in Jesus "there is no male and female," with obvious reference to Galatians 3:28. If Christ is the primary form of humanity, however, the prototype on which all other expressions of humanity are grounded, transformed, and redeemed, and if sexual differentiation is excluded from the humanity revealed by the prototype, then sexual differentiation cannot be a part of essential humanity.

In the very next paragraph, Gregory strengthens that christological logic by appealing to the nature of God himself: "Thus the creation of our nature is in a sense twofold: one made like to God, one divided according to this distinction: for something like this the passage darkly conveys by its arrangement, where it first says, 'God created man, in the image of God created He him,' and then, adding to what has been said, 'male and female created He them,'—a thing which is alien from our conceptions of God."[58] Gregory articulates here a conviction common to most of the early church theologians: God is not gendered. Despite the use of gendered language to describe him, God is neither male nor female. This does not mean that he somehow encompasses *both* male and female in

55. See the excellent discussion in Ludlow, *Gregory of Nyssa, Ancient and (Post)modern,* 166–75.

56. E.g., Gerhart B. Ladner, "The Philosophical Anthropology of Saint Gregory of Nyssa," *Dumbarton Oaks Papers* 12 (1958): 90; and Martien Parmentier, "Greek Patristic Foundations for a Theological Anthropology of Women in Their Distinctiveness as Human Beings," *Anglican Theological Review* 84, no. 3 (2002).

57. Ladner, "The Philosophical Anthropology of Saint Gregory of Nyssa," 90.

58. *On the Making of Man,* 16.8.

himself, but that he is *neither* male nor female.[59] Sexual differentiation is a creaturely reality, not a divine one.

For Gregory, though, this has implications for understanding essential humanity.[60] Although Gregory does not unpack every step in his thinking, the logic appears to move something like this:

1. The *imago Dei* is what is most essential to being human.
2. The *imago Dei* is fundamentally about human persons participating in and manifesting God's goodness, which includes all of his divine attributes.
3. God does not include sexual differentiation as one of his good attributes.
4. Therefore, sexual differentiation is not a part of the *imago Dei*.
5. Therefore, sexual differentiation is not a part of essential humanity.

All of this raises the question of why God would add sexual differentiation to his original creative vision for humanity in the first place. And this brings us to Gregory's second, though clearly related, argument for the transformative removal of biological sexuality. For Gregory, biological sexuality is closely related to the fall, and is, therefore, something that must be transcended in the resurrection. Although Gregory did not think that sexuality came as a temporal consequence of the fall, he does present it as a logical consequence. In his foreknowledge, God knew that humanity would fall into sin and that the fall would endanger their continuation as his creatures.[61] As an act of grace, then, God decided in advance to create human persons as sexually differentiated beings so that, once fallen, we would have a means of procreation appropriate to that fallen condition.[62] Thus, biological sexuality was created entirely for the purpose of enabling biological procreation and will be done away with in the

---

59. Verna E. F. Harrison, "Gender, Generation, and Virginity in Cappadocian Theology," *Journal of Theological Studies* 47 (1996): 68.

60. For the purposes of this discussion, we can take "essential" to mean any property or set of properties without which an entity (e.g., human) can no longer be the kind of entity that it is. In other words, something is essential to being human if you would no longer be human if you lost that property.

61. With regard to how humanity would have procreated if the fall never happened, Gregory speculated that there is an angelic mode of procreation proper to rational creatures, although one that is "unspeakable and inconceivable by human conjectures, except that it assuredly exists" (*On the Making of Man*, 17.2).

62. Ibid.

resurrection.[63] As Harrison explains, "In the eschaton, this mode of generation, which is inextricably bound to division, limitation, and decay, will no longer occur, nor will the gender distinction which exists for its sake."[64] Consequently, Gregory views biological sexuality, like the garments of skin, as an aspect of our current humanity that is a penultimate good: necessary for now, but ultimately to be transcended in Christ.[65]

Finally, as we discussed above, Gregory places a strong emphasis on the creational and eschatological unity of humanity. Thus, anything that serves to divide human persons from each other must be overcome in the christological transformation so that we can all be one in Christ. Thus, Gregory's third argument for the necessity of the transformation of sexual differentiation is precisely that it serves as one of those factors that divide humanity. We see this in the creation account where Gregory explicitly contrasted the unity of humanity in the *imago Dei* with our creation as "male and female, a phrase that "declares that man is thus divided."[66] As Harrison explains, "Thus, for Gregory the differences based on gender and class are less central to what it is to be human than intellect, freedom and the capacity for virtue and communion with God, properties that manifest the divine image and are shared by all human beings."[67] Gregory's third argument for the necessity of a christological transformation of humanity's biological sexuality is that it is among those things that divides us and prevents our complete unity in Christ. And as we saw in our discussion of the resurrected body, any such divisive features will be "shed" as we put on Christ's transformed humanity.

Transposing Gender: The Eschatological Significance of Sexuality

All of this would seem to suggest that for Gregory human sexuality will have no role to play in the resurrection. Since there is "neither male nor female in Christ," biological sexuality is completely removed through our

---

63. As Peter Brown rightly comments, "Sexuality, for him, meant reproduction" ("Marriage and Mortality: Gregory of Nyssa," in *The Body and Society: Men, Women, and Sexual Renunciation in Early Christianity* [New York: Columbia University Press, 1988], 296).

64. Harrison, "Gender, Generation, and Virginity in Cappadocian Theology," 56.

65. Gregory clearly distinguished between "moral evil" and biological sexuality (*The Great Catechism*, 28), the latter of which serves to maintain human existence as God brings humanity to its *telos*, albeit now as if "by a long detour" (Ladner, "The Philosophical Anthropology of Saint Gregory of Nyssa," 85).

66. *On the Making of Man*, 16.7.

67. Harrison, "Gregory of Nyssa on Human Unity and Diversity," 339.

christological transformation, and sexuality will no longer be one of those things that divides humanity. Hans Boersma thus concludes, "The eschatological life in Christ is angelic, and therefore genderless, in character,"[68] describing this as the "christological overcoming of gender."[69] And this idea that true humanity lies in some sexless human nature has raised considerable skepticism among some feminist theologians who rightly point out that visions of a sexless or androgynous humanity have historically been used to make some vision of a perfect *male* humanity normative for all humans.[70]

Although it is clear that at least certain aspects of human sexuality are transcended and "overcome" in the resurrected state, we should not presume that Gregory's theology entails the complete elimination of all the implications of human sexuality. Instead, Gregory affirmed both explicitly and implicitly some continuing significance for human gender.

With respect to Gregory's explicit statements, we need to account for the fact that Gregory continued to use gendered language and symbols to describe resurrected humanity. As several scholars have pointed out, Gregory's vision of eschatological humanity is not de-gendered; instead, he presents human persons as constituted by a kind of gender fluidity in which they take on a variety of gendered characteristics as they move through the various stages of ascent toward God.[71] Thus, Sarah Coakley concludes,

> In all these transferences and reversals, the message Gregory evidently wishes to convey is that gender stereotypes must be reversed, undermined and transcended if the soul is to advance to supreme intimacy with the Trinitarian God; and that the language of sexuality and

---

68. Boersma, *Embodiment and Virtue in Gregory of Nyssa*, 114.

69. Ibid., 113.

70. Ludlow, *Gregory of Nyssa, Ancient and (Post)modern*, 169. Several feminist theologians have consequently argued in favor of Augustine's theology of the resurrection in which human persons retain their biological gender, even while objecting to his gender hierarchicalism (e.g., Rosemary Radford Ruether, "Misogynism and Virginal Feminism in the Fathers of the Church," in *Religion and Sexism* [New York: Simon and Schuster, 1974], 156–58; and Kari Elisabeth Børresen, "God's Image, Man's Image? Patristic Interpretation of Gen 1,27 and I Cor 11,7," in *Image of God and Gender Models in Judaeo-Christian Tradition* [Oslo: Solum Forlag, 1991], 199–205.

71. See esp. Harrison, "Gender, Generation, and Virginity in Cappadocian Theology"; Coakley, "The Eschatological Body"; Valerie A. Karras, "Sex/gender in Gregory of Nyssa's Eschatology: Irrelevant or Non-Existent?" in *Studia Patristica Vol 41, Orientalia; Clement, Origen, Athanasius; the Cappadocians; Chrysostom* (Leuven: Peeters, 2006), 363–68; Virginia Burrus, "Queer Father: Gregory of Nyssa and the Subversion of Identity," in *Queer Theology* (Oxford: Blackwell, 2007), 147–62.

gender, far from being an optional aside or mere rhetorical flourish in the process, is somehow necessary and intrinsic to the epistemological deepening that Gregory seeks to describe.[72]

The challenge of Gregory's anthropological vision, then, is not that gender has been removed, but that there seems to be so much of it!

Boersma contends that in Gregory's view of eschatological humanity, we need to give primacy to his understanding of Galatians 3:28 in which there is neither male nor female in Christ. Thus, we should see his gender-switching language as a metaphorical allusion to the bodily instability that results from our transposition in Christ.[73] From this perspective, it is entirely possible to make sense of Gregory's gendered anthropological language in the resurrection without viewing it as entailing the kind of real gender, and the corresponding gender fluidity, proposed by some interpreters.

However, although Boersma is correct to note the primacy of Galatians 3:28 in Gregory's anthropology, it is not necessary to assume that the christological transformation of biological sexuality necessarily undermines the significance of human sexuality entirely. As Kevin Corrigan rightly argues, "Just because physical sexuality and genitalia are accidental [i.e. nonessential], this does not mean that everything resulting from them is accidental."[74] In other words, it is entirely possible to make a distinction between the physical/biological aspects of sexuality and the gendered identities and characteristics that result from having lived as biologically sexual beings. In other words, we can distinguish between one's "sex" and one's "gender."[75] With that distinction in mind, we can agree with Boersma that Gregory envisions a complete transposition of biological sexuality such that there is neither male nor female, while still affirming the possibility that gendered characteristics and identities continue in the eschaton. Thus, as Morwenna Ludlow argues,

---

72. Sarah Coakley, "'Persons' in the 'Social Doctrine of the Trinity: A Critique of Current Analytic Discussion," in *The Trinity: An Interdisciplinary Symposium on the Trinity*, ed. Stephen T. Davis, Daniel Kendall, and Gerald O'Collins (Oxford: Oxford University Press, 2001), 128.

73. Boersma, *Embodiment and Virtue in Gregory of Nyssa*, 114.

74. Kevin Corrigan, *Evagrius and Gregory: Mind, Soul, and Body in the Fourth Century*, Ashgate Studies in Philosophy and Theology in Late Antiquity (Farnham: Ashgate, 2009), 139.

75. It would be anachronistic to suggest that Gregory intended a clear distinction between biological and cultural aspects of sexuality as often seen in modern literature on the subject (see footnote 4). Nonetheless, as we will see, we can make a loose distinction in Gregory's theology between aspects of sexuality rooted in the present, material body (biological sexuality) and the corresponding sexual identities that have enduring significance even after the eschatological transformation of the body (gender).

> Not only does his view not deny the goodness and necessity of human materiality (whilst allowing for its healing and transformation in the eschatological body), but it also, in the distinction between physical sex and emotional, moral, and spiritual expressions of gender, does not require men and women to abandon *all* notions of femininity or masculinity in their present and eschatological journey into God.[76]

In other words, it is possible that eschatological humanity is "degenitalized" but not de-gendered.[77]

Consistent with his emphasis on the eschatological unity of humanity, Gregory then argues that the qualities we typically associate with sexual differentiation (i.e., the qualities of being *masculine* or *feminine*) are no longer distributed and divided between the sexes, but human persons come to participate in and manifest all of these virtues. Thus, Gregory's argument does not seem to entail the conclusion that we will no longer be gendered, but that we will be even more robustly gendered, sharing all the qualities/virtues of human nature.

According to some of his interpreters, the fluidity of Gregory's gender language for eschatological humanity suggests that he does not think resurrected persons have any kind of stable gender identity. Indeed, some have concluded that he affirms a kind of "homosexual" humanity in which we are multiply sexed rather than androgynously non-sexed.[78] Although such an approach takes Gregory's gendered language seriously, it errs in not appreciating the important link that Gregory establishes between embodied personal identity in this life and in the resurrected state. For Gregory, the physical body that I have in this life, which would include its sexuality, has significance for my identity even in the eschaton. Remember that Gregory views the body and soul of the human person as interdependent in such a way that the soul marks the body as its own and is in turn "stamped" by its body, indelibly marked so that body and soul belong together. Although Gregory thinks that my body will be radically transformed through union with Christ, it will still be *my* body and I will still be formed by the bodily experiences that shaped my body and marked my soul.

---

76. Ludlow, *Gregory of Nyssa, Ancient and (Post)modern*, 178.

77. Sarah Coakley proposes this as an apt way of describing Gregory's vision of protological humanity, but the language serves here as well (*Powers and Submissions: Spirituality, Philosophy, and Gender* [Oxford: Blackwell, 2002], 163).

78. E.g., Gerard Loughlin, *Queer Theology: Rethinking the Western Body* (Oxford: Blackwell, 2007), 279.

Consider, for example, what Gregory says about his sister Macrina. In his *Life of Macrina*, Gregory described his sister as having lived such a life of virtue that her body has already begun to be reshaped and transformed in preparation for its continual and ultimate transformation in the resurrection.[79] At her funeral, he discovered a small scar on her body, the result of God miraculously healing her from a life-threatening tumor. Although the body's transformation had already begun, the scar remains. For Gregory this is a reminder of divine intervention, "an occasion and reminder of perpetual thanksgiving to God."

So the partially transformed body of Macrina continues to bear a physical mark as a memorial of her faithfulness and God's grace. Gregory may think that the scar would have disappeared in Macrina's resurrected and fully transformed state, but there is room in Gregory's theology for maintaining that even Macrina's resurrection body would in some way be marked by this "token of God's powerful help."[80] Given the continuity that Gregory affirmed between the pre- and post-resurrection bodies, it is entirely possible that whatever form the resurrection body takes in its transformed state, some aspect of its shape will manifest the physical realities of the pre-resurrection body. Thus, even if the resurrection body is radically different from our current bodies, making it impossible to say precisely how Macrina's resurrection body would bear that scar, some aspect of the resurrection body may serve to manifest the reality of having-been-scarred.[81]

There is a second possibility, however, for understanding how Macrina might be marked by this scar in her resurrected state. Here we return to Gregory's notion that personal identity in the eschaton has more to do with our particular virtues than our physical divisions. Whatever form Macrina's body takes in the resurrection, she will continue to bear the virtue of having-been-scarred by God's gracious healing. This embodied reality shapes who Macrina was, and, insofar as she continues to be Macrina in the eschaton, it will continue to shape her identity forever. She will always have an identity shaped and particularized by the virtue of having-

---

79. Thus, he described her body as already glowing so brightly that "she was resplendent even in the dark robe, divine power having added, as I think, this final grace to the body, so that, as in the vision of my dream, rays actually seemed to shine forth from her beauty" (Gregory of Nyssa, *The Life of Saint Macrina*, trans. Kevin Corrigan [Eugene, Ore.: Wipf & Stock, 2005], 48).

80. Ibid., 47.

81. If correct, this would also provide resources for dealing with disabilities in the eschaton. We will not be disabled, but we will be embodied in ways that manifest/reflect the reality of disability.

been-scarred. In that sense, the physical characteristics of Macrina's pre-resurrection body continue to particularize Macrina's identity even after they have been transformed through her incorporation into Christ.

Drawing on Macrina as an example of how the features of pre-resurrection bodies might continue to shape personal identities in the eschaton, then, it seems entirely consistent with Gregory's christological vision for resurrected humanity to say that the particularities of having-been-biologically-gendered will continue to shape our identities even if biological sexuality has been eliminated in the resurrection. If this is a viable interpretation, then Gregory's understanding of human sexuality in the eschaton involves the following claims:

1. Biological sexuality is nonessential to human nature and is transcended through the christological transformation of humanity.
2. In the unity of humanity in Christ, we overcome the division of sexual differentiation as all humans participate in all of the divine virtues.
3. Nonetheless, we will retain the gender identities entailed by our current embodiment as those who will always have the virtue of having-been-gendered in particular ways.

In this way, Gregory manages to retain a place for human sexuality in the eschaton even as he radically overturns much of what we typically associate with embodied sexuality.

CHRISTOLOGY, SEXUALITY, AND ESCHATOLOGICAL HUMANITY

From what we have seen, Hans Boersma is surely correct when he exclaims, "One of the most striking elements of Gregory's views on gender and virginity is their christological grounding."[82] Gregory offers a theological vision for the human person that is shaped by Christology throughout. He does not discount the reality that the historical humanity of Christ was biologically male, but neither does he see that as decisive for understanding the eschatological *telos* of human nature. Starting with the *imago Dei*, the incarnation, and the resurrection, Gregory argues that at each step we see humanity reshaped and transformed through union with Christ. Although this ultimately requires a strong dose of apophaticism when seeking to understand true humanity as we will experience it

---

82. Boersma, *Embodiment and Virtue in Gregory of Nyssa*, 87.

in the resurrection, Gregory shows how such a christological framework has implications for how we understand the nature of the human person today. Without denigrating or demonizing the material and particularizing features of human nature as we currently experience it, Gregory argues that anything that appears incompatible with the true humanity revealed in his three theological loci must eventually be eliminated or at least *transposed* into a new anthropological key.

Regardless of whether we are inclined to agree, such a christologically shaped anthropology necessarily challenges the modern assumption that biological sexuality is a fundamental feature of real humanity. It allows us to think again about the relationship of sexuality and gender to the essence of a humanity interpreted through the lens of Christology. All three stages of Gregory's christological argument raise questions about the significance of sexuality: the fact that human persons were created to image a God who transcends sexual distinctions, the conviction that in Christ there is neither male nor female, and the hope that in the resurrection we will all "put on Christ" and be joined together as we participate in and manifest the divine virtues forever. Thus, Gregory believes that his christological starting point requires that we bracket out biological sexuality as a nonessential feature of historical humanity.

The fact that Gregory views biological sexuality as "nonessential," however, does not entail the conclusion that it is unimportant. Much of what shapes our identities as human persons is nonessential in the same way. For example, my relationship with my wife is nonessential (I would still have been human without it) yet fundamentally important (it is now an irreplaceable aspect of my particular identity). And Gregory presents biological sexuality in much the same way. Neither does the nonessential nature of biological sexuality mean, for Gregory, the loss of any enduring significance for sexuality in the eschaton. As we have seen, his theology has resources for maintaining that resurrected persons will still be shaped by the material realities of the present body. Just as Macrina will always be marked by having-been-scarred, so I will always be shaped by having-been-male, even as my identity continues to be reshaped and transformed eternally as well. Sarah Coakley thus rightly observes that Gregory has an "eschatologically oriented theory of gender,"[83] though only through an eschatological vision that is thoroughly christological as well.

---

83. Coakley, *Powers and Submissions*, 164.

CHAPTER 2

All Will Be Well

Suffering and Redemption in Julian of Norwich's Cross-Shaped Anthropology

———•———

Sin is necessary, but all will be well, and all will be well,
and every kind of thing will be well.

Julian of Norwich, *Showings*[1]

AFTER LANGUISHING IN RELATIVE OBSCURITY for centuries, Julian of Norwich has received significant attention in recent years, with scholarly editions of her writings in the original Middle English,[2] multiple modernized versions,[3] and several book-length introductions to her life and theology.[4] Describing Julian's significance among English authors, one commenta-

---

1. *Julian of Norwich: Showings*, trans. Edmund Colledge and James Walsh, The Classics of Western Spirituality (New York: Paulist, 1978), 225. All further quotations from *Showings* are from this edition and will be cited within the text by chapter and page number (e.g., 51:267–68).

2. E.g., Edmund Colledge and James Walsh, eds., *A Book of Showings to the Anchoress Julian of Norwich*, 2 vols. (Toronto: Pontifical Institute of Mediaeval Studies, 1978); Nicholas Watson and Jacqueline Jenkins, eds., *The Writings of Julian of Norwich: A Vision Showed to a Devout Woman and A Revelation of Love* (University Park, Pa.: Penn State University Press, 2006).

3. In addition to the Colledge and Walsh translation referenced above, see, e.g., Father John-Julian, *A Lesson of Love: The Revelations of Julian of Norwich* (New York: Walker, 1988); M. L. Del Mastro, ed., *The Revelation of Divine Love in Sixteen Showings Made to Dame Julian of Norwich* (Liguori, Mo.: Triumph, 1994); Elizabeth Spearing, *Revelations of Divine Love (Short and Long Text)* (New York: Penguin, 1998); Simon Parke, ed., *Revelations of Divine Love* (Hove, UK: White Crow Books, 2011).

4. See esp. Joan M. Nuth, *Wisdom's Daughter: The Theology of Julian of Norwich* (New York: Crossroad, 1991); Denise Nowakowski Baker, *Julian of Norwich's Showings: From Vision to Book* (Princeton, N.J.: Princeton University Press, 1994); Sandra J. McEntire, ed., *Julian of Norwich: A Book of Essays* (New York: Garland, 1998); Christopher Abbott, *Julian of Norwich: Autobiography and Theology*, Studies in Medieval Mysticism (Cambridge: D. S. Brewer, 1999); Grace Jantzen, *Julian of Norwich: Mystic and Theologian*, new ed. (New York: Paulist, 2000); Denys Turner, *Julian of Norwich, Theologian* (New Haven, Conn.: Yale University Press, 2011).

tor states that the literature dedicated to Julian "far outstrips that of any other religious or, with the exception of Chaucer, secular writer from the fourteenth century."[5] And this despite the fact that Julian's only known work, A Book of Showings to the Anchoress Julian of Norwich (hereafter Showings), has been described by one scholar as "by far the most profound and difficult of all mediaeval English spiritual writings."[6]

For our purposes, though, Julian's significance derives from her unique approach to understanding the human person, one that takes as its point of departure a series of visions Julian received of the crucified Messiah. As a young woman, Julian prayed that she might receive "a bodily sight, in which I might have more knowledge of our saviour's bodily pains" (2:178), a prayer that was eventually fulfilled when she received a series of thirteen "showings" while suffering from a life-threatening illness.[7] It is in Julian's reflections on these revelations that we find her unique perspective on how Christology informs what it means to be human. According to her, we only come to understand humanity rightly by gazing intently at the humanity of Christ revealed on the cross. There we see that our true essence, the "substance" of the human person, has been firmly grounded in Christ, thoroughly enveloped in divine love, and made so secure that no sin or evil can possibly threaten it. To be human is to be inseparably united in Christ with the very being of God himself.

Although this might lead one to believe that Julian offers an overly optimistic picture of humanity, one that neglects the lived experiences of real humans in a broken world, Julian actually demonstrates a keen interest in the reality of pain and suffering, as well as how we must understand those tragic realities in light of the crucified Messiah. Indeed, for Julian, a theology that begins with the cross of Christ *must* take seriously the reality of sin and suffering in the world. Although she will ultimately present an anthropology of hope, one that looks forward to

---

5. Frederick C. Bauerschmidt, "Order, Freedom, and 'Kindness': Julian of Norwich on the Edge of Modernity," *Theology Today* 60, no. 1 (2003): 63.

6. Colledge and Walsh, eds., *Julian of Norwich: Showings*, 22. Grace Jantzen notes that this results at least partly from "the astonishingly complex" structure of *Showings*, with each vision informing the others and Julian constantly moving back and forth between issues to clarify or qualify issues addressed elsewhere (Jantzen, *Julian of Norwich*, 89).

7. The fact that these visions came during a period of intense illness might well lead one to wonder about the reliability of the visions themselves. Julian herself struggled with this, confessing at one point to "a man of religion" that she thought she had been "raving" (66:310). In the end, though, Julian concluded that her visions, and the corresponding insights, were legitimate to the extent that they lead to the love of God and the well-being of other Christians (9:191).

the day in which God will both *redeem* humanity and *explain* the reason for all the pain and suffering his people have experienced, Julian refuses to use this as a way of avoiding the very real and difficult questions that revolve around the problem of evil.

The first part of our study focuses on what it means for Julian to develop a christological anthropology around her visions of the crucified Messiah. In what way can such visionary experiences truly ground a christological understanding of the human person? The second part of the study presses into Julian's understanding of sin and suffering, using this as an opportunity to reflect on the extent to which christological anthropologies can avoid the temptation to become abstract reflections on "ideal" humanity and instead engage the real, and often painful, experiences of everyday humans.

"READING" THE CRUCIFIED CHRIST: JULIAN'S THEOLOGICAL METHOD

Anyone reading *Showings* for the first time will be immediately struck by the vivid and even gruesome depictions of the crucified Christ, many of which fixated on Christ's blood that flowed freely from his many wounds.[8] At other times she saw details of Christ's suffering—for example, the "contempt, foul spitting, buffeting, and many long-drawn pains" (10:193)—even receiving an explicit vision of Christ's dying and desiccated body (16:206). Although these descriptions are particularly prominent in the early chapters, the whole work is thoroughly shaped by these images of Christ's crucified body in all its painful brokenness.[9]

The crucified Messiah thus serves as the inescapable focus of Julian's theological reflections. Indeed, this is so critical for Julian that she refuses to countenance any possibility that she might *begin* by focusing on the broken humanity of Jesus, only to turn her attention later to loftier and more heavenly truths (19:211–212). As Denys Turner notes, "The Cross for Julian is no mere topos of her Revelation. It is not even as little as its most important topos. It is the embodiment of her theological epistemology as such; for Julian theological knowledge itself is cruciform."[10]

---

8. E.g., 3:181; 10:193; 12:200. Indeed, the fourth vision contains so much blood that Julian concludes, "If it had in fact and in substance been happening there, the bed and everything all around it would have been soaked in blood" (12:200).

9. It is important to note that Julian did not think she was viewing the crucifixion itself, but her "visionary insight ... into the Passion's implications" (Barry Windeatt, "Julian's Second Thoughts: The Long Text Tradition," in *A Companion to Julian of Norwich*, ed. Liz Herbert McAvoy [Cambridge: D. S. Brewer, 2008], 102).

10. Turner, *Julian of Norwich*, 22.

Nonetheless, it would be overly simplistic to suggest that *Showings* is merely a record of what Julian saw during her visionary experiences. Indeed, Julian herself distinguishes between three modes of "revelation" that take place in the *Showings*: "by bodily vision and by words formed in my understanding and by spiritual vision" (9:192). The "bodily vision" refers to the concrete images that she saw during the vision, most often, as we have seen, of Christ's suffering body. But these visions were often accompanied by "words formed in my understanding," which were interpretive insights given to Julian that allowed her to understand more of the theological significance of the visions. In other words, Julian received more than mere images in these visions, but often received instruction as to how these visions might properly be understood. To these was added the "spiritual vision," which borders on a mystical insight that transcends complete understanding.[11] And this last element is the one Julian found the most difficult to convey through her written account, acknowledging that she "may not and cannot show the spiritual visions as plainly and fully as I should wish" (9:192). Julian's theological methodology thus required more than simply writing down what she observed in her visions and reflecting on its theological significance. The visions themselves comprise a complex interweaving of visual, intellectual, and mystical elements that must be accounted for in any attempt to understand her theology.[12]

At the same time, we must not downplay the importance of Julian's own attempts to understand and articulate the significance of her visions. Indeed, it is not even possible to distinguish neatly between the visions and Julian's interpretations of them. If the visions comprise the "text" of Julian's theology, then it shares in the same "fundamental interpretive ambiguity and indeterminacy of any text; it must be interpreted."[13]

---

11. As Kevin Magill argues, though, Julian does not present any of her visionary experiences as ineffable, and thus incommunicable, "mystic" experiences. Although she struggles to understand and articulate the full meaning of her visions in places, she clearly thinks that they *can* be understood and talked about. Magill thus argues that Julian qualifies as a "visionary" but not a "mystic" (Kevin J. Magill, *Julian of Norwich: Mystic or Visionary?* [New York: Routledge, 2006]).

12. According to Nicholas Watson, Julian's visions thus involve "a disparate series of glimpses of Christ's Passion, strung like beads along her life-saving gaze at a crucifix, and interspersed with other, more abstract sights, as well as with a few pregnant words passed from Christ to her and sometimes back again" (Nicholas Watson, "The Trinitarian Hermeneutic of Julian of Norwich's *Revelation of Love*," in *Julian of Norwich: A Book of Essays*, ed. Sandra J. McEntire [New York: Garland, 1998], 84).

13. Frederick C. Bauerschmidt, "Julian of Norwich—Incorporated," *Modern Theology* 13, no. 1 (1997): 85.

Comparing the short version of the text, which she compiled shortly after receiving her visions, and the long version written nearly twenty years later, we can see the extent to which Julian deepened and elaborated her account as she sought to understand more clearly the significance of what she experienced.[14] Julian was not merely describing her experiences. Instead, she was using them constructively to develop and deepen her understanding of God and his creation.[15] Put simply, Julian was a theologian.

Thus, *Showings* is far more than a mere summary of sixteen visions about the crucifixion. It includes a complex interweaving of the visual images themselves, the deeper revelatory significance of these visions given to Julian at that same time, and Julian's own extended reflections on the theological significance of these visions and how they relate to the Christian life in general.[16] For Julian, then, Christ's crucified body is the essential center of theological reflection, but one that unfolds rapidly into a broad vision that encompasses the entire range of human existence.

AN ONTOLOGY OF LOVE: THE REAL SUBSTANCE OF THE HUMAN

Having seen that Julian built her theology on the basis of her crucicentric methodology, we can move on to consider what this means for her theological anthropology. And she was quite clear that such an approach requires a robustly christological understanding of the human person.[17]

---

14. See esp. Watson, "Trinitarian Hermeneutic." According to Colledge and Walsh, "The whole tone and temper" of the text changed, moving from the cautious apprehension of the short text to the long text in which Julian is "serene, balanced and at peace with herself" (Edmund Colledge and James Walsh, eds., *A Book of Showings to the Anchoress Julian of Norwich*, vol. 1 [Toronto: Pontifical Institute of Mediaeval Studies, 1978], 80). Jantzen similarly describes the later Julian as "more intellectually confident" (Jantzen, *Julian of Norwich*, 175). Others have argued that the differences have been overemphasized and that we need to pay more attention to the short text (see esp. Nicholas Watson, "The Composition of Julian of Norwich's *Revelation of Love*," *Speculum* 68, no. 3 [1993]: 637–83; Windeatt, "Julian's Second Thoughts: The Long Text Tradition").

15. As Watson explains elsewhere, the long text is "a full-scale reworking" of the short text, and it is "part expansion, part commentary, part theological *summa*" (Carolyn Dinshaw, David Wallace, and Nicholas Watson, eds., "Julian of Norwich," in *The Cambridge Companion to Medieval Women's Writing* [New York: Cambridge University Press, 2003], 213).

16. To assess her own reflections, Julian relies on a fairly standard set of theological sources: reason, the traditional teachings of the church, and the inward work of the Spirit (80:335).

17. Grace Jantzen thus argues that Julian's theology in general is Christocentric, "if by this is meant that a true understanding of Christ gives a true understanding of all other doctrines. In him divine and human nature are united; in him human wholeness is perfected, and in him the entire Trinity is comprehended" (*Julian of Norwich*, 109).

"Love Was His Meaning"

In one important sense, the cross itself is not the actual center of Julian's theology. Instead, Julian views the cross primarily as the supreme demonstration of divine love. Although the cross is the irreplaceable focus of Julian's theology, its primary role is to direct our attention toward the one who acted on the cross and the love demonstrated in that act. This is why, as Grace Jantzen points out, "She did not say that she had had a revelation of the passion of Christ; she says, 'This is a revelation of *love* which Jesus Christ ... made in sixteen showings'."[18] In the very first chapter we hear that this will be "a revelation of love" (1:175), and "all the revelations which follow are founded and connected" in the revelation of divine love that we see in the crucified Messiah (1:175). The concluding chapter returned to this theme, making it clear that this has remained her focus throughout: "What, do you wish to know your Lord's meaning in this thing? Know it well, love was his meaning. Who reveals it to you? Love. What did he reveal to you? Love. Why does he reveal it to you? For love. Remain in this, and you will know more of the same. But you will never know different, without end" (86:342). Julian's crucicentric theology, then, is inescapably a theology of love, the love displayed on the cross.

Critical for Julian's theology, though, is the Trinitarian shape of the love revealed on the cross. Since Jesus was "both God and man," Julian contends, "where Jesus appears the blessed Trinity is understood" (4:181). In other words, as Bauerschmidt points out, "The corporeal, suffering humanity of Jesus, in all its categorical particularity, is not simply a symbolic wrapping around an ineffable, transcendental experience, but is the actual appearance in history of the triune life of God, the mutual indwelling love of Father, Son, and Spirit."[19] Indeed, Denys Turner argues that it is in "that connection between the Cross and the Trinity alone that the theological unity of Julian's work is to be found."[20] Thus, although the first half of *Showings* is more explicitly christological, with the focus shifting to the Trinity in the second half, Julian would not have recognized any significant distinction between those two foci. For her, a christocentric approach to theology is always thoroughly Trinitarian; and any Trinitarian theology will be necessarily christocentric.

---

18. Ibid., 91. See 1:175.

19. Bauerschmidt, "Julian of Norwich," 84.

20. Turner, *Julian of Norwich,* 22–23. He thus contends that Julian's theology is aptly characterized as a *theologia crucis* (ibid., 133).

At first glance, this declaration that the cross reveals the wondrous love of God hardly sounds groundbreaking or revolutionary. Indeed, it borders on the pedantic. For Julian, though, the cruciform love of God remains one of the most profound mysteries of the universe. How can it be that the infinite God of the universe would deign to suffer and die for human persons? And in light of this tremendous and terrifying reality, what must we conclude about the nature of both God and those same human persons? Who are we that God should love us in this way? Wrestling with these questions leads Julian to the conclusion that we need to view "love" itself as an ontological reality.

Seeing the eternal Son joined to a suffering and dying humanity on the cross, along with the implication that in some way the entire Trinity has participated in this kind of self-sacrificing love for the sake of creation,[21] has radical implications for how Julian understands the essence of creation. In one famous scene, Julian saw all of creation as "something small, no bigger than a hazelnut, lying in the palm of my hand" (5:183), and she was amazed by the fact that something so small and insignificant could possibly remain in existence. It was revealed to her that it "lasts and always will because God loves it; and thus everything has being through the love of God" (5:183). Thus, she contends that God's love is the "ground," "substance," "essence," or "nature" of creation itself since God is "the true Father and the true Mother of natures" (62:302).

When Julian says that "everything has being through the love of God," though, she has in mind more than the notion that God sustains all things in existence because of his fondness for creation. Instead, Julian views love as more of an ontological reality than a psychological state.[22] She certainly thinks this is true of the Trinity itself, where each person of the Trinity has his being in virtue of the constitutive relations shared with the other persons. What is surprising, though, is that all of creation similarly finds its being in this same triune love. At one point, Julian distinguishes between an "uncreated charity," which "is God," and a "created charity" which is "our soul in God" (84:341). Julian thus sees charity as essential to both divine and human being, differentiating them exclusively in terms of *how* they have their being rather than *what* fundamentally grounds their

---

21. As Julian clearly affirms, "All the Trinity worked in Christ's Passion" (23:219). But she still maintains the uniqueness of the Son's role in that "only the virgin's Son suffered" (ibid.).

22. Brant Pelphrey, "Leaving the Womb of Christ: Love, Doomsday, and Space/Time in Julian of Norwich and Eastern Orthodox Mysticism," in *Julian of Norwich: A Book of Essays*, ed. Sandra J. McEntire (New York: Garland, 1998), 292.

existence. Elsewhere, Julian expresses the same idea using the language of goodness. According to Julian, God's goodness "fills all his creatures ... and endlessly overflows in them" (5:184). God's creatures are "clad and enclosed in the goodness of God" (6:186) such that God simply is "nature's substance" (56:290). And it is important to notice here, as Jantzen does, that "Julian does not say merely that God is the *cause* of everything that is good, or that the goodness it has is *from* God: she makes a much stronger identification. God *is* everything good; its goodness *is* God."[23] Thus, when Julian says that created things are grounded in God's love, she is articulating the long-standing notion that created things do not have an existence of their own; instead, they only exist insofar as they participate in the being of God, which is itself constituted by love.[24]

Although all created things are included in this ontology of love, Julian particularly emphasizes the unique status of the human person. The human soul is the "noblest thing" made by God (53:284), and is "so wholly united to God ... that between God and our soul nothing can interpose" (46:259). Indeed, the union of divine and human established by divine love is so close that Julian sees "no difference between God and our substance, but as it were, all God" (54:285).[25] As startling as this declaration of the soul's identity with God might be, Jantzen rightly notes that "Julian is here affirming the same position as that held by many another mystic."[26] Like those other medieval thinkers, Julian quickly emphasizes that this framework does not eliminate *every* distinction between Creator and creature, affirming that "God is God, and our substance is a creature in God" (54:285). Beyond this, though, human nature is completely enveloped by divine love such that "our nature is wholly in God" (57:291).

---

23. Jantzen, *Julian of Norwich*, 129.

24. See Pelphrey, "Leaving the Womb of Christ." This does not mean, however, that Julian's theology entails some form of pantheism. Although Julian clearly affirms that God is the substance of everything that exists, she also makes clear distinctions between created and uncreated being, and it also seems she would have rejected any sense in which creation was a necessary outflow of the divine being.

25. For a good discussion of this passage, see Denys Turner, *The Darkness of God: Negativity in Christian Mysticism* (New York: Cambridge University Press, 1998), 159–62. According to Turner, Julian's language cannot capture adequately the distinction between created and uncreated being, "not because there is none but because the gulf is too wide" (161).

26. Jantzen, *Julian of Norwich*, 140.

The Lord, the Servant, and the Fall

Julian's ontology of love thus grounds the being of humanity in the eternal love of the triune God. Although she presents this as something that has shaped all creation from the beginning, her famous allegory of the lord and the servant makes it clear that, for humans at least, this is an explicitly christological reality. Indeed, this allegory plays such a central role in Julian's argument that it has been described as "the hinge on which the long text . . . pivots,"[27] the "crux of the whole book and the key to understanding it."[28]

In this part of Julian's vision, she saw a loving and kind lord sending his servant on an errand. The servant is so faithful and dedicated that he quickly rushes off to do his lord's will. Unfortunately, he "falls into a dell and is greatly injured" (51:267). Even more tragically, the servant is so wracked by pain that he cannot turn his face "to look on his loving lord, who was very close to him, in whom is all consolation" (51:267). Through it all, though, Julian can find no fault in the servant. His fall is presented entirely as an accident, a consequence of rushing so eagerly to do the will of his lord.

Julian saw this as the most complex and challenging of all her visions, one that she did not include in the short version of the text, waiting until after twenty years of "inward instruction" before she felt ready to explain its meaning (51:270). And her consternation stemmed from her conviction that the servant symbolized Adam and his fall in the Garden, "and yet at the same time . . . I saw many different characteristics which could in no way be attributed to Adam" (51:269). How could this allegory describe Adam's fall into sin, which the Bible portrays as stemming from Adam's willful disobedience, when the allegory so clearly presents the servant as one who fell through eagerness to obey? Correspondingly, where is the blame and guilt that is supposed to follow from Adam's sin? Where is God's legitimate wrath toward his unfaithful creatures, and the judgment that inevitably accompanies such a transgression? Since this allegory seemed contrary to so many of the clear teachings of church tradition, Julian wrestled with its implications for years.

Ultimately, Julian found the answer in the realization that the allegory has a double significance: the servant was both Adam *and* Christ:

---

27. Bauerschmidt, "Julian of Norwich," 90.

28. Jantzen, *Julian of Norwich*, 149. The allegory and Julian's explanation comprise the entirety of chapter 51.

"In the servant is comprehended the second person of the Trinity, and in the servant is comprehended Adam, that is to say all men" (51:274). On the one hand, then, the servant represents Adam and his fall into the painfully debilitating condition of sin: "This man was injured in his powers and made most feeble" and although "his will was preserved in God's sight," the servant "was blinded and hindered from knowing this will" (51:270). Thus, Adam is the servant lying in the ditch, feeble and hurting, unable to turn and see the gracious, consoling face of God. His substance remains secure in God's love, but he can no longer see that truth. Even more, Julian recognizes that this is true of all humans. Although the vision focuses on a single servant, Julian sees in this very singularity the corporate reality of all humanity: "For in the sight of God all men are one man, and one man is all men" (51:270). She later affirms that "the love of God creates in us such a unity that when it is truly seen, no man can separate himself from another" (65:309). Thus, the servant allegory presents all humanity as rushing eagerly to do God's will and falling headlong into its currently sinful state.

During Julian's twenty years of reflection, though, she came to realize that interpreting the allegory properly requires seeing it as a reference to the incarnate Son as well. In the allegory we see both the fall of Adam "from life to death, into the valley of this wretched world" (51:274) *and* the "fall" of the Son, not into sin, but "into the valley of the womb of the maiden" (51:275). Although these two events are obviously far removed in time, from God's eternal perspective the two are one. In the eagerness of the servant, then, we see the faithful obedience of the Son as he hurries off to save God's creatures. And in the painful state of the servant in the ditch, we see the Son falling into our material condition and experiencing the pains of living and dying in this fallen world.[29]

For Julian, though, the falling of Adam and the Son share a more intimate union than just that of two temporally disconnected events viewed from the same eternal perspective. As she explains, the humanity of Jesus is the "true Adam," and this is what has been intimately joined to the divine nature in Jesus Christ (51:274). Thus, "When Adam fell, God's Son fell" specifically because "the union which was made in heaven" was such that "God's Son could not be separated from Adam" (ibid.).

---

29. We will see in the next section, though, that there is a sense in which the "godly will" that remains unfallen in the human person can be viewed as eagerly obedient to the will of the Father.

Consequently, there is some kind of union between the eternal Son and the human nature that logically *precedes* his "fall" into the incarnation. Understanding this union begins with returning to Julian's ontology of love. Since the love of God that grounds human nature is eternal, there is a sense in which humanity "has been known and loved in God's prescience without beginning in his righteous intent" (53:283). "God never *began* to love mankind" (ibid.) because God's love is as eternal as God himself.[30] As Turner explains, "We are eternally thought before we are made; we are eternally loved as we are thought; and God's thought and love for us are God."[31] The fundamental unity between humanity and God is therefore grounded in the eternality of divine love.

This unity finds its supreme historical expression in the incarnation, but in such a way that it also includes humanity itself in this union with the divine. In Jesus, humanity was intimately united to God "by a knot so subtle and so mighty" such that it became "endlessly holy" (53:284). This union has significance for all human persons because "all the souls which will be saved in heaven without end are knit in this knot, and united in this union, and made holy in this holiness" (ibid). Thus, we are somehow included in the uniting of Jesus' human soul to the divine essence such that "where the blessed soul of Christ is, there is the substance of all the souls which will be saved by Christ" (54:285). The incarnation demonstrates that true humanity involves human persons united with the divine being, and all of this revolves around the love of the Trinity. Consequently, Jesus Christ is the one in whom all of God's people have their being. The Son "wanted to be the foundation and the head of this fair nature" that includes all human persons, and he is thus the one "out of whom we have all come, in whom we are all enclosed, into whom we shall all go" (53:283).[32]

---

30. Emphasis added.

31. Turner, *Julian of Norwich*, 173.

32. Julian thus emphasized to a remarkable extent the idea that Christ is the "mother" of humanity, offering an extended reflection on this image in chapters 57 through 60. For additional information on this aspect of Julian's theology, see Caroline Walker Bynum, *Jesus as Mother: Studies in the Spirituality of the High Middle Ages* (Berkeley: University of California, 1982); Brant Pelphrey, *Christ Our Mother: Julian of Norwich*, Way of the Christian Mystics (Wilmington, Del.: Michael Glazier, 1989); Margaret Ann Palliser, *Christ, Our Mother of Mercy: Divine Mercy and Compassion in the Theology of the "Shewings" of Julian of Norwich* (New York: Walter de Gruyter, 1992); Marilyn McCord Adams, "Julian of Norwich on the Tender Loving Care of Mother Jesus" in *Our Knowledge of God* (Dordrecht, Netherlands: Kluwer, 1992), 197–213; Kerry Dearborn, "The Crucified Christ as the Motherly God: The Theology of Julian of Norwich," *Scottish Journal of Theology* 55, no. 3 (2002): 283–302.

One of the key functions of the servant allegory, then, is to establish the fundamental unity of human persons in Jesus Christ. Although Adam has a role to play in anthropology, Julian's understanding of the human person is far more christological than protological. And this takes us at least some distance toward resolving the nagging features of the allegory. The eagerness of the servant and the lack of any blame placed upon him after his "fall," refer partly to the eagerness and blamelessness of the Son who is the head and source of all humanity.

However, this still does not tell the entire story. If this were all Julian has in mind, we would not have a parable with a truly "double" aspect. Instead, the allegory would simply focus on Jesus as the true and faithful servant. What about the other aspect? For Julian, there is an important sense in which the allegory teaches truths about other human persons as well. Adam and all other humans are in some way "eager" to do God's will and "blameless" even after our fall into the tragic condition of sin. We now turn to understanding that claim and its significance for Julian's theological anthropology.

Eager and Blameless

To Julian's great astonishment, then, she saw God "showing no more blame to us than if we were as pure and holy as the angels are in heaven" (50:266). Despite our very real fall into a sinful condition that is clearly contrary to God's desire for his creatures, he still does not look on us with any blame, wrath, or judgment. Indeed, according to Julian, "our Lord was never angry, and never will be" (46:259). Julian was well aware that such a conclusion runs contrary both to the official teachings of the church and to our own existential experiences of being sinful and guilty. She thus wrestled extensively with what it could mean to say that even sinful humans are blameless before God. Her response involves seeing that even fallen humans are sheltered in the divine love.

The reason God will never be angry is that "he *cannot* be angry" (49:263, emphasis added). This is because "our life is all founded and rooted in love, and without love we cannot live" (ibid.). Remember that Julian viewed love more as an ontological category in which all things find their being in relationship than a psychological state expressing some kind of divine emotion toward creation. The same appears to hold true for her understanding of anger. For Julian, *anger* denotes primarily a state of being in which two parties have become fundamentally alienated from each other and only secondarily the affective condition of the two parties that results from this separation. For God to be angry in this ontological sense would be for him to somehow become alienated from a creation that can only exist insofar as it continually participates in God's love. But this is simply impossible for a God who is himself constituted in the love of the three persons and who freely unites himself to humanity in Jesus. Since God's own being is fundamentally constituted by friendship, he cannot simultaneously be the kind of God who would reject friendship and condemn his creation to non-being, which would be the inevitable consequence of being cut off from love (49:264). Indeed, the very fact that we still exist serves to demonstrate the fact that God is not angry with us: "For truly, as I see it, if God could be angry for any time, we should neither have life nor place nor being" (ibid.). Instead, we have an "endless friendship" with God that "protects us when we sin so that we do not perish" (ibid.). Both the incarnation and the crucifixion similarly declare the enduring nature of this friendship. Since we are united with Christ, and since he took all the wounds of humanity to himself, God does not, indeed *cannot*, assign any more blame to us than he would to his own Son (51:275). "In this endless love man's soul is kept whole" (53:284).

This provides the necessary context for understanding Julian's claim that there is a "godly will" in the human person which "is so good that it can never will evil, but always constantly it wills good and it does good in the sight of God" (53:282). Just as the true substance of the human person is sheltered by God's love, sustained by the unbreakable relationship God establishes with his creatures, so there is a true will of the human person, one that continues to desire what God desires regardless of what we see and experience on the surface. That godly will corresponds to the "eagerness" of the servant rushing to do the will of the beloved lord, and it continues to characterize our deepest desires even now.

All of this, of course, stands in sharp tension to humanity as we actually see and experience it. And Julian is well aware that any adequate anthropology needs to address the reality of human pain, brokenness, and guilt, those things that correspond to the injuries of the servant lying in the ditch. Although we remain God's creatures, and our deepest selves are therefore sheltered in God's love, that does not diminish the fact that we lie broken in the ditch, wracked with pain and unable to see God's compassionate face. For Julian, then, postlapsarian humanity is characterized by "fundamental cleavage within the self" between our true humanity and the humanity that we actually experience.[33]

---

33. Bauerschmidt, "Julian of Norwich," 87.

She explains this cleavage by making a distinction between two aspects of the human soul: "we are double by God's creating, that is to say substantial and sensual" (58:294). *Substance* refers to the higher part of the soul that exists in perfect union with God, while *sensuality* denotes the lower part of the soul, that which is "the soul in contact with the body and affected by the vagaries of time and space."[34] Both of those are part of the created nature of the human person, and thus sensuality itself is not a consequence of the fall.[35] Instead, the human person was always intended to exist with substance and sensuality functioning in complete harmony along with the body as a psychosomatic unity. The entrance of sin disrupts this harmony, destroying the peace that was God's creational plan for human persons. "And so in our substance we are full and in our sensuality we are lacking" (57:291).

According to this account, we have to view the condition of humanity from two perspectives. On the one hand, our *substance* remains unfallen and unblemished, united to God in Christ. And this is the basis for Julian's claim that God "puts away all our blame, and regards us with pity and compassion as innocent and guiltless children" (28:227). From another perspective, though, we see that our *sensuality* has become disrupted by sin, throwing our lives into the pain and confusion that necessarily results. We thus condemn ourselves as guilty, discerning that our sins "deserve" the corresponding pains (ibid.). Both perspectives are legitimate, and express judgments on different aspects of postlapsarian humanity.[36]

Julian's theology thus retains a strong emphasis on the significance of sin and its devastating impact on humanity, while still affirming that the true core of the human person remains at one with God and desires to do his will. Sin primarily involves the pain that results from this cleavage. Some might wonder at this point whether Julian's theology entails some form of universalism.[37] And Julian herself recognized that her visions

---

34. Joan M. Nuth, "Two Medieval Soteriologies: Anselm of Canterbury and Julian of Norwich," *Theological Studies* 53, no. 4 (1992): 633.

35. It is important to note that Julian's substance/sensuality distinction is not the same as the body/soul distinction. For Julian, both substance and sensuality together comprise the "one soul" of the human person (55:288). Sensuality, though, is the part of the soul that interacts with the person's bodily nature.

36. Thus, "God judges us in our natural substance, which is always kept one in him, whole and safe, without end; and this judgment is out of his justice. And man judges us in our changeable sensuality, which now seems one thing and now another, as it derives from parts and presents an external appearance" (45:256).

37. Those arguing that Julian's theology suggests some of universalism include Clifton

pressed in this direction, leading her to wonder how her visions could be consistent with the traditional teachings of the church on the reality of hell.[38] However, Julian consistently affirms her intention of remaining faithful to the church's teachings on this issue, regularly stating that her emphasis on the blamelessness and fundamental purity of the soul applied primarily to "those who will be saved" (9:192).[39] And in at least a few places, she clearly affirms the existence of a hell and the possibility that some will end up there.[40] Although she clearly hopes that the circle of those joined to Christ will be broader than it might appear, she refuses to speak dogmatically on the issue.[41]

Still, the issue of universalism presses us toward the questions that we will address in the next part of this chapter. Given her strong emphasis on God's love pervading and grounding the entire universe in such a way that it seems almost impossible for anything to disrupt that relationship, does Julian's theology provide an adequate framework for under-

---

Wolters, "Introduction," in *Revelations of Divine Love* (London: Penguin, 1966), 36; Nuth, "Two Medieval Soteriologies," 192; Spearing, *Revelations of Divine Love (Short and Long Text)*, xxv; Nicholas Watson and Jacqueline Jenkins, eds., *The Writings of Julian of Norwich*: A Vision Showed to a Devout Woman *and* A Revelation of Love (University Park, Pa.: Penn State University Press, 2006), 92. But others rightly point out that Julian's intentionally guarded language suggests caution on this point. (e.g., Reneé Neu Watkins, "Two Women Visionaries and Death: Catherine of Siena and Julian of Norwich," *Numen* 30, no. 2 [1983]: 643; Jantzen, *Julian of Norwich*, 178–79; Turner, *Julian of Norwich*, 103–9). Bauerschmidt probably comes closest to the truth when he affirms an "impulse toward universal salvation" in Julian's theology as well as a clear rejection of universalism as a certainty ("Julian of Norwich," 96).

38. See esp. 32:233; 33:234.

39. See also 52:284; 54:285. Sandra McEntire contends that we need to understand Julian's avowals of orthodoxy as "a strategy, or a screen" designed to protect her teachings, which lie on "the margins of heterodoxy," from the condemnations of the church ("The Likeness of God and the Restoration of Humanity in Julian of Norwich's *Showings*," in *Julian of Norwich: A Book of Essays*, ed. Sandra J. McEntire [New York: Garland, 1998], 25; for a similar conclusion, see Abram Van Engen, "Shifting Perspectives: Sin and Salvation in Julian's *A Revelation of Love*," *Literature and Theology* 23, no. 1 [2009]: 1–17). Although we certainly need to be sensitive to the difficulties of writing theology as a woman in medieval England, we should also be careful about suggesting that we can confidently extract Julian's intentions from the text, particularly when they run contrary to the grain of the text itself.

40. See esp. 16:209; 33:234.

41. The hopeful aspects of Julian's views on the salvation of all humans come out most clearly in chapter 32. After wondering about the fate of those "who die out of the faith of Holy Church" and how it could be possible that "every kind of thing should be well" if they are damned for eternity, Julian receives the answer: "What is impossible to you is not impossible to me. I shall preserve my word in everything, and I shall make everything well" (32:233). Julian never hears exactly what this possibility might be, but many interpret her on this point as suggesting at least an openness to universal salvation.

standing the very real brokenness that is part of everyday humanity? Or does she offer an overly optimistic and idealist view of the human person that offers little help to those seeking to understand what it means to be human in the real world?

IT JUST FITS: LOCATING SIN IN A LOVE-SHAPED WORLD

Julian's anthropological methodology thus begins by reflecting on the marvelous revelation of divine love that we see in the cross. More than just the self-giving sacrifice of one human for the well-being of others, the cross manifests God's intimate love for creation in general, that which establishes the being of all creatures, and his special care and concern for human persons in particular. On the cross, we see that God not only takes human nature into intimate union with himself, but that God's love also protects and preserves humanity, looking upon fallen humans with care and compassion rather than blame and anger. Thus, God's love envelops all of creation so that no matter how difficult things may appear from a creaturely perspective, we know that "all will be well" (27:225).

Yet this very assurance raises some of the most difficult questions in Julian's theology. If God is all goodness, if he is present in all things, and if he truly loves and protects his creation to the extent that Julian's revelation suggests, what sense can we make of all the sin and suffering we see in the world around us? How can God be this intimately joined to his creation and still permit the kinds of evil we witness on a daily basis? Such questions bring us to the second half of this study, as we seek to understand what resources Julian's christological anthropology has for understanding humanity as it actually exists in a broken world.

The Reality and Mystery of Suffering

We must first recognize that Julian herself was no stranger to misery. She was no ivory tower theologian reflecting on human misery from the safety of her study. Indeed, one of the most striking features of Julian's *Showings* is that she experienced these visions in the midst of great personal pain and suffering. She describes the first vision as coming when "God sent me a bodily sickness in which I lay for three days and three nights," a sickness so severe that on the third night she "received all the rites of Holy Church, and did not expect to live until day" (3:179). Julian would have also experienced all the difficulties of living in medieval Norwich, not the least of which would have included the deprivations of medieval warfare and the ravages of the plague. As Veronica Rolf describes, "Life expectancy was short at best in the Middle Ages, and the fear of death had always been high; the plague magnified that fear a thousandfold. Daily life became even more morbid, a constant waiting for the sword of death to strike. There was a marked increase in pilgrimages to saints' tombs, days of fasting and penance, attendance at Mass, promises made to patron saints and town protectors."[42] Consequently, medieval thinkers like Julian well understood the significance of coming to terms with death and suffering rather than pretending that all was well in the world.

In addition to her personal experiences with misery, Julian's theological method virtually requires her to wrestle with sin and suffering. As Grace Jantzen notes, "If Christian belief takes its point of departure from the cross of Christ, as Julian emphasized, then it is theology which must be done 'within earshot of the dying cry of Jesus.'"[43] Indeed, if the cross is necessary for understanding of human existence, then we must wrestle with the fact that pain and suffering are normative human experiences. Suffering simply is part of the human condition as we now know it. Although Julian's response to sin and suffering will emphasize the hope that sin and suffering will eventually be redeemed and overcome, she never downplays the reality of such suffering in our present experience.

For Julian, then, a Christian vision of the human person must include human suffering. Neither her personal experience nor her cross-centered methodology will allow her to lose sight of our concrete circumstances in search of an understanding of true humanity. That is precisely why sin and suffering constitute such a problem in Julian's theology. Having emphasized *both* that God is intimately involved in creation *and* that creation as we know it is wracked by sin and suffering, Julian found herself backed into a difficult corner: "it seemed to me that if there had been no sin, we should all have been pure and as like our Lord as he created us. And so in my folly before this time I often wondered why, through the great prescient wisdom of God, the beginning of sin was not prevented. For then it seemed to me that all would have been well" (27:224). As Jantzen suggests, this is in many ways "the central question of the book."[44] Yet it remained one that Julian found almost impossible to answer. "Ah, good Lord, how could all things be well, because of the

---

42. Veronica Mary Rolf, *Julian's Gospel: Illuminating the Life and Revelations of Julian of Norwich* (Maryknoll, N.Y.: Orbis, 2013), 80.

43. Jantzen, *Julian of Norwich*, 168.

44. Ibid., 167.

great harm which has come through sin to your creatures? And here I wished, so far as I dared, for some plainer explanation through which I might be at ease about this matter" (29:227).

At one level, the only answer Julian received is that the resolution to this problem is a mystery that will not be unveiled before the eschaton. There remained "some great thing which was to come" in which God will make everything right (36:239), but "what the deed will be and how it will be performed is unknown to every creature who is inferior to Christ, and it will be until the deed is done" (32:232). At another point Julian "saw hidden in God an exalted and wonderful mystery, which he will make plain and we shall know in heaven," and this is the mystery of "why he allowed sin to come" (27:226). For now, though, such mysteries remain a part of God's "privy counsel," and it is only fitting for God's servants "out of obedience and respect not to wish to know his counsel" (30:228).

From one perspective, then, Julian simply held fast to God's promise that "all will be well." *How* all will be well, she could not conceive; *that* all will be well she took as the firm promise of God, a God who has consistently demonstrated his unshakeable love for creation. A God who would suffer and die for his creation is a God who can be trusted to make everything right. Thus, "we ought to rejoice in him for everything which he reveals and for everything which he conceals; and if we do so, willingly and meekly, we shall find great comfort in it, and we shall have endless thanks from him for it" (36:239).

With this answer in hand, we might expect that Julian would have stopped wrestling with the question entirely. After all, she had clearly been told not to pry into God's "privy counsel" and to accept "willingly and meekly" the fact that the resolution to this problem will not be given until the eschaton. Yet that is precisely what Julian did *not* do. Indeed, the differences between the short and long texts indicate that much of Julian's theological development in the twenty-year interim was spent wrestling with precisely this issue.[45] Even within the text, Julian continues to ask about the reason for sin's existence despite having been told not to pry into such mysteries. So either Julian was willfully disobedient to the instruction she received, something that would run contrary to the entire grain of *Showings*, or she did not see these statements as a prohibition on *any* kind of inquiry into mystery. Jantzen helpfully suggests that the explanation may reside in the distinction Julian drew between the

---

45. Ibid., 175.

general and the specific.[46] According to Julian there is a fundamental difference between seeking to understand the existence of sin and suffering in general and trying to discern the meaning of any particular instance of sin or suffering.[47] Although both remain shrouded in mystery, Julian felt perfectly free to pry into the former, seeking to understand better the reasons that God might have for allowing sin in general to enter his good creation. Yet she never seeks to explain away any instance of suffering, as though we might be able to offer insight as to why a particular individual has gotten sick or is experiencing some other trauma. Clearly the two issues are related, and Julian remains hopeful that in the end we will see why God allowed every instance of suffering, yet her inquiries always focused on suffering in general.

For Julian, then, the fact that sin and suffering are wrapped in mystery does not preclude us from pressing on toward greater understanding. Instead, Julian views theological mysteries more as opportunities to reflect more deeply on the amazing world that God has created than as clear boundaries that we should not cross.

Sin Is Behovely

One of the more difficult statements in *Showings* comes in the thirteenth revelation where Julian wrestles with idea that it would seem better if sin had never entered the world. In response, Jesus informs her that "sin is necessary [behovely]" (27:225). Since this was given as a direct response to the problem, understanding what it means to say that sin is "behovely" should take us some way toward understanding how Julian dealt with this great mystery.

Denys Turner argues convincingly that we need to differentiate Julian's concept of the behovely from modern notions of necessity.[48] According to Turner, Julian used the term *behovely* in much the same way that many medieval theologians used the term *conveniens*—i.e., as a way of describing something that is "fitting" in a particular context.[49] In other

---

46. Ibid., 175–78.

47. See 35:236–38.

48. See Denys Turner, "'Sin Is Behovely' in Julian of Norwich's *Revelations of Divine Love*," *Modern Theology* 20, no. 3 (2004): 407–22; Turner, *Julian of Norwich*, 32–53.

49. Watson and Jenkins note that the word is often used to "express satisfaction at a good fit with something," and they suggest that Julian may be drawing on the words of the Easter liturgy: *O felix culpa, O necessariusm peccatum Ade* ("O happy fault, O necessary sin of Adam!") (Watson and Jenkins, *The Writings of Julian of Norwich*, 208).

words, *behovely/conveniens* strikes a middle ground between that which is strictly *necessary* and that which is merely *arbitrary*. On this account, to say that sin is behovely is specifically to say that there is an important way in which sin "fits" into the divine economy, but without making the stronger claim that sin is strictly necessary in God's plan.[50] From this perspective, Turner argues that sin "fits" in the same way that certain events fit into a narrative or certain modulations into a song:

> "When a cadence or a modulation is completed in an unexpected way, you are *both* surprised *and* know immediately why it had to be just so, and how its being just so reveals anew everything that precedes it. Stories and music ... in the end make the surprising turn of events to be obvious, as if after the event we can see how we might have predicted it, even though, before the event, in no wise could we have done so."[51]

The element of unpredictability means we usually cannot see what makes something behovely until we have reached the end of the story. Looking back on the entire narrative, we discern how the various pieces fit together to produce the whole. So there is a sense in which this way merely repeats the eschatological hope discussed in the previous section. Yet for Julian the behoveliness of sin also entails that sin is a necessary part of precisely *this* story. In other words, although God certainly could have created a world in which sin did not exist, he chose to write a different story, one that includes the fall and redemption of human persons. And since sin is part of how God chose to write *this* story, it is a necessary part of the story. Contingently necessary, but necessary nonetheless.[52] And this becomes particularly clear when we return again to the cross. Since for Julian the cross is the central element of the story that God chose to enact, sin must be a part of the story. The story simply cannot exist as precisely this story apart from the existence of sin.

At this point, though, we might begin to wonder whether Julian really does take sin as seriously as she ought. If sin is a necessary part of God's greater story, does this not suggest that sin is part of God's design, and, therefore, not as terrible as we might think? For Julian such a

---

50. Turner thus uses the incarnation itself as an analogous situation: "The Incarnation was neither a necessity imposed upon God, nor just a divine whim. It was meet and just, conveniens—or, had you been writing in Julian's Middle English, behovely" (Turner, *Julian of Norwich*, 41).

51. Ibid., 45.

52. Ibid., 51.

conclusion was unthinkable. She boldly stated that "we must hate sin" (40:247) because it is the cause of all the pain and suffering that we see around us. Put simply sin is "all which is not good" (27:225), including all of the pains that Jesus suffered for his creatures. Indeed, the cross itself is a powerful declaration that God takes sin seriously. If the cross reveals the amazing depths of God's love, it also demonstrates that at its core sin is a rejection of God's love. However, since love is the substance of all that exists, sin by its very nature rends the fabric of creation. That is why Julian calls Adam's sin "the greatest harm ever done or ever to be done until the end of the world" (29:228). Far from downplaying the sinfulness of sin, Julian viewed even a single sin as a destructive act of cosmic proportions.

However, this seems only to make the original question even more difficult. How can it be behovely for God to allow something so destructive to take place in his creation? Rather than answering the question, appealing to the contingent necessity of sin seems only to leave us caught in the dilemma of affirming that all will be well despite the truly heinous nature of sin, and the suffering that it inevitably introduces into the world.

God Does Everything

One possible way of making sin "fit" into the story would be to appeal to some kind of free will theodicy in which sin and suffering are a consequence of God giving his creatures sufficient "space" in which to exercise their free wills and then for them to experience the painful consequences of using their freedom unwisely. And according to Jantzen, Julian seems to have something similar in mind. Jantzen argues that a fundamental aspect of Julian's theology is the concept of "reciprocal desire" in which God's love for us elicits our love response to him.[53] For a relationship to be grounded in reciprocal desire like this, however, God must "impose restraints upon himself" so that his creatures can be "genuinely differentiated beings."[54] Jantzen continues, "Thus creatures, to be creatures in their own right at all, are increasingly dependent on God's self-limitation which allows them the freedom to act according to their nature, even while their substance and the very possibility of their acting at all is rooted in the being of God."[55] She sees confirmation of this in Julian's

---

53. Jantzen, *Julian of Norwich*, ix.

54. Ibid., 133.

55. Ibid., 134.

distinction between the substance of humanity and our sensuality. Although the former is characterized by the unfaltering godly will, the latter "constitutes our God-given independence."[56] Thus, despite the fact that God could have exercised his sovereign rule over us in such a way that sin would have been impossible, he courteously limits himself to the extent that on the cross we see him "giving himself up to the freedom of the very human beings he had himself created."[57]

Regardless of whether such a free will theodicy would be successful at answering Julian's questions about the problem of sin and suffering, however, it does not seem that such a response is entirely consistent with her broader theology. Remember that in Jesus humanity is knit to the divine being in a union so close that Julian saw "no difference between God and our substance, but as it were, all God" (54:285). For Julian, this involves the corresponding conclusion that God is so intimately involved in everything that happens in creation that "he does everything which is done" (11:197). And she goes on to strengthen this further, claiming that "God does everything, however small it may be, and that nothing is done by chance" (ibid.). Given this strong emphasis on divine involvement in all creaturely events, it becomes difficult to see how there could be any conceptual space for a free will theodicy.[58]

Another possibility would be to note Julian's statement that "nothing is done by chance, but all by God's prescient wisdom" (11:197). The idea that God is causally active in the world by means of his "prescient wisdom" might suggest that Julian is merely affirming God's general sovereignty over all things, guiding creaturely realities toward his intended purposes. God may cause some of these events himself, but many others he merely permits, foreknowing in his wisdom how they will fit into his divine plan. Tempting as this might be, though, Julian seems to have something far more robust in mind. For Julian, everything that is done in

---

56. Ibid., 142. Jantzen uses a similar argument to contend that Julian could not have been a universalist: "This is why it is impossible for Julian to be a universalist: it would trivialize the freedom which God has given us, and the courtesy and humility by which he allows us not to be in his presence" (ibid., 179).

57. Jantzen, *Julian of Norwich*, 134.

58. Based on such statements, it seems likely that Julian held to some form of theistic compatibilism, maintaining that it is entirely compatible for humans to have a form of free will even if God determines everything that happens in creation. Turner argues that Julian operates with a Thomistic concept of dual causation. Although this is an intriguing proposal, and Julian may well have been sufficiently familiar with the broad outlines of Thomas's theology to have been influenced by him in this area, it is difficult to find clear indications in *Showings* that this is the case (Turner, *Julian of Norwich*, 53–58).

creation "has the property of being of God's doing" (11:198), which suggests a closer relationship between creaturely events and divine agency than that of mere permission. That all creaturely events have the property of having been "ordained" by God (ibid.) means that God has determined precisely what would happen as an expression of his active providence.

It might be possible to contend that, despite her rhetoric, Julian does not have free will actions in mind, envisioning only that God does everything in the world *except* for the free will actions of human persons. As Denys Turner rightly notes, though, this seems unlikely, especially given the difficulties this would create for understanding Julian's soteriology: "It would rend apart the unities of Julian's theology as a whole were we to seek a way out of the problem of the relationship between God's causal sway over each and every free act and her soteriology, of such kind as to attribute to God a salvific role in regard to history as a whole but no causal agency in regard to those human free acts."[59] At the very least, Julian's emphasis on God "doing" everything in creation "however small it may be," suggests that she would not view even human action as somehow standing apart from divine agency. And the idea that God sovereignly determines to allow sufficient "space" for creaturely action runs directly contrary to Julian's emphasis on the intimate union of the divine and human established in Christ and characteristic of all creation, a union so close that Julian cannot see any real "space" between the two.[60]

However Julian understood the nature of the human will in its relationship to the divine will, an issue on which Julian does not offer a clear position, it seems clear that the two are sufficiently intertwined that no response to the problem of evil can be offered through appeal to the human will alone. Indeed, her theology seems to entail a kind of divine omnicausality that risks making God himself culpable for sin and suffering. Although Julian herself surely rejected any such conclusion, she still recognized that God's ever-present agency raised questions about what it means to say that some action is "sin" (11:197). God is "at the centre of everything, and he does everything" (11:197). Thus, for Julian, the problem is not merely that God allows bad things to happen, but that he presents himself to her as causally involved in the most minute details of the universe such that it is a marvel to her how "sin" could have any real meaning.

---

59. Ibid., 53.

60. Julian's explanation for the continuing differentiation between divine and human does not rely on the concept of causal or ontological "space" between the two, but only on the distinction between created and uncreated substance (e.g., 84:341).

For the Greater Good

That leads to a final way of understanding what it means to say that sin is "behovely," one that Julian herself raises explicitly to explain how sin fits into God's story. As destructive and devastating as sin might be, Julian argues that those who have been wounded by its depravity and healed through God's love come out the other side in a higher and better state than if they had never fallen into sin in the first place.

Looking at the pivotal allegory of the lord and the servant, Julian concludes that even though the servant's fall was painful and debilitating, once he has been raised up and healed, he will be "blessedly rewarded forever, above what he would have been if he had not fallen" (51:269). Similarly, Julian argues that having fallen into sin and been redeemed by Jesus' self-giving love on the cross, we learn a kind of humility and meekness that would not have been available to us otherwise, such that "we are raised very high in God's sight by his grace" (39:244). In other words, as important as it is to wrestle with the pain and suffering that we see on the cross, God's declaration of steadfast love is even more important. And when we see the latter in light of the former, something only possible in a world broken by sin, we arrive at an even higher state than would have been possible in an unfallen world. Thus, in the end, "the reward which we shall receive will not be small, but it will be great, glorious and honourable. And so all shame will be turned into honour and joy" (39:245). For Julian, as tragic and painful as this world might be, she still thinks that there is at least some sense in which we are better off living in a world characterized by sin than we would have been in a world without sin.

From one perspective, this seems entirely unhelpful as a response to sin, nothing more than a superficial assurance that all this pain and suffering will make you into a better person in the end. Remember, though, that Julian's response is grounded in her christological account of the human person, one that views human nature as fundamentally grounded in the divine love that characterizes and constitutes God's own being. Her conviction that sin, along with the misery that results from sin, cannot threaten our existence at this fundamental level does not come from downplaying these painful realities but from her hopeful confidence that the God she saw displayed on the cross, the one who entered into our painful condition as an expression of his love, will in fact make all things well. Like a mother who uses painful life circumstances to help a child develop toward greater maturity without allowing them to suffer lasting harm, God walks alongside us and shelters us in his love. Although we are generally blinded by our own sin and unable to see God's gracious compassion, the cross assures us that it is always there.

Jantzen thus notes that Julian's approach to pain and suffering differs in one important respect from what we see in many modern approaches. Although Julian would agree that theology must begin with a close and honest consideration of empirical realities, which necessarily includes all the brutal realities of the everyday world, she would contend that this is only part of the story: "the other half is the personally experienced overwhelming love of God in Christ. When these two are brought together, it is indeed a great mystery, but the mystery is the source of insight as she ponders it more and more fully."[61] And Jantzen goes on to recognize that Julian's theology is not "a complete response to the problem of sin and pain, and Julian never pretends that it is."[62] Turner similarly concludes that Julian never offers a real theodicy, if by that we mean "a comprehensive manner of explaining away God's responsibility for sin or, more generally, evil."[63] Although Julian is shocked by sin and certainly seeks to understand how it fits into a world thoroughly shaped by divine love, she eschews any "solution" that approaches the difficulty as a conceptual inconsistency that needs to be resolved through theological argument. Instead, she offers a way of understanding the very real pain and suffering of life in the world around us, while at the same time arguing that there is a deeper and more fundamental reality that is grounded in the love of the triune God, the intimate union of divinity and humanity that we see in Jesus Christ, and the amazing declaration of God's continued friendship demonstrated on the cross. None of this removes the pain of sin, but it does offer a glimpse of hope.

JULIAN'S LOVE-CENTERED ANTHROPOLOGY

At the beginning of *Showings*, Julian tells us precisely where her theological project is heading: "This is a revelation of the love of Jesus Christ ... made in sixteen showings, of which the first is about his precious crowning of thorns; and in this was contained and specified the blessed Trinity, with

---

61. Jantzen, *Julian of Norwich*, 176.

62. Ibid., 189. Gatta similarly concludes that although Julian's approach is "admittedly inconclusive from a philosophical standpoint, the soothing refrain that 'alle shalle be wele' is nonetheless satisfying in literary and psychological terms" (Julia Gatta, "Julian of Norwich: Theodicy as Pastoral Art," *Anglican Theological Review* 63, no. 2 [1981]: 176).

63. Turner, *The Darkness of God*, 34.

the incarnation and the union between God and man's soul" (1:175). Here we see both Julian's methodology and her core theological commitments *in nuce*. Beginning with the amazing display of love that is Jesus on the cross, she quickly moves on to emphasize that this reveals to us the love of the Trinity that grounds all creation, and the incarnation that establishes an intimate and seemingly unbreakable bond between the human soul and God himself. For Julian, then, the cross shows us what it means to be human: creatures united to Christ and sheltered in God's love.

At the same time, though, the cross also reveals a world broken and ravaged by sin. Indeed, in the crucified Messiah we see that pain and suffering are part of the normal condition of human existence in this world. Julian's methodology does not allow her to shy away from all of this misery, taking refuge in the theological niceties of God's love. Instead, the cross directs her attention to a God who powerfully displays his love in the midst of life's most brutal realities. This, and this alone, offers Julian comfort in her struggle to understand the existence of sin. Even if the cross does not answer all the questions the way she might like, it provides "the only story that to Julian could be credible."[64] On the cross we see a God who entered into our broken condition, indeed he *united* himself to us in our brokenness, falling into the ditch along with us and experiencing the agony that can only be produced by a sin-shaped world. God does not wrathfully inflict this pain upon us, nor does he abandon us to it; instead, he takes it to himself, compassionately healing his creatures, and like a loving mother, using every painful circumstance as an opportunity to lead us toward greater Christlikeness.

Julian well knew that "all will be well" is not a *solution* to the problem of suffering. It is an expression of hope, an act of faith. In the crucified Messiah, Julian saw the truth that God has united himself to humanity and that he will not let us go. In the end, she saw all of this as less a way of answering an impossibly difficult theological issue than as an exhortation to avoid despair: "And he wants us to see that his pains and his tribulation exceed all that we may suffer so far that it cannot be comprehended in full. And if we well contemplate his will in this, it keeps us from lamenting and despairing as we experience our pains" (28:227).

In the end, then, Julian offers a thoroughly christological understanding of the human person, one decisively informed by her visions of Christ's broken body and the pain that he experienced on our behalf.

---

64. Turner, *Julian of Norwich*, 20.

Her christological anthropology, then, reflects simultaneously on the true humanity that we see only in Christ and the very real suffering that all humans experience. In the process, she offers an interesting model, one that locates pain and sorrow within a cross-shaped vision of the human person in which God's infinite love provides the sure ground for human nature.

CHAPTER 3

The Chief Article of Our Humanity

Justification and Vocation in
Martin Luther's Anthropological Vision

———————

Paul ... briefly sums up the definition of man, saying,
"Man is justified by faith."

Martin Luther, *The Disputation Concerning Man, Luther's Works*[1]

IN THE OPENING THESES OF his *The Disputation Concerning Man* (1536), Martin Luther goes right to the heart of the question that is the focus of our current study: What is the proper vantage point from which to develop a right understanding of the human person? In response, he quickly identifies and refutes what he sees as the primary candidate for a nontheological understanding of humanity in his day: the philosophical vision of the human person as a rational animal. Although Luther found much to appreciate in this definition, going so far as to say that that such a perspective can "name the essential difference" between humans and other creatures, namely reason, he ultimately contends that philosophical perspectives like this "know almost nothing about man."[2] This is partly because the human person must be seen as a creature made in the image of the Creator, and one who has fallen into sin and corrupted his original creative design. As valuable as nontheological perspectives might be, they are necessarily precluded from arriving at any full understanding of the human person. In the end, nontheological anthropologies "neither understand what man is nor do they know what they are talking about,"[3]

---

1. Martin Luther, *The Disputation Concerning Man, Luther's Works* (Saint Louis: Concordia, 1958–1986), 34:135–44 (henceforth *LW*).

2. *LW* 34:137.

3. *LW* 34:139. It is in this context that Luther leveled his strong critique of Aristotle, stating that he "knows nothing of theological man" (ibid.). Although the overall context suggests

83

offering perspectives that are at best "fragmentary, fleeting, and exceedingly material."[4]

In the middle of the disputation, Luther sharpens the critique further. It is not simply philosophy's failure to understand creation and the fall that renders it unable to understand the essence of humanity. Rather, philosophy's anthropological inadequacy stems from its inability to view humanity from the only theologically appropriate starting point: justification. According to Luther, Paul's statement that "man is justified by faith" should be understood as a brief "definition" of humanity.[5] The fact that philosophy necessarily seeks knowledge of the human apart from the doctrine of justification means it cannot understand the essential meaning of humanity.

Luther has thus clearly identified the fundamental starting point for his theological anthropology in the doctrine of justification. This means that in Luther's theology, we do not first arrive at some understanding of humanity, and only subsequently appeal to justification as a doctrine that explains how human persons get saved. Instead, justification in some way informs what it means to *be* human. Luther understands justification in a way that, rather than focusing on solely soteriological issues, sheds light on the entire spectrum of human existence from creation through the eschaton. Thus, Luther does not *reduce* theological anthropology to justification; instead, he presents the human person as a being who must be understood first through the lens of justification, which alone provides an accurate picture of true humanity. Only then can we understand correctly the complex reality of humanity in its various circumstances and relationships.

At this point, however, we might legitimately wonder: if *justification* is the true center of Luther's theological anthropology, does it really qualify as *christological*? In other words, does this not suggest that his anthropology is really grounded in soteriology rather than Christology? Although the answer to this question needs to unfold through the course of this chapter, we should note at the beginning that Luther would probably argue that this is a false distinction. As we will see, Luther presents justification as a fundamentally christological reality. Justification is not merely something that Christ *does*, and the faith that actualizes

---

appreciation for what Aristotle's philosophy offers our understanding of what we might call "natural" man, it is precisely his inability to see the human person both as creature and as sinfully fallen that prevents him from having any true theological insight (*LW* 34:139, 143).

4. *LW* 34:138.

5. *LW* 34:139.

justification for the human person is not merely something that we *believe* about what Christ has accomplished. According to Luther, justification by faith is *receiving Christ himself*. Thus, when Luther says that justification defines humanity he is claiming that the essence of what it means to be human is to be righteous in Christ. This is both revealed and actualized in Jesus as the truly righteous one who enables the righteousness of all who participate in his justification. For Luther, justification is not merely about how Jesus saves us; it is about how Jesus makes us human.

A comprehensive study of Luther's theology of justification clearly lies beyond the scope of this study. Fortunately, the general outlines of his theology of justification are well known and have been ably summarized by others.[6] So we can focus our attention on identifying those aspects of his theology of justification that are most relevant to his theological anthropology. Even here, though, we cannot be comprehensive. If Luther was correct and justification really is the center of his anthropology, it should be possible to look at *any* aspect of his theological anthropology and discern how it finds its center in justification (directly or indirectly). Thus, even addressing the implications of justification for anthropology would require too broad a study. Instead, we will focus on identifying several important implications of justification for understanding the human person, using those to gesture toward what it means for Luther to say that justification is a summary definition of humanity.

Having done that, we will turn our attention to Luther's theology of vocation as a way of studying his anthropology in action. As we will see, Luther's justification-centered anthropology has pressing implications for the practical realities of living humanly in the everyday world. Indeed, it is quite possible to say that for Luther, being human *is* our vocation, one that gets particularized in various ways depending on our specific circumstances. For Luther, the way we are saved (justification) declares fundamental truths about who we are (anthropology) which in turn has vital implications for how we are to live (vocation).

---

6. Among the many excellent studies, see Bengt Hägglund, *The Background of Luther's Doctrine of Justification in Late Medieval Theology* (Philadelphia: Fortress, 1971); Gerhard O. Forde, *Justification by Faith: A Matter of Death and Life* (Philadelphia: Fortress, 1982); Jared Wicks, "Justification and Faith in Luther's Theology," *Theological Studies* 44, no. 1 (1983): 3–29; Oswald Bayer, *Living by Faith: Justification and Sanctification* (Grand Rapids: Eerdmans, 2003); Alister E. McGrath, *Iustitia Dei: A History of the Christian Doctrine of Justification*, 3rd ed. (New York: Cambridge University Press, 2005); Carl Trueman, "*Simul Peccator et Justus*: Martin Luther and Justification," in *Justification in Perspective: Historical Developments and Contemporary Challenges*, ed. Bruce L. McCormack (Grand Rapids: Baker Academic, 2006), 73–98.

THE CHIEF ARTICLE OF OUR FAITH

The importance of justification for Luther's theology as a whole cannot be underestimated, and Luther himself refers to it as "the central article of our teaching,"[7] claiming elsewhere that it "preserves and guides all churchly teaching."[8] To understand how Luther's theology of justification shapes his theological anthropology in particular, we will first need to take a quick look at several key aspects of his teaching on justification.

Anyone attempting to summarize Luther's theology of justification, though, faces the immediate difficulty that Luther's views on the subject developed over time. Although Luther himself famously described his tower experience as a sudden and radical conversion to a new understanding of justification, most agree that Luther's theological development was more complex, with many identifying the writings of 1519/1520 as the real turning point in Luther's understanding of justification. In his earlier writings, although Luther was beginning to develop some of the motifs that would characterize his more mature theology, he had not yet developed those concepts with the precision that would characterize his later writings.[9] Most importantly, his earliest writings on justification included a promissory or proleptic understanding of justification. In other words, the declaration of justification at the beginning of the Christian life was given on the basis of a promise that the believer would in fact become righteous through the process of personal transformation. The righteous transformation of the believer was, consequently, the ground for the declaration of justification. And this proleptic view stood in uneasy tension with other strands in Luther's developing theology of justification, the latter of which would come to characterize Luther's more mature theology and will be the focus of our discussion here.

Luther's theology has traditionally been interpreted with a strong emphasis on the *forensic* nature of justification and the *alien* nature of our righteousness in Christ.[10] According to Luther, humans cannot stand

---

7. *D. Martin Luthers Werke: kritische Gesamtausgabe* (Weimar: H. Böhlau, 1883), 40 III, 335, 5–10. Hereafter, *WA*.

8. *WA* 39, I, 205, 2–5.

9. See esp. Berndt Hamm, *The Early Luther: Stages in a Reformation Reorientation* (Grand Rapids: Eerdmans, 2014).

10. This traditional interpretation, though, has received significant criticism in the modern era, most importantly for our purposes from the "New Finnish" school of interpretation (see esp. Carl E. Braaten and Robert W. Jenson, eds., *Union with Christ: The New Finnish Interpretation of Luther* [Grand Rapids: Eerdmans, 1998]; Tuomo Mannermaa, *Christ Present in Faith: Luther's View of Justification* [Minneapolis: Fortress, 2005]; Olli-Pekka Vainio, *Justification and Participation in Christ: The Development of the Lutheran Doctrine of Justification from*

righteous before God (*coram Deo*) on account of their own works, but only as they are united to Christ and his righteousness is imputed to them: "By this fortunate exchange with us He took upon Himself our sinful person and granted us His innocent and victorious Person. Clothed and dressed in this, we are freed from the curse of the Law, because Christ Himself voluntarily became a curse for us."[11] This is what Luther means when he says that we are saved by a righteousness that is "outside of us and . . . foreign to us."[12] Thus, Luther adamantly rejects any notion that righteousness can be understood in terms of such intrinsic moral qualities. Instead, the startling declaration of "Justified!" pronounced over sinful human beings can only be on the basis of the imputation of an alien, extrinsic righteousness that is ours in Christ.[13]

This, then, is the basis for Luther's frequent declarations that such justification is "passive" and entirely apart from "works."[14] He does not mean by this that justification is entirely apart from works, only that meritorious works have no role to play as the ground or basis upon which the eschatological judgment "Justified!" is finally pronounced over a human person. As Paul Althaus summarizes,

> Man cannot earn this for himself but can only permit it to be granted to him through God's free grace for Christ's sake. The situation with our righteousness is no different from our entry into heaven on the Last Day. Christ will take us from earth and put us into heaven (1 Thessalonians

---

Luther to the Formula of Concord (1580) [Leiden: Brill, 2008]). On this view, both traditional and modern interpretations of Luther have been unduly influenced by an anti-metaphysical bias that is inappropriate to Luther's late-medieval context. For Luther, justification is about more than a "mere" declaration about the human person; it involves a "real-ontic" transformation in which the human person actually becomes righteous through union with Christ and the outpouring of the Spirit. Although this approach has helpfully recovered a number of vital concepts, critics have pointed out a tendency to overemphasize Luther's early writings, to neglect the importance of themes like the two kinds of righteousness, and to disregard important developments in Luther scholarship (see esp. R. Scott Clark, "*Iustitia Imputata Christi*: Alien or Proper to Luther's Doctrine of Justification?" *Concordia Theological Quarterly* 70, no. 3–4 [2006]: 272–84).

11. *LW* 26:284. For the historic background of "imputation" and its use in Luther's theology, see Sibylle Rolf, "Luther's Understanding of *Imputatio* in the Context of His Doctrine of Justification and Its Consequences for the Preaching of the Gospel," *International Journal of Systematic Theology* 12, no. 4 (2010): 435–51; Clark, "*Iustitia Imputata Christi*."

12. *LW* 34:153.

13. As Paul Althaus declares, "Righteousness is not a quality of man as philosophy and the scholastic theology determined it to be; rather it consists in being righteous only through God's gracious imputation of Christ's righteousness" (*The Theology of Martin Luther* [Philadelphia: Fortress, 1966], 227).

14. E.g., *LW* 26:7.

4:16), and we will not do it for ourselves. We are completely passive in this process and cannot do anything toward it. The same is true here. Something happens to us; and we can only let it happen to us, without being actively involved in it in any way.[15]

Thus, our righteousness *coram Deo* is always a passive and alien righteousness, one in which "God sees the sinner as one with Christ. He forgives his sin and considers the sinner to be righteous for Christ's sake."[16]

The fact that our righteousness before God is always passive and alien, however, does not mean that we are completely uninvolved. Indeed, Luther clearly emphasized the importance of our faith response to the word of grace. However, this does not mean that Luther somehow grounded justification in the strength and sincerity of our own faith. Further, he was deeply suspicious of any attempt to understand faith as the one "work" we can perform that merits justification. "Faith, then, is not a work, since it looks only toward the promise. The promise, however, is that kind of a gift, that we bring nothing to faith, because the promise came earlier and because reason turns away from faith. It is up to God alone to give faith contrary to nature, and ability to believe contrary to reason. That I love God is the work of God alone."[17] Consequently, the righteousness of faith that we receive through imputation comes entirely without works. It is rightly called a "passive" righteousness because we contribute nothing, merely permitting someone else to work in us.

Even more importantly, Luther focuses not on the quality or nature of the individual's faith, but on the one received *through* faith: "Faith justifies because it takes hold of and possesses this treasure, the present Christ."[18] In other words, according to Bernard Lohse, "the decisive content" of justification simply is that "in faith Christ is present."[19] Christ is not merely the *object* of faith, but the one who himself becomes present in faith through the power of the Spirit. As Althaus explains, "Thus in matters of justification, Christ and faith cannot be treated as

---

15. Althaus, *Theology of Martin Luther*, 228. According to Bernard Lohse, it was primarily Albrecht Peters who established the importance of always viewing Luther's writings on justification against the backdrop of eschatological judgment (*Martin Luther's Theology: Its Historical and Systematic Development* [Minneapolis: Fortress, 1999], 259).

16. Althaus, *Theology of Martin Luther*, 227.

17. *LW* 34:160.

18. *LW* 26:130.

19. Lohse, *Martin Luther's Theology*, 261. Similarly, Althaus says that "Luther sees the essence of justifying faith in the fact that it grasps Christ" (*Theology of Martin Luther*, 230).

two different things and set in opposition to each other. Christ is what he is for me in God's judgment only in that faith in which I 'grasp' him; and that faith is meaningful in God's judgment only because Christ is present with a man."[20] This is precisely what makes Luther's understanding of justification so thoroughly christological. It is not merely that Jesus is the one who makes justification possible; to be justified simply *is* to receive Christ himself through faith. In the end, then, "the article of justification is nothing else than faith in Christ, when this is properly understood."[21]

Thus far we have spoken of justification exclusively as something that conditions our standing *coram Deo*. For Luther, though, this is only half the picture. Ultimately, Luther viewed righteousness as the state in which we are most fully human. In other words, we are righteous when we are operating according to God's creational intentions for humanity.[22] Although our relationship with God has obvious importance for being fully human, Luther contended that we are only fully righteous (i.e., fully human) when we stand rightly before the rest of creation (*coram mundo*), including most importantly our standing before our fellow humans (*coram hominibus*). This is the basis of Luther's distinction between the "two kinds of righteousness" that characterize the human person.[23] As he explains at the beginning of his *Lectures on Galatians* (1535), "This is our theology, by which we teach a precise distinction between these two kinds of righteousness, the active and the passive, so that morality and faith, works and grace, secular society and religion may not be confused. Both are necessary, but both must be kept within their limits."[24] A little later, Luther declares that these two kinds of righteousness distinguish two different "worlds," the heavenly and the earthly.[25] The heavenly world involves a passive righteousness that has to do with faith, grace, and true religion, while the earthly world

---

20. Althaus, *Theology of Martin Luther*, 231.

21. Ibid., 225.

22. Robert Kolb, "Luther on the Two Kinds of Righteousness; Reflections on His Two-Dimensional Definition of Humanity at the Heart of His Theology," *Lutheran Quarterly* 13, no. 4 (1999): 449–66.

23. For more on this see David A. Lumpp, "Luther's 'Two Kinds of Righteousness': A Brief Historical Introduction," *Concordia Journal* 23, no. 1 (1997): 27–38; Kolb, "Luther on the Two Kinds of Righteousness."

24. *LW* 26:7.

25. *LW* 26:8.

deals with an active righteousness involving morality, works, and society. Thus, although Luther recognized the gift-dimension of all human relationships, his primary emphasis was on the fact that our standing *coram mundo* is established on the basis of our works. This is an active righteousness that is properly ours in the sense that we perform it. Both kinds of righteousness are essential for a proper understanding of salvation and the Christian life, but so is maintaining a proper distinction between them.

Although these are two fundamentally different kinds of righteousness, however, they are interrelated in that the secondary righteousness we have *coram mundo* "is the product of the righteousness of the first type, actually its fruit and consequence."[26] As Luther explains, "And indeed, we are reborn not only for life but also for righteousness, because faith acquires Christ's merit and knows that through Christ's death we have been set free. From this source our other righteousness has its origin, namely, that newness of life through which we are zealous to obey God as we are taught by the Word and aided by the Holy Spirit."[27] Our righteousness *coram hominibus* is thus fully a gift of God as it proceeds from our primary righteousness *coram Deo* aided by both Word and Spirit, but it remains our own active righteousness, something that we strive after and accomplish.

Luther's rejection of antinomianism, as well as his emphasis on the active righteousness that should characterize Christian living *coram mundo*, should caution us against thinking that Luther's theology of justification has no room for any real transformation of the human person. One of the important developments in modern Luther scholarship has been the growing appreciation of the fact that forensic justification is entirely compatible with the notion that human persons are in fact changed and transformed as a result. Luther himself affirms a progressive aspect to justification when he says, "Every one who believes in Christ is righteous, not yet fully in point of fact, but in hope. For he has begun to be justified and healed."[28] Such a person is "not yet a righteous man, but is in the very movement or journey toward righteousness."[29] He even explicitly affirms that faith involves "a divine work in us which

---

26. *LW* 31:297–300.
27. *LW* 1:64.
28. *LW* 27:227.
29. *LW* 34:152.

changes us."[30] Such statements sprinkled throughout both his early and his more mature writings suggest that, although Luther prioritizes the declarative aspect of justification, he always says this is compatible with the real transformation of the human person. This is because, as Althaus rightly notes, there is no necessary contradiction in emphasizing both alien righteousness and transformation: "This concern for the beginning of renewal and of faith's battle against sin does not replace concern for Christ. 'On account of the beginning of the new creation' does not compete with and certainly does not substitute for 'on account of Christ.'"[31] Thus, transformation in Christ is the "indispensable condition" of justification, but not its "sufficient basis."[32]

Consequently, we need to move beyond viewing justification as a "mere" declaration, as though in the act of justification God did no more than make an observation about the condition of humanity. For Luther, God's speech is always an efficacious reality. In justification, as in creation, God's words bring new realities into existence. Thus, as Robert Kolb and Charles Arand explain, when God promises that he will justify, this "is not an announcement that will be fulfilled only in the future; it is a creative word that takes immediate and present effect. In the here and now it brings about the very thing that it announces about the future."[33] Just as a marriage vow enacts a reality rather than merely describing one, so God's declaration "Justified!" makes it the case that we are in fact in a right relationship with him. It creates its own reality. That is why, as Gerhard Forde explained, it is a false dichotomy to suggest that Luther had to choose between "forensic" and "essential" righteousness.[34] It is the very forensic/declarative nature of justification that renders it effective: "the more forensic it is, the more effective it is!"[35]

JUSTIFICATION AND THE NATURE OF HUMANITY

With that brief outline of Luther's theology of justification in mind, we can begin to see some of the implications this has for Luther's theological anthropology.

---

30. *LW* 35:370.

31. Althaus, *Theology of Martin Luther*, 239.

32. Ibid., 241–42.

33. Robert Kolb and Charles P. Arand, *The Genius of Luther's Theology: A Wittenberg Way of Thinking for the Contemporary Church* (Grand Rapids: Baker Academic, 2008), 42.

34. Forde, *Justification by Faith*, 36.

35. Ibid.

Reversing the Narrative

One critical question has to do with the relationship between justification and creation in Luther's theological anthropology. Although we might worry that some justification-centered anthropologies might unnecessarily downplay the importance of creation in understanding the human person, such is clearly not the case for Luther, who wrote extensively on the doctrine of creation and its anthropological significance.[36] Instead, a different concern arises for Luther. Could it be that despite the justification-centered definition he offers in *The Disputation Concerning Man*, his understanding of the human person was actually grounded in the doctrine of creation rather than justification? In his lectures on Genesis, Luther offers a robust notion of humanity made in the image of God and thus constituted by its two-fold relationality: *coram Deo* and *coram mundo*.[37] Luther appears to develop some of the key themes of his anthropology independently of justification and, even more importantly for our purposes, independently of any explicitly christological considerations. On this account, Luther's emphasis on justification arrives on the scene only *after* he has already determined what it means to be human. If this were to prove accurate, we might say that Luther's soteriology was christocentric, but not his anthropology. His christocentrism would be focused more on *redeeming* true humanity than *revealing* it.

However, Luther's arguments elsewhere suggest that he did *not* think creation itself could provide an adequate definition of what it means to be human. On the one hand, Luther argues negatively that one of the consequences of the fall is that sin has obscured our vision of original humanity and precluded our ability to generate a definition of humanity from that perspective. Although Luther exercises some freedom in speculating about the condition of Adam's pre-fall capacities,[38] he ultimately concludes we simply cannot know anything about the true nature

---

36. For good summaries, see Johannes Schwanke, "Luther on Creation," in *Harvesting Martin Luther's Reflections on Theology, Ethics, and the Church*, ed. Timothy J. Wengert (Grand Rapids: Eerdmans, 2004), 78–98; Theo Bell, "Man Is a Microcosmos: Adam and Eve in Luther's Lectures on Genesis (1535–1545)," *Concordia Theological Quarterly* 69, no. 2 (2005): 159–84; Johannes Schwanke, "Luther's Theology of Creation," in *The Oxford Handbook of Martin Luther's Theology*, ed. Robert Kolb, Irene Dingel, and Lubomir Batka (New York: Oxford University Press, 2014), 201–11.

37. See esp. *LW* 1:60ff.

38. E.g., "I am fully convinced that before Adam's sin his eyes were so sharp and clear that they surpassed those of the lynx and eagle. He was stronger than the lions and the bears" (*LW* 1:62).

of human persons created in the image of God.[39] On the other hand, and less explicitly, Luther suggests a more positive reason for thinking that creation alone cannot define true humanity. Although the creation accounts say much about human origins, they say little about the eschatological *telos* of humanity—the end toward which we are heading—and, therefore, that which constitutes God's ultimate purpose for creating humanity. In other words, creation focuses on protology to the exclusion of eschatology. Although Luther did not deal with the question extensively, it appears in places that he thought eschatological humanity would transcend its original condition, thus suggesting there is more to true humanity than we see in the Garden.[40] Because true humanity has been obscured by the fall and because true humanity is an eschatological reality not yet revealed in the creation accounts, Luther does not seem to think that those of us living in the interim between the fall and our eschatological redemption can use the creation accounts to define true humanity.

At this point, it may seem that Luther is beginning to lean in the direction of an eschatological apophaticism akin to what we witnessed in Gregory of Nyssa. But Luther draws a different conclusion, arguing that the doctrine of justification is what binds together the creational and eschatological perspectives on the human person. Justification allows us to see through the obscurity of sin and catch a glimpse of God's creational purposes for humanity. Because Luther was convinced that God's redemptive purposes are fully consistent with his creative purposes, it is not as though he thinks justification will reveal a humanity completely distinct from our created state. Instead, the redemptive action of God that we see in justification is the lens through which we should understand the creation narratives themselves.[41] That is why Luther freely uses the language of justification when interpreting the creation accounts. For

---

39. "Therefore, when we speak about that image, we are speaking about something unknown. Not only have we had no experience of it, but we continually experience the opposite; and so we hear nothing but bare words" (*LW* 1:63).

40. Thus, Luther argues that even before the fall we were "created for a better life" such that even if Adam and Eve had not fallen we still would have needed to be transformed into our eternal state (*LW* 1:56).

41. Niels Gregersen thus concludes, "Luther depicts God's work of creation after the model of God's work of salvation, so that the first article of faith (about creation) is permeated by the insights that flow out the gospel message of the second and third articles of faith (about the work of Christ and the Holy Spirit)" ("Grace in Nature and History: Luther's Doctrine of Creation Revisited," *Dialog* 44, no. 1 [2005]: 20).

example, in the Small Catechism, Luther argues that it was by "divine goodness and mercy" that we were created, completely "without any merit or worthiness in me."[42]

Although it might seem intuitively obvious that *creatio ex nihilo* entails a kind of passive righteousness in which humanity receives its standing before God as pure gift, that is not something emphasized or even clearly suggested by the creation narratives themselves. Instead, it appears that Luther uses the logic of justification to draw from the doctrine of creation ideas that are only implicit in the narrative. In other words, it is not that Luther thinks we can realize a fully developed understanding of the human person as constituted before God by grace apart from merit on the doctrine of creation alone, an understanding that just happens to cohere with a similar account offered in the doctrine of justification. Instead, it is when God acted to *re*-create humanity through justification that we truly see what it means to stand as a human person *coram Deo*. Based on this and the conviction that God's actions in redemption will be consistent with his actions in creation, Luther *then* draws the conclusion that the condition of humanity in creation can be understood in light of our standing *coram Deo* in justification.[43] On this ground, we can see that true humanity before God is always created *ex nihilo*: "God established the relationship between himself and his human creatures as that of unconstrained giver to absolute receiver."[44]

And as Robert Kolb explains, the conceptual framework of justification informed Luther's emphasis on the passive righteousness that characterized humanity before the fall as well:

> Adam and Eve, Luther believed, had also possessed only this passive righteousness. They were human in God's sight not because they had proved their humanity through specific activities which had won God's favor. Instead, they had been created by his breath and hand because he wanted them as his children. His love and mercy expressed themselves by forming his creatures as right and righteous in his sight. He formed

---

42. Martin Luther, "Small Catechism," in *Book of Concord*, http://bookofconcord.org/smallcatechism.php (accessed June 20, 2015).

43. "In his explanation of the first article of the Creed, Luther intensifies this point about creation theology and anthropology in a concept based expressly on the doctrine of justification: 'I believe that God has created me together with all that exists ... apart from my merit or worthiness'" (Oswald Bayer, "Being in the Image of God," *Lutheran Quarterly* 27, no. 1 [2013]: 77).

44. Kolb and Arand, *The Genius of Luther's Theology*, 37.

them with the expectation that they would perform as his children in relationship to the rest of his creation as they trusted in him and showed him their love.[45]

Thus, Luther freely uses the conceptual framework of justification to understand the creation narratives.

In addition to providing a glimpse through the veil of the fall, justification also offers a perspective on the eschatological *telos* of humanity. Like the doctrine of creation, justification is limited in that even here we do not actually see humanity in its fullest sense. The fullness of humanity is something that awaits its final revelation in the eschaton. Nonetheless, in justification we see God's intent to bring about true humanity by *redeeming*, rather than *replacing*, fallen humanity. As Luther argues, "Therefore, man in this life is the simple material for the form of his future life. Just as the whole creation which is now subject to vanity (Rom. 8:20) is for God the material for its future glorious form."[46] Thus, although the full truth of humanity has yet to be revealed, the act of redemption becomes a signpost toward the ultimate *telos* of the human person, an interpretive lens that offers insight into our eschatological destiny.

Luther thus resists any attempt to separate the doctrines of creation and justification in understanding the human person. As Bengt Hägglund explains, "Theological anthropology does not consist of isolated remarks on humans' conditions and qualities, which then are used as building blocks in theology, but it is integrated into the entire doctrine of creation and redemption."[47] Since the God who created is also the God who redeemed, we should expect there to be an inseparable relationship between the insights provided by both perspectives. Consequently, we cannot arrive at a definition of what it means to be human from a creational perspective alone. Although the doctrine of creation was one of the more significant loci in Luther's theology, as testified by the extent of his lectures and writings on that subject,[48] it is actually the doctrine of justification that provides the theological starting point for any such endeavor.

---

45. Kolb, "Luther on the Two Kinds of Righteousness," 463.

46. *LW* 34:139.

47. Bengt Hägglund, "Luthers Anthropologie," in *Leben Und Werk Martin Luthers von 1526 bis 1546: Festgabe Zu Seinem 500 Geburtstag*, vol. 1 (Göttingen: Vandenhoeck & Ruprecht, 1983), 63, translation mine.

48. Indeed, in Luther's writings on the Old Testament, only Psalms receives more attention than Genesis (Bell, "Man Is a Microcosmos: Adam and Eve in Luther's Lectures on Genesis (1535–1545)," 159–84).

A Gifted Humanity

Luther thus established his grace-based definition of the human person on the doctrine of justification, and this in turn serves as the lens through which he views every aspect of the human person. And this had implications for how Luther described the very essence of the human person. According to Luther, a justification-centered anthropology must conclude that humans "do not have their essence from themselves, and even when their essence has been bestowed, they do not have any power of their own."[49] The fundamental ontological truth of a human person is not found in any kind of abstract essence by which we determine the features necessary for a being to qualify as human. Instead, the essence of humanity is grounded in the reality of our standing *coram Deo*. And since our standing *coram Deo* is always an act of grace, a relationship gifted to us by our maker, then human persons receive their essence, their very being, as a gift.

Even in their pre-fall state, Adam and Eve did not have some kind of autonomous essence that enabled them to stand as creatures before God. They too stood *coram Deo* only as a gift of God's gracious favor. And as Luther argues, this applies to even the smallest aspects of human existence: "It is not at all in his hand but only in God's hand. For just as I believe that he created the entire world out of nothing, and that everything has come only from his word and command, so I have to confess, that I am a part of the word and his creation. Therefore, it must follow that in my power there is no ability to raise my hand, but God alone does and effects everything in me."[50] Looking at Luther's sermons on Genesis (1523), Robert Kolb explains, "This righteousness is comparable to the identity that a person has because it has been bestowed on them by birth, a total gift (*natalis*). It is a righteousness that is essential, that is, that determines the core identity of a person (*essentialis*)."[51]

This provides the basic shape of Luther's understanding of the *imago Dei*. Unlike most theologians before him, Luther did not define the image as capacity or set of capacities inherent in the human person.[52] Instead,

---

49. *WA* 24:36, 22–24.

50. *WA* 24:27–22.8.

51. Robert Kolb, "God and His Human Creatures in Luther's Sermons on Genesis: The Reformer's Early Use of His Distinction of Two Kinds of Righteousness," *Concordia Journal* 33, no. 2 (2007): 172.

52. Luther described the efforts of earlier theologians to identify the requisite capacities as "dangerous opinions" that threaten to lead us away from a true understanding of humanity (*LW 1:61*).

Luther thought of the image primarily in terms of our righteous relationship with God. As he says in his exegesis of Genesis 1:26: "Therefore my understanding of the image of God is this: that Adam had it in his being and that he not only knew God and believed that He was good, but that he also lived in a life that was wholly godly; that is, he was without the fear of death or of any other danger, and was content with God's favor."[53] Later, in *The Disputation on Justification*, he basically equates the image with righteousness: "Man was created in the image of God, in the image of righteousness, of course, of divine holiness and truth, but in such a way that he could lose it."[54] Throughout, then, the image deals primarily with the kind of relationship that human persons were supposed to have with their gracious Creator, one characterized by trust, love, and obedience. And this is why Luther often talks about the image as completely lost after the fall when that relationship was devastatingly severed.[55]

For Luther, then, we misunderstand the essence of the human person when we fail to see human nature fundamentally as a *gift*. Although we will see in the next section that Luther also emphasized the importance of humanity's faith response, thus affirming that humans have some role to play in being constituted as *human*, it would be a fatal mistake to think that humanity's existential response to grace is the fundamental ground of Luther's theological anthropology. For Luther, insofar as human persons are created *ex nihilo*, both in justification and in creation, the essence of humanity is entirely passive, received as a gift of God's grace. Any role that we play in constituting our own humanity must be subsequent to and always based upon that initial gracious act.

A Faithful Humanity

A corollary to Luther's conviction that humanity is constituted by the divine Word of grace is the fact that human identity is therefore constituted in the faith response (or lack thereof) that we offer to that Word.[56] As Otto Pesch writes, "If human being is defined by justifying faith, then faith—or, more precisely, the *call* to faith—is a constituent part

---

53. *LW* 1:63.

54. *LW* 34:177.

55. E.g., *LW* 1:61–63.

56. Heinz Bluhm demonstrates that this emphasis on a faith-shaped humanity can be traced back to Luther's earliest writings ("Luther's View of Man in His First Published Work," *Harvard Theological Review* 41, no. 2 [1948]: 103–22).

of human nature."[57] For Luther, then, that which most fundamentally identifies us as humans and distinguishes us from other creatures is not a particular ontology (e.g., possessing an immaterial soul) or a unique capacity (e.g., reason). Instead, that which most fundamentally makes us the kind of creature that we are is the fact that we are the ones who have been addressed by God and who necessarily respond. Thus, in many ways, Luther's anthropology is "an anthropology of responding."[58]

It is critical to remember here that Luther does not construe faith as any kind of *work* by which we contribute to our own existence. Otherwise, we would in a sense be *self*-constituted in the act of faith, undermining Luther's emphasis on the *creatio ex nihilo*. As Luther explains in *The Freedom of a Christian*, faith involves clinging to the promises of God and trusting that the one who gave the promises is "one who is true, just, and wise [and] will act in a way so that all will be well."[59] That is why, as we noted earlier, Luther views faith more as an orientation of the whole person than any particular act executed by the person. Faith is the shape of human existence. Thus, as Bayer concludes, "Faith is not something *in* the human in addition to it but rather is its being itself."[60]

According to Luther, the essence of being human is grounded in the prior act of God such that both creation and re-creation are *ex nihilo* events, which means that humanity is something passively received from another rather than something that we actively create through our own efforts, consciously or otherwise. This does not mean, however, that faith accomplishes nothing of real significance. Instead, Luther presents faith as "determinative and even decisive" for human living.[61] That is because the *coram Deo* relationship is not one in which the human can stand with any kind of uncommitted neutrality. To stand *coram Deo* is to be summoned into a particular kind of relationship, one that demands and necessarily elicits a response: whether of faith or unfaith. And given the fundamental importance of the *coram Deo* relationship for establishing what it means to be human, one's faith response to that relationship

57. Otto Hermann Pesch, "Free by Faith: Luther's Contribution to a Theological Anthropology," in *Martin Luther and the Modern Mind: Freedom, Conscience, Toleration, Rights*, ed. Manfred Hoffmann (Lewiston, N.Y.: Mellen, 1985), 37.

58. Bayer, "Being in the Image of God," 78.

59. Martin Luther, *The Freedom of a Christian* (Minneapolis: Fortress, 2008), 60.

60. Bayer, "Being in the Image of God," 77.

61. Gerhard Ebeling, "Luther's Understanding of Reality," trans. Scott A. Celsor, *Lutheran Quarterly* 27, no. 1 (2013): 60.

determines the shape of one's entire existence. "Faith and unfaith are therefore," according to Bayer, "more than mere interpretations of reality. In both cases, something effective *happens*."[62] To use one of Luther's analogies, faith is that which "unites the soul with Christ just as a bride is united with her bridegroom."[63] True humanity thus comes into being as the human person is united to Christ in faith. Responding in unfaith, on the other hand, necessarily separates the person from Christ, fundamentally alienating the person from the only relationship in which we are constituted as true humans.[64] Thus, as Luther says, "God the Father has made all things depend on faith so that whoever has faith has everything, while the one who lacks faith has nothing."[65]

This is the point at which Luther reintroduces the question of human capacities. Although we have already seen that the basic moves in Luther's anthropology shift attention away from the intrinsic attributes or capacities a human possesses, placing the focus on humanity's standing before God understood primarily through the lens of *gift* and *faith*, Luther does not ignore human capacities entirely. Instead, he presents them as secondary, though still important, aspects of anthropology, focusing on those capacities necessary for humans to be the kinds of beings that we see in this faith response. In other words, we first establish that the fundamental *meaning* of humanity is found in the *coram Deo* relationship and humanity's necessary faith response to that already existing relationship. Only then do we turn our attention to the capacities that seem necessary for us to be the kinds of beings who can exist in and respond to that kind of relationship.

And for Luther, the most important capacities have to do with our ability to communicate. Thus, Luther declares, "There is no mightier or nobler work of the human than speech."[66] But he does not develop this out of a mere comparison with non-human creatures, concluding that speech is that which sets humans apart from the animals. Instead, speech is the noblest work of humanity because speech is a communicative response to another, and such a capacity for communicative response

62. Bayer, "Being in the Image of God," 86, emphasis in original.

63. Luther, *The Freedom of a Christian*, 62.

64. This raises the important question of whether Luther thought that only Christians qualified as truly human. Although to my knowledge Luther never addressed this question directly, the idea that true humanity is only that which stands before God in faith surely suggests this conclusion.

65. Ibid., 58.

66. *LW* 35:254.

is necessary for humanity to be what it is before God.[67] Similarly, for Luther the "ear" is a fundamental capacity of humanity because hearing represents the proper posture of the human person before God: passively receiving the active Word that confronts us and demands a response.[68] He also describes human reason, which is necessary for any meaningful faith response, as "the most important and the highest rank among all things and, in comparison with other things of this life, the best and something divine."[69] Thus, Luther does not deny the importance of human capacities, but he does relativize their significance somewhat by locating them within a broader and more fundamental emphasis on humanity's faith response *coram Deo*.

Kolb and Arand rightly note, then, that for Luther, "Faith lies at the core of human existence."[70] Although the gracious divine action always has precedence over our faith response, Luther still views the human person as fundamentally shaped by the powerful realities of faith and unfaith.

A Relational Humanity

By now the third aspect of Luther's justification-centered theological anthropology should be relatively apparent. For Luther, the human person is a fundamentally relational being. We have already seen that this is necessarily the case given the constitutive significance of the *coram Deo* relationship. However, Luther does not focus solely on the divine/human relationship. Consistent with the two kinds of righteousness, Luther also emphasizes the importance of creaturely relationships for true humanity. And, although the divine/human relationship is the most basic relationship that constitutes our humanity, Luther does not think this can or should be separated from creaturely relationships. Instead, creaturely relationships constitute the sphere in and through which God establishes the fundamental *coram Deo* relationship with human persons. Thus, as Oswald Bayer summarizes, "Relative to its Creator, the believing self finds

---

67. As far as I am aware, Luther does not address the question of humans who cannot speak for whatever reason. As a speculation, it seems entirely consistent with Luther's theology to emphasize that humans only need the capacity to respond to God in some way, verbal or otherwise, to ground his theology of responding.

68. Margaret R. Miles, "'The Rope Breaks When It Is Tightest': Luther on the Body, Consciousness, and the Word," *Harvard Theological Review* 77, no. 3–4 (1984): 248.

69. *LW* 34:137.

70. Kolb and Arand, *The Genius of Luther's Theology*, 38.

itself not isolated and immediate but instead mediated through worldly means. God speaks to humans in a 'speech to the creature through the creature' ... The fellow creatures, first and foremost one's parents, are the means through which God calls us into life and gives everything."[71] Thus, the divine/human relationship, although always established by divine initiative and grounded in grace, is nonetheless often mediated through creaturely relationships.

We should pause here for a moment and reflect again on the relationship between creation and justification in the logic of Luther's theology. From one perspective, Luther's relational anthropology hardly seems like a unique contribution of a justification-centered anthropology. Even though Christian anthropologies have sometimes tended toward an overly individualistic understanding of the human person, particularly when defining the *imago Dei* in terms of particular human capacities, they still appreciated the significance of the creational emphasis on humanity as it stands in relation to God and one another. It thus seems difficult to conclude that justification is really driving this aspect of Luther's theology, again raising questions about whether Luther's anthropology is truly grounded in Christology and justification as he claims. Remember, though, that Luther can maintain justification as the fundamental *starting point* that orients every aspect of theological anthropology while still drawing anthropological insights from creation. The key is that those insights must be shaped by the perspective provided by justification.

Of equal importance, though, is the fact that Luther did not affirm some kind of generic relationality, as if we could determine purely on the basis of human plurality or even sexual differentiation the kind of relationality that is in view. Indeed, although Luther is sometimes associated with the modern emphasis on relational humanity,[72] it is difficult to find "relationality" itself functioning as an anthropological category in Luther's theology. Instead, Luther emphasized human relationships shaped by grace, faith, and responsibility as providing the necessary framework for human existence. It is only in this sense that Luther qualifies as a "relational" theologian.

Some of Luther's interpreters have concluded that Luther's emphasis on relationality indicates an attempt to develop an entirely new ontology

---

71. Bayer, "Being in the Image of God," 78.

72. Lewis William Spitz, "Luther's Impact on Modern Views of Man," *Concordia Theological Quarterly* 41, no. 1 (1977): 26–43.

on the basis of these constitutive relations. From this perspective, Luther sought to replace the static *substance ontology* of medieval scholasticism with a more dynamic *relational ontology*.[73] Luther is thus viewed as staging an "ontological revolution" and paving the way for those modern anthropologies that view relations as having a kind of ontological primacy over particular things/substances.[74]

Despite the value of this interpretation and its clear recognition of how important the category of relationship is in Luther's anthropology, it would be a mistake to separate Luther too sharply from his medieval context.[75] Luther is perfectly willing to talk about body and soul as the discrete substances that comprise the human person, speaking in terms that would be familiar to any medieval theologian.[76] For Luther, though, these were secondary considerations when it comes to understanding the whole person (*totus homo*) before God and the rest of creation. Thus, Luther's emphasis on constitutive relations marginalizes the ontological considerations of earlier anthropologies, but without rejecting them entirely. For understanding the whole person, such issues are "insufficient, if not irrelevant."[77] Rather, any theological anthropology that is faithful to the humanity revealed in the doctrine of justification must emphasize grace, faith, and relationality. Those are the foundational building blocks of true humanity.

CALLED TO BE HUMAN: THE VOCATION OF BEING HUMAN

The truth of what it means to be human, according to Luther, is most clearly revealed in the doctrine of justification. Only there do we see the unmistakable beauty of the human person constituted by her relationships with God and creation, and brought into union with Christ through faith so that her entire life is shaped by the dynamic of receiving and responding. And this means that Luther's justification-centered anthropology reveals not only what we *are* as human beings, but also what we are *called to be*. If true humanity, the humanity that we see expressed in the doctrine of justification, includes not only the passive

---

73. See esp. Wilfried Joest, *Ontologie der Person bei Luther* (Göttingen: Vandenhoeck & Ruprecht, 1967); Gerhard Ebeling, *Luther; an Introduction to His Thought* (Philadelphia: Fortress, 1970).

74. Ebeling, "Luther's Understanding of Reality," 69.

75. See esp. the work of Heiko Oberman, Steven Ozment, and David Steinmetz.

76. E.g., Luther, *The Freedom of a Christian*, 51.

77. Pesch, "Free by Faith," 37.

righteousness that is ours *coram Deo* but also the active righteousness that obtains between humans and the rest of creation, then it necessarily follows that true humanity, although fundamentally constituted by the gift of God's grace, is also something toward which we must strive. In other words, true humanity is a *vocation*, something to which we are called when God summons us to our own humanity in the Word of grace.

Luther's theology of vocation is complex and studying it in depth would require understanding a variety of interrelated concepts including the two kingdoms/governments, the law/gospel relationship, the three estates, the orders of creation, and more.[78] So we will not attempt to cover everything in this short section. Instead, I want to highlight a few ways in which Luther's justification-centered anthropology shapes his theology of vocation. In this way, we will see that this is not some abstract theological issue. For Luther, our vision of humanity's *essence* shapes our vision of humanity's *calling*.

The Universal Vocation of Christians *coram Deo*

To begin, it may help to clarify the term *vocation* itself. One weakness of talking about vocation—or, as it is often translated, "calling"—is that such English terms carry with them inherently religious overtones. In other words, the English terms suggest that certain kinds of human work qualify as vocations, but not others. Thus we end up with a distinction between sacred and secular work, with the theological notion of vocation restricted only to the former. And it is precisely this sacred/secular distinction and the corresponding limitation of vocation to the sacred alone that Luther rejects. To see why, we will need to view Luther's arguments against the background of his criticism of medieval monasticism.[79]

---

78. Gustaf Wingren's 1942 dissertation remains the most influential study of Luther's theology of vocation (Gustaf Wingren, *Luther on Vocation*, trans. Carl C. Rasmussen, repr. [Philadelphia, Muhlenberg, 1957; repr., Eugene, Ore.: Wipf & Stock, 2004]; but see also Philip S. Watson, "Luther's Doctrine of Vocation," *Scottish Journal of Theology* 2, no. 4 [1949]: 364–77; Martin J. Heinecken, "Luther and the 'Orders of Creation' in Relation to a Doctrine of Work and Vocation," *Lutheran Quarterly* 4, no. 4 [952]: 393–414; John S. Feinberg, "Luther's Doctrine of Vocation: Some Problems of Interpretation and Application," *Fides et Historia* 12, no. 1 [1979]: 50–67; Karlfried Froehlich, "Luther on Vocation," *Lutheran Quarterly* 13, no. 2 [1999]: 195–207; Kenneth Hagen, "A Critique of Wingren on Luther on Vocation," *Lutheran Quarterly* 16, no. 3 [2002]: 249–73; Robert Kolb, "Called to Milk Cows and Govern Kingdoms: Martin Luther's Teaching on the Christian's Vocations," *Concordia Journal* 39, no. 2 [2013]: 133–41.

79. In this section, I am drawing largely on the historical summary offered in Froehlich, "Luther on Vocation."

The Latin term *vocatio* is simply a Latin translation of the Greek *klēsis*, which refers primarily to the salvific call that all believers receive and to which they respond in faith. Thus, the term originally referred to a calling that necessarily applies to all Christians. As the early church moved from its status as a persecuted minority to being the established church of the Roman Empire, they encountered a new challenge in that most people began life as a Christian and never experienced the kinds of divine calling and conversion so powerfully described in the New Testament. This led, among other factors, to the rise of monasticism as a way of expressing and experiencing that kind of transformational commitment. As a result, certain biblical terms that were originally applied to all Christians underwent a kind of restriction:

> After the fourth century, "to convert" meant to leave the world and embrace the monastic "vocation"; the term *vocation* itself now referred exclusively to the divine call to the monastic "profession," and "profession" was now the word for the solemn act of taking the monastic vows. Most tellingly, "religion" no longer meant the totality of the Christian faith or other faiths but served simply as the technical term for monasticism.[80]

This is the historical background against which Luther registered his objection that all Christians have a calling/vocation, a particular sphere of life in which they are to live lives shaped by their faith response before God and other creatures. There is no "higher calling" in the Christian life such that we can distinguish between sacred and secular vocations. Instead, all Christians are called to live justification-shaped lives wherever they are.

And for Luther this is more than merely recapturing the biblical language of calling and its applicability to all Christians. Instead, Luther saw this as a necessary extension of his theology of justification. All Christians have the same standing *coram Deo* regardless of the particular nature of our work in the world. This does not diminish the value of human work, which Luther will argue is an important expression of justification. But it does level the playing field: "Therefore, just as those who are now called 'spiritual,' that is, priests, bishops, or popes, are neither different from other Christians nor superior to them, except that they are charged with the administration of the word of God and the sacraments, which is

---

80. Ibid., 198.

their work and office ... A cobbler, a smith, a peasant—each has the work and office of his trade, and yet they are all alike consecrated priests and bishops."[81] Without downplaying the significant differences that exist between a priest and a cobbler, Luther argues on the basis of our equal standing before God that all vocations are equally spiritual.[82] "Christian liberty is not tied to any specific work. On the contrary, all works are the same to a Christian, no matter what they are."[83] Thus, Luther's sermons and writings are filled with "righteous haulers of manure, brewers of beer, and changers of diapers."[84] Luther's understanding of the Christian life has little to do with making distinctions between fundamentally different kinds of human work. Instead, he focuses on the extent to which any given work has been shaped by the constitutive gift-relationship and correlative faith-response that make us truly *human*.

Particular Vocations in Particular Locations

Luther's emphasis on the oneness of Christian vocation does not mean, however, that he was unable to distinguish between various kinds of Christian action. Indeed, Luther's own theology of justification with its emphasis on the two kinds of righteousness creates the possibility of affirming the essential equality of all humans *coram Deo* while also affirming the particular differences that exist *coram mundo* and *coram hominibus*. Although all Christians share the same relationship to God, we all stand in different relationships to other people and the world in general. These particularities constitute our unique location in society, which Luther referred to as our station (*Stand*). And within this station, each Christian has a particular occupation (*Beruf*) to perform, and typically more than one. It is this combination of station and occupation that constitutes the particularities of our calling *coram mundo*, which we engage as an outworking of our universal calling *coram Deo*. Thus, Kolb and Arand conclude, "The passive righteousness of faith provides the core identity of a person; the active righteousness of love flows from that core identity into the world."[85]

---

81. *LW* 44:130.

82. As early as the 1520 *Address to Christian Nobility*, Luther argued that all Christians are equally a part of the "spiritual estate" and not just priests and monks (*LW* 44:127).

83. *LW* 52:37.

84. Timothy J. Wengert, "Introduction," in *Harvesting Martin Luther's Reflections on Theology, Ethics, and the Church*, ed. Timothy J. Wengert (Grand Rapids: Eerdmans, 2004), 10.

85. Kolb and Arand, *The Genius of Luther's Theology*, 26.

For Luther, then, the doctrine of justification—and the corresponding idea of the two kinds of righteousness—provides the lens through which we view the entire Christian life. Here alone do we clearly see the human person passively receiving the gift of righteousness *coram Deo* and actively working out the implications of that core identity *coram mundo*. This means that the particular shape of our vocation must always be that of love and service: "We owe nobody anything but to love (Romans 13:8) and to serve our neighbor through love."[86] This is consistent with Luther's famous dictum regarding the nature of the Christian life as freedom in service to the neighbor: "A Christian is Lord of all, completely free of everything. A Christian is a servant, completely attentive to the needs of all."[87]

Luther's understanding of the two kinds of righteousness also shapes his vision of what we are doing when we serve the neighbor as an expression of vocation. Remember that although Luther distinguished between the two kinds of righteousness, he refused to separate them. One of the ways in which they are interrelated is that God establishes our relationship with him in the sphere of and through the means of creaturely relationships. And this is what we see in Luther's theology of vocation, where, according to Gustaf Wingren, he maintains that "with persons as his 'hands' or 'coworkers,' God gives his gifts through the earthly vocations."[88] Christian vocation is already a high calling when viewed exclusively as our calling to serve our neighbor. For Luther, though, it is even more. In vocation, we participate in God's own providential action of sustaining and blessing his good creation.

Since vocation is constituted by a particular situation, which includes all of the various relationships in which the human person stands, vocations are necessarily unique. No one stands in precisely the same place with regard to all of their various relationships. Luther thus critiqued the medieval emphasis on imitation as an appropriate category for understanding vocation. Although we may be able look to other Christians as examples of living faithfully in their particular circumstances, there is no straightforward way in which they provide an example that we can simply imitate in our own circumstances. Luther even critiqued the *imitatio Christi* as an inadequate basis for the Christian life. Jesus does provide a

---

86. *LW* 28:46.

87. Luther, *The Freedom of a Christian*, 50.

88. Wingren, *Luther on Vocation*, 27. See also Niels Henrik Gregersen, "Grace in Nature and History."

model (*exemplum*) that demonstrates the kind of Christian faithfulness we are called to exhibit, and an impulse (*motivatio*) for living out that faithfulness, but neither of these suggests a kind of imitation in which we can simply repeat Jesus' actions in our own circumstances.[89] Such mere imitation would actually be a betrayal of *my* neighbor and *my* location.[90]

Vocation, Law, and Gospel

Christians thus have a duty to live out their vocations in service to the neighbor. And this emphasis on the duty and responsibility of Christian vocation suggests a relationship between vocation and the law in Luther's theology. Our particular vocations involve something we are called to *do* (law) rather than a promise that we merely *receive* (gospel). As John Feinberg points out, "If it is a command to do something that God wants, it cannot be based on the Gospel."[91] And since vocation is an expression of *active* righteousness, it seems clearly to fall in the category of law.

Viewed from this perspective, vocation serves two purposes in the Christian life. In the first place, the duty of vocation and the consequences associated with failing to submit to the divine command provide a check on human selfishness, driving us to do that which we ordinarily would not. God thus secures the distribution of his good gifts in the world, most of which would be lost if we were left without the kind of command that can force us from our self-interested isolation. The second function of vocation as an expression of law is to reveal our own sinfulness. Christian vocation demands that we love our neighbors truly and sincerely, consistently placing their needs above our own, and that quickly reveals to us our own selfishness and inadequacy. We simply do not love the neighbor as we ought. Indeed, on our own, we *cannot* love the neighbor as we ought. So the very nature of the Christian "call" is to demand that we do what we cannot do. This is what Wingren refers to as the "cross" of vocation, a daily struggle in which our old selves are crucified so that we can be made alive again in the gospel.[92]

We should be careful, however, about focusing too much on this aspect of vocation, as important as it is in Luther's theology. At the very

---

89. Bernd Wannenwetsch, "Luther's Moral Theology," in *The Cambridge Companion to Martin Luther*, ed. Donald K. McKim (Cambridge: Cambridge University Press, 2003), 134.

90. See esp. Wingren, *Luther on Vocation*, 171–84.

91. Feinberg, "Luther's Doctrine of Vocation," 59.

92. Wingren, *Luther on Vocation*, 29.

least, this could easily lead to a rather negative view of vocation. Although Luther viewed vocation as a daily struggle that should drive us to the cross, we have also seen that he views vocation as participating in God's own work to sustain and bless his creation. And this means that vocation is a function of creation and not merely a consequence of the fall. Thus, Luther routinely associated vocation with the "orders of creation"—i.e., those stations of life that are rooted in creational realities like family, government, and ministry.[93] Consequently, while the task might be difficult, we should not miss its essential goodness as well.[94] As Johannes Schwanke states, "Luther's discovery of the world as a given, promised domain extricates him from a monastic denial of life and corresponding flight from the world. As a reformer living entirely out of joy in creation, he discovers worldliness as a theological category. Everything that the human being is and possesses is 'God's gift,' which should be 'used' by human beings."[95] Similarly, to the extent that our vocations are simply expressions of living as God's creatures in God's creation, vocation too should be viewed as a gift of God to be used joyously by his people.

We should also be careful not to overemphasize the impossibility of vocation. Although the demand of vocation drives us to our knees before the cross as we realize our inadequacies, that is precisely where we receive the grace necessary to fulfill the vocation. John Feinberg says it well: "the grounds or the basis for one's earthly vocation is Law, God's command to love and serve our neighbor. Gospel, however, is necessary as the *energizing factor* which enables us to fulfill the command God has given us to love our neighbor. Such an explanation is consistent with Luther's basic distinction between Law and Gospel, for the Law tells us what we must but cannot do, and the Gospel tells us how we can fulfill the command of God. In this case, faith (Gospel) becomes active in love and thereby fulfills the command (Law) to love and serve our neighbor."[96]

The promise of the gospel, then, is that God will give us the faith and love that we lack so that we can serve the neighbor as we ought. And this is only good and right given what we have already said about vocation participating in God's own action of pouring out his good gifts

93. *LW* 5:135–39.

94. This is the focus of Kenneth Hagen's critique of Wingren's study (Hagen, "A Critique of Wingren on Luther on Vocation").

95. Schwanke, "Luther on Creation," 92.

96. Feinberg, "Luther's Doctrine of Vocation," 60.

on creation. From the perspective of law, of course a finite and fallen human person cannot accomplish God's divine purposes, no matter how hard he strives. Down that road lies only frustration and failure. In his goodness, however, God provides what we lack so that our efforts can be taken up and made part of his own gracious action toward creation. As Luther said when offering advice to his barber: "You are God's creation, his handiwork, his workmanship. That is, of yourself and in yourself you are nothing, can do nothing, know nothing, are capable of nothing ... But what you are, know, can do, and can achieve is God's creation ... Here is the soul's garden of pleasure, along whose paths we enjoy the works of God."[97] In Christian vocation we see both law and gospel, striving and receiving.

BEYOND SALVATION: JUSTIFIED IN CHRIST AS A DEFINITION OF HUMANITY

We began this chapter with Luther's claim that the fundamental definition of what it means to be human is the fact that "man is justified by faith."[98] So we traced this claim through the contours of Luther's theology to see what he meant and how justification defines the essence of humanity. Along the way, we saw that, in Luther's view, justification orients every aspect of anthropology around God's grace, humanity's faith response, and the inherently relational nature of living *coram Deo* and *coram mundo*. According to Luther, justification is not primarily a doctrine about how human persons get saved. As important as this might be, justification goes further. In justification, we see the truth that righteousness (both *coram Deo* and *coram mundo*) is the essence of being human. Thus, any attempt to view humanity apart from justification necessarily creates a false image of the human person that leads toward destruction.

We have also seen that Luther's emphasis on justification does not detract from the inherently christological focus of his anthropology. For Luther, justification itself is thoroughly christological. To be righteous is to be united with Christ. This means that if justification defines what it means to be human, then Luther is claiming that the most fundamental reality of humanity is to be united with Christ through faith. This is no mere definition of how we *fix* broken humanity, as though there were some deeper definition of humanity that justification merely restored. Instead, being united with Christ through faith simply *is* what it means to be human.

---

97. *LW* 43:210.
98. *LW* 34:135–44.

Thus, rather than being one doctrine among many, justification in Christ becomes a "metatheological criterion," something that provides "a universal vantage point" from which to view all of Christian life and doctrine, as well as the framework within which we must interpret any non-theological perspectives on humanity (e.g., Aristotelian philosophy).[99] On this basis, Luther offered a creative and challenging vision of what it means to be human, one that marginalized many aspects of earlier theological anthropologies and established trajectories that remain influential to this day.

---

99. Stephen Duffy, *The Dynamics of Grace* (Collegeville, Minn.: Liturgical, 1993), 193.

CHAPTER 4

The Feeling of Being Human

Friedrich Schleiermacher and the Ecclesial Mediation of True Humanity

——•——

The feeling of absolute dependence ... is ... an essential element of human nature.

Friedrich Schleiermacher, *The Christian Faith*[1]

SCHLEIERMACHER FAMOUSLY VIEWED CHRISTIAN DOGMATICS as an empirical discipline that begins not with revealed doctrine, whether located in Scripture or tradition, but with the redemption that is actually experienced by Christians through Jesus. "The reference to redemption is in every Christian consciousness simply because the originator of the Christian communion is the Redeemer; and Jesus is Founder of a religious community simply in the sense that its members become conscious of redemption through him" (§11). Schleiermacher thus took it as the necessary starting point of Christian theology that all Christians have in fact experienced redemption, that this redemption came about through the person and work of Jesus of Nazareth, and that it is possible to reflect upon the redemptive experience as it has been understood by the Christian community throughout the centuries to draw theological conclusions about the nature of redemption, the redeemed, and the Redeemer. Consequently, "all doctrines properly so called must be extracted from the Christian religious self-consciousness, *i.e.* the inward experience of Christian people" (§64) such that Christian doctrines simply are "accounts of the Christian religious affections set forth in speech" (§15). In the context of his theological anthropology, then, Schleiermacher's theology involves

---

1. Friedrich Schleiermacher, *The Christian Faith*, ed. H. R. Mackintosh and J. S. Stewart (Berkeley: Apocryphile, 2011), §6.1. Hereafter, I will cite *The Christian Faith* in text by section number (e.g., §88.2).

working through the implications of this experience of redemption for understanding the nature of the redeemed.

For Schleiermacher, that understanding of theology emphasizes the importance of Christology. If theology takes redemptive experience as its necessary starting point, and if it is not possible to understand redemption apart from some understanding of the Redeemer, then we should expect that Schleiermacher's approach to theology, and consequently to anthropology, will be shaped by Christology in some meaningful way. Indeed, for Schleiermacher, everything about Christian theology must be "related to the redemption accomplished by Jesus of Nazareth" (§11). The same holds for Schleiermacher's view of the human person. The Redeemer Jesus came both as a revelation of true humanity and as the one who makes true humanity possible for all others. To see humanity rightly, we must begin with Christology.

However, having said that, Schleiermacher's methodology still raises important questions about what stands at the center of his theology. Despite the obvious importance of Christology throughout his theology, some of his interpreters claim that his theology is thoroughly *anthropo-* centric. Since he begins with the individual *experience* of redemption and only on that basis begins to reflect on the reality of God and Jesus Christ, many theologians have worried that the robustly christological content of Schleiermacher's theology serves to camouflage its inherently anthropological basis.[2] In other words, does the essential logic of Schleiermacher's theology move *from* anthropology *to* Christology? If it does, in what sense does his theological anthropology qualify as meaningfully christological?

In this chapter we will explore Schleiermacher's understanding of the human person as viewed through his particular account of the Christian experience of redemption. In so doing, we will see that Schleiermacher presents the human person as fundamentally shaped by particular ways of experiencing, knowing, and acting in the world. But it is only as the human person enters the sphere of Jesus' own consciousness that the full capacities of the person are awakened and he or she can begin making steady progress toward the life of blessedness that is the true goal of humanity. This in turn is made possible only as Jesus' redemptive influence is mediated to the person through the fellowship of those who have already been

---

2. The most influential example of this critique has been that of Karl Barth. See esp. Karl Barth, *Protestant Theology in the Nineteenth Century: Its Background and History* (Grand Rapids: Eerdmans, 2002), 411–59.

redeemed—i.e., the church. Schleiermacher's theological anthropology thus develops through the complex interaction of Christology, ecclesiology, soteriology, and ethics. Understanding how those theological loci combine to inform Schleiermacher's theological anthropology will help us see how he understands the human person and the extent to which that account is particularly informed by the person and work of Jesus Christ.

THE EXPERIENCE OF REDEMPTION IN SCHLEIERMACHER'S CHRISTOLOGICAL ANTHROPOLOGY

Since Schleiermacher's theology centers on the Christian experience of redemption, our analysis must begin there as well. Borrowing somewhat loosely from Barth's famous three-fold description of revelation as involving a revealer, a revealed, and a revealedness,[3] we might say that Schleiermacher's theology of redemption involves a similar tripartite emphasis: Redeemer, redeemed, and redeemedness. The Christian experience of redemption itself comprises the redeemedness, which revolves around Schleiermacher's particular account of the "feeling of absolute dependence" and the corresponding "God-consciousness." At the same time, though, Schleiermacher contends that we cannot have a Christian experience of redemption without some concept of a Redeemer. Thus, although the experience of redemption is the necessary starting point for theological reflection, Schleiermacher contends that this experience is always thoroughly christological. Redeemer and redemption are inseparable in Christian experience. Finally, none of this would have any purchase on reality if not for some account of those redeemed. This immediately presses us toward some concept of the human person and, for Schleiermacher, the Christian communities in which those human persons experience redemption.

With that threefold framework for Schleiermacher's redemptive theology in mind, we will address in this section the nature of redeemedness and the Redeemer. Together, those will help us see how Schleiermacher understands the nature of redemption and why he contends that it is inherently and thoroughly christological. In the latter half of the chapter, we will turn our attention to the nature of the redeemed, focusing here on Schleiermacher's particular understanding of how the individual human is constituted by the community. This will lead in turn to some reflections on the nature of Christian action. For Schleiermacher, redemption should not be understood as an exclusively "inner" experience. Instead,

---

3. Karl Barth, *Church Dogmatics*, vol. I/1 (London: T&T Clark, 2004), 299.

Schleiermacher presents redemption as a person-forming experience that leads to world-forming action. Schleiermacher's vision of true humanity, then, is formed through redemption in Christ that comes through the Christian community and expresses itself in Christian action.

The Feeling of Absolute Dependence

Schleiermacher famously grounds his understanding of Christianity in his concept of piety, which he defines as "the consciousness of being absolutely dependent, or, which is the same thing, of being in relation with God" (§4). Understanding what Schleiermacher means by terms like "consciousness" and "absolutely dependent" will take us into the heart of his account of the Christian religion and its conception of the human person.[4]

In *The Christian Faith* Schleiermacher makes important distinctions between "feeling," which is a kind of pre-reflective awareness of some state of affairs; "consciousness," which is a mode of experiencing the world in which we become aware of our feelings and able to reflect upon them and how they shape human living; "and self-consciousness," which is a mode of knowing in which "the self is present to itself."[5] Thus, as Catherine Kelsey says, feelings involve "the awareness we have *before* we think," while consciousness is what we have when that intuitive awareness arises to a more reflective level.[6] To

---

4. This does not mean that Schleiermacher thinks that only Christians have a concept of true humanity. Instead, as we will see, Schleiermacher contends that humans have an inherent capacity for God-consciousness that expresses itself in a limited manner in all humans before redemption and also finds expression in non-Christian religions (§6–9). At the very least, Schleiermacher would say that we catch glimpses of true humanity wherever there are humans, but that the full completion of human nature comes about only through Jesus.

5. Richard R. Niebuhr, *Schleiermacher on Christ and Religion: A New Introduction* (New York: Scribner's, 1964), 182. Schleiermacher develops his vision of what it means to be human throughout his writings. As Clements says when describing Schleiermacher's speeches, "They comprise a positive, new vision of what it is to be truly human, in a wholeness, richness and freedom not known by the passing wisdom of the age" (K. W. Clements, *Friedrich Schleiermacher: Pioneer of Modern Theology*, The Making of Modern Theology [London: Collins, 1987], 37). Thus, although we will be focusing largely on *The Christian Faith* as the most mature and sustained articulation of Schleiermacher's anthropological vision, anthropology was something Schleiermacher addressed in most of his theological writings.

6. Catherine L. Kelsey, *Thinking about Christ with Schleiermacher* (Louisville: Westminster John Knox, 2003), 72. According to Kevin Hector, Schleiermacher's concept of "feeling" is best understood as a kind of "attunement" with one's surroundings, "the innumerable ways in which one is affected by, and copes with, various circumstances prior to and apart from conscious reflection and judgment" (Kevin W. Hector, "Attunement and Explicitation: A Pragmatist Reading of Schleiermacher's 'Theology of Feeling,'" in *Schleiermacher, the Study of Religion, and the Future of Theology: A Transatlantic Dialogue*, ed. Brent W. Sockness and Wilhelm Gräb [New York: Walter de Gruyter, 2010], 223).

see what this means, let us consider what Schleiermacher has to say about the kinds of conscious experiences that infuse everyday living.

According to Schleiermacher, all of our everyday conscious experiences involve both an active and a passive component. Conscious experiences are never entirely self-generated, as though we could have thoughts and experiences completely independent of the particular objects that we are experiencing and thinking about. Even when I am thinking about my own self, I am still having an experience of a particular object (my "self" in this case) that serves as the occasion for the experience. At the same time, though, it seems unlikely that I could have any of those experiences if not for some aspect of my subjectivity that somehow preceded the experiences themselves and served as the condition of their possibility. In other words, according to Schleiermacher, our own subjective experiences require us to make a distinction between something that is "self-caused"—i.e., that which is immediate to the self and (at least logically) prior to particular experiences—and that which is "non-self-caused"—i.e., that which is mediated through particular objects of experience. Conscious experiences thus have both an active/productive and a passive/receptive aspect, or as Schleiermacher explained, "a Being and a Having-by-some-means-come-to-be" (§4.1).

Schleiermacher contends, though, that if we dig more deeply into these experiences, we will discover an immediate, pre-reflective feeling that corresponds to each of these poles. On the one hand, we have a "feeling of dependence" (§4.2), an intuitive sense that we require something other than ourselves to be the kinds of persons that we are. But we also experience a "feeling of freedom," which is the intuitive sense that we are discernible individuals who have the power both to respond to the given and to influence the being of the given, even if in a very small way. In other words, in the feelings of freedom and dependence, we have an intuitive sense that we are significant individuals embedded in a larger network of mutually informing relations, in which we play a small but not insignificant role in shaping the identities of the beings with whom we stand in relation.[7] We experience ourselves as both free and dependent, active agents and passive recipients.

---

7. This means there is a reciprocal relationship between the self and the object of experience. It is not merely that the object acts on the self, but that the self also serves to constitute the object, even if only minutely. Even in our experiences of heavenly bodies "we ourselves do, in the same sense in which they influence us, exercise a counter-influence, however minute" (§4.2).

Yet Schleiermacher presses even further. In addition to these pre-reflective feelings of dependence and freedom, he contends that we can also discern in our conscious experiences an even deeper "feeling of absolute dependence" (§4.3). This is a pre-reflective intuition that there is one being who influences us, but whom we do not influence in return, the awareness of a kind of consciousness that can only come from outside of us, indeed from outside the created order itself. To this being alone we have a feeling of dependence to which there is no corresponding feeling of freedom, and, thus, it is a feeling of *absolute* dependence.[8] Schleiermacher argues that "God" is the only adequate word for describing such a feeling of absolute dependence.[9] He is the only possible "*Whence*" of such an experience (§4.4).

The kind of consciousness that corresponds to this feeling of absolute dependence is what Schleiermacher calls "God-consciousness" (§11.2). Despite what the name might suggest, though, Schleiermacher does not intend to suggest by this that God-consciousness refers to the conscious experiences that we have of God himself. For Schleiermacher, God is not an "object" of experience like an apple or a table. Instead, like the feelings of relative dependence and freedom, the feeling of absolute dependence arises in the context of my experiences with natural objects like tables and apples. Even as I experience such items, I can discern within those experiences a deeper feeling, one that points toward a kind of dependence more fundamental than my "Being and Having-by-some-means-come-to-be" with respect to the apple and the table. Indeed, it is a feeling of dependence so absolute that I come to realize that its source lies beyond the entire web of mutually involving relations itself. It is that on which the entire world order depends. Thus, according to Schleiermacher, God-consciousness occurs in and through the "lower" forms of consciousness

---

8. Georg Behrens has pointed out that Schleiermacher frequently talks about "the absolute feeling of dependence" rather than "the feeling of absolute dependence," contending on the basis of these varying grammatical constructions that Schleiermacher actually had two very different ideas in mind with this phrase (Georg Behrens, "Feeling of Absolute Dependence or Absolute Feeling of Dependence? (What Schleiermacher Really Said and Why It Matters)," *Religious Studies* 34, no. 4 [1998]: 471–81). Yet Hueston Finlay argues convincingly that despite the apparent grammatical support for such an interpretation, Schleiermacher used the two phrases interchangeably to describe the absoluteness of our dependency relationship with God (Hueston E. Finlay, "'Feeling of Absolute Dependence' 'Absolute Feeling of Dependence'? A Question Revisited," *Religious Studies* 41, no. 01 [2005]: 81–94).

9. Schleiermacher rejects the possibility that such an experience could come from our interaction with any particular object within creation, or even the entirety of creation itself, since all such relationships involve both influence and counterinfluence (§4.3).

(§5). The God-consciousness "does not constitute by itself alone an actual moment in religious experience, but always in connexion with other particular determinations" (§32) and "only under the general form of self-consciousness" (§62).

God-Forgetfulness, God-Consciousness, and Human Development

With all of this as background, we can now address what Schleiermacher means by the experience of redemption and how it relates to his discussion of the various modes of consciousness. According to Schleiermacher, when we say that Christians have experienced redemption, we are saying at least that they are conscious of some prior (bad) state from which they needed to be redeemed (the consciousness of sin) and that they have also experienced the transition into some new (better) condition that constitutes the state of redemption (the consciousness of grace). Although Schleiermacher contends that the consciousness of sin and grace are inseparable in our experience—i.e., we never become aware of grace without a prior awareness of sin, but our awareness of sin as *sin* requires some intuition of grace—he nonetheless contends that it is legitimate to separate them in the order of presentation for the sake of clarity (§64). The antithesis between sin and grace thus comprises the basic structure of the entire second half of *The Christian Faith*.

The problem that creates the need for redemption is that of *"Godlessness, or, better, God-forgetfulness"* (§11.2). Even though God-consciousness always comes about in conjunction with other forms of self-consciousness, this is far from an instantaneous process. Indeed, if we again allow our actual experiences to guide our discussion, we discover that they vacillate between those often fleeting moments in which we experience God-consciousness and those more frequent moments in which we do not. Instead of facilitating God-consciousness, then, the lower consciousness often serves to inhibit it and prevent it from becoming actualized in our experience.[10] Thus, the essence of sin for Schleiermacher is anything that "has arrested the free development of the God-consciousness" (§66.1). This state of resistance to God-consciousness is the bad condition from which human persons need redemption.

---

10. As Walter Wyman explains, "[T]he higher self-consciousness must enter into a relationship with the sensible self-consciousness to form a moment of consciousness; the inhibition of the God-consciousness by the sensible self-consciousness constitutes the 'bad condition'" (Walter E. Wyman, "Sin and Redemption," in *The Cambridge Companion to Friedrich Schleiermacher*, ed. Jacqueline Mariña [New York: Cambridge University Press, 2005], 132).

The reference to the "free development" of God-consciousness sig-
nals the fact that Schleiermacher views God-consciousness as a natural
expression of what it means to be human. It is "an essential element of
human nature" (§6.1). Indeed, he rejects any suggestion that redemption should be understood as a merely external addition to or altera-
tion of humanity rather than a perfection of how God created humanity
from the beginning. Such "magical" views of redemption actually entail
a form of re-creation that denies our humanity and eliminates the possibility of a true redemption (§11.2). In his account, then, grace perfects
nature; prior to redemption every human person has the seed of the God-
consciousness operating within them, even if it is entirely impercepti-
ble.[11] This is what Schleiermacher refers to as the "original perfection" of
human nature (§68). By this, he is not referring to the supposedly pre-fall
condition of Adam and Eve, but to the fact that human nature has been
created for God-consciousness and, despite the hindrances of the sensible self-consciousness, remains capable of having the God-consciousness
restored through the work of the Redeemer.[12]

The fact that Schleiermacher emphasizes the necessity of a Redeemer
means he also rejects the alternative of viewing the God-consciousness as
such a natural outgrowth of already-existing human capacities that no real
redemption is even necessary. On this account, human nature contains
within itself the solution to its own problem. All we need is a model or
example of true humanity that we can follow through our own efforts to
bring about our own redemption. Yet Schleiermacher rejected any such
opinion with no uncertainty: "But this view, in nullifying as it does not
only the reality of sin but also the need of redemption, leaves so little
room anywhere for the peculiar work of a Redeemer that it can scarcely
be regarded as a Christian view at all" (§68). As we will see in the next
section, Schleiermacher maintains the absolute uniqueness of Jesus in the
redemption of humanity. Thus, despite his emphasis on "original perfection," humanity as we actually experience it has "a complete incapacity for
good" (§70) as a result of the "derangement of our nature" (§68).

---

11. See esp. §13 and §60.

12. According to Nelson, Schleiermacher understood the "goodness" of created state as
"a framework for moral possibility. Creation is 'perfect' when it is, in principle, perfect-
ible" (Derek Nelson, "Schleiermacher and Ritschl on Individual and Social Sin," *Zeitschrift
für Neuere Theologiegeschichte* 16, no. 2 [2009]: 134). For a nice survey of Schleiermacher's
rejection of the fall, see David Nelson Duke, "Schleiermacher: Theology without a Fall,"
Perspectives in Religious Studies 9, no. 1 (1982): 21–37.

This is not, however, because our natures themselves have been fundamentally altered, something that Schleiermacher thought would entail sin causing us to become something non-human. Instead, Schleiermacher associates the inevitability and universality of human sinfulness with two factors. As he says, "We are conscious of sin partly as having its source in ourselves, partly as having its source outside our own being" (§69). With regard to the source of sin in ourselves, Schleiermacher describes the relationship between the sensible self-consciousness and God-consciousness in developmental terms. In human development, the sensible self-consciousness arises first, as evidenced by the fact that even very small children have conscious experiences of the world around them. God-consciousness, on the other hand, comes at a later stage in human development. Although this two-stage development of human consciousness is natural to the human condition, it still results in the historic reality that the sensible self-consciousness gets a head start in human experience (§67.2). As a result, when the human person develops to the point where the God-consciousness begins to manifest itself, "resistance takes place" (ibid.). Thus, "the strength of the resistance made by the flesh and manifested in the consciousness of sin, is due to the advantage gained by the flesh during the prior time" (ibid.).

However, this account of sin might suggest that sin itself is natural to the human condition—i.e., the inevitable consequence of human development. Yet Schleiermacher contends that sin is also sourced in something outside of us, namely the human communities that shape and define us as human persons. Schleiermacher thus argues that "the sinfulness which is prior to all action operates in every individual through the sin and sinfulness of others" (§71.2). Just as each generation of human persons is formed by the one preceding it, "so the sinful self-assertiveness of sense, proceeding as it does from its earlier development has a more remote source than the individual's life" (§69.3). This is what Schleiermacher refers to as the "corporate character" of sin (§71.2). Schleiermacher refused to speculate on how this might have worked if we had not fallen into sin, since this would require us to theologize beyond what we can know on the basis of the experience of redemption, yet Schleiermacher's account seems to suggest something like the following. In such a hypothetical world, the developing human person would have been guided through the process of moving from the lower consciousness toward God-consciousness by the entire community of human persons in whom that developmental process was already under way.[13] In the world in which we actually find ourselves, however, these human communities shape human persons such that the lower consciousness dominates and necessarily inhibits the formation of God-consciousness. In such a state, we find in ourselves a desire for "harmony with the God-consciousness" (§68.2), but with no possibility of actualizing that desire ourselves. Consequently, "sin is inevitable for us, in so far at least as that it is not in our power at any particular moment to be sinless" (§86.2). In this condition, human persons would never have experienced redemption. For this, we need a Redeemer.

The Unique Dignity of the Redeemer

According to Schleiermacher, our experience of redemption includes not only the consciousness of sin, but also the consciousness of grace in Jesus. As we saw earlier, Schleiermacher defines the essence of Christianity around the experience of "the redemption accomplished by Jesus of Nazareth." In the latter half of *The Christian Faith* he systematically unpacks that conviction, arguing that Jesus is the Redeemer who accomplishes the redemption and reconciliation of humanity by transmitting his sinless perfection to humanity through the corporate life of the redeemed.

To understand Jesus' role as the redeemer, we need to discuss Schleiermacher's distinction between redemption and reconciliation. Properly speaking, redemption refers specifically to "the removal of sin" (§100.3). Since we have already seen that *sin* is simply whatever inhibits the God-consciousness, it stands to reason that redemption involves the implantation of the God-consciousness in humanity as "a vital new principle" that overcomes the inhibitions of the lower consciousness and transforms both individuals and communities into humans empowered by God's own presence. As we will see in a moment, although the capacity for God-consciousness has been a part of humanity from the beginning, it only arrives in its true form through the sinless perfection of Jesus. Thus, redemption involves the "communication of Christ's sinless perfection" to the rest of humanity (§88). In this way, "the God-consciousness already present in human nature,

---

13. This is confirmed by Schleiermacher's account of Jesus' own development (§93.3-4; see also Friedrich Schleiermacher, *The Life of Jesus*, ed. Jack C. Verheyden, trans. S. Maclean Gilmour [Philadelphia: Fortress, 1975], 99). Although Schleiermacher argues that Jesus always experienced perfect God-consciousness, he contends that this is consistent with saying that Jesus' God-consciousness developed over time. As a child, his God-consciousness was perfect in the sense that it was as well developed as a child's God-consciousness could be, not that it was the complete and full expression of all that God-consciousness can be.

though feeble and repressed, becomes stimulated and made dominant by the entrance of the living influence of Christ" (§106.1).

Reconciliation, on the other hand, is a consequence of redemption in which believers are assumed into Jesus' "unclouded blessedness" (§101), which involves eliminating the impact of sin on the redeemed. Prior to redemption, human consciousness is marred by strife and turmoil, riven with pain, guilt, and evil. Blessedness is the condition of living in the world without experiencing this turmoil. This does not mean that the "natural imperfections" of the world that we currently experience as evil are themselves eliminated, only that they are now experienced as "merely incentives" for growing in God-consciousness (§84.4). Jesus' state of "unclouded blessedness" thus describes the perfect peace of his conscious state, a peace that is untroubled by any conflict or strife despite the vicissitudes of life (§98). Jesus thus transmits not merely God-consciousness as the power to live the redeemed life, but also the inner peace that corresponds to this new state.[14] Each of these involves growth and development such that although we do not currently experience perfect redemption (God-consciousness) or reconciliation (blessedness), we do experience their increase, pointing toward a future reality in which the perfection witnessed in Christ becomes a reality for all humans.[15]

As these explanations of redemption and reconciliation have already made clear, Schleiermacher thought that neither becomes a reality for humanity apart from Jesus Christ. He alone has the sinless perfection and unclouded blessedness that enables redemption and reconciliation to become realities in the world (§91).[16] As I mentioned earlier, though, one important criticism of Schleiermacher is that his approach to theology

---

14. As Catherine Kelsey explains, "Redemption is not primarily about forgiveness of sin; that understanding of the effect of Christ is too narrow. Redemption is a transformation of human nature" (Kelsey, *Thinking about Christ with Schleiermacher*, 63).

15. This raises the question of universalism in Schleiermacher's theology. If he thinks that all humans will eventually be transformed through the ever-expanding influence of Jesus' God-consciousness, does this mean that Schleiermacher thinks that all humans will eventually be saved? Although Schleiermacher prefers not to speculate about eschatological truths since they cannot be extrapolated from the Christian experience of redemption (§157.2), he does think that it is more reasonable to believe "that through the power of redemption there will one day be a universal restoration of all souls" (§163, appendix).

16. Consequently, Schleiermacher ends up with several "actualizations" of God-consciousness in the world. First, there is the fleeting experience of God-consciousness that human persons can have prior to redemption. Second, there is the perfect actualization of God-consciousness that occurs only in Jesus. And finally, we have the actualization of God-consciousness in redemption, which is real but partial, and thus involves growth and development.

is essentially anthropocentric. Karl Barth famously described Schleiermacher's theology as comprising "an ellipse with two foci," by which he means the human and the divine.[17] Yet the two foci exert an "attractive power" on each other such that the ellipse "tends to become a circle, so that its two foci have the tendency to coincide in one centre point."[18] Barth contended that the anthropological pole exerted the greater influence; thus, the divine tends to be collapsed entirely within this new anthropological center. Barth was sensitive enough to Schleiermacher's theology to recognize that this was never his intent. Indeed, Barth describes him as wanting to be a "Christocentric theologian."[19] Yet in the end he concluded that the trajectory of Schleiermacher's theology is such that an anthropocentric outcome seems nearly inevitable.

Even more vitally for our purposes, Barth argued that Schleiermacher's Christology itself was tainted by this anthropological approach. According to Barth, Schleiermacher viewed Jesus as mere *exemplar* of true humanity.[20] Although Schleiermacher identified Jesus as the most perfect expression of God-consciousness, Barth contended that this only establishes that Jesus is *quantitatively* different than the rest of humanity.[21] Thus, Jesus stands at one end of a continuous spectrum that includes all human persons. As a result, despite Schleiermacher's high appreciation for the significance of Jesus Christ, he cannot account for the *essential uniqueness* of Jesus.[22]

If Barth's interpretation of Schleiermacher is correct, and it is one that has exercised considerable influence on the reception of Schleiermacher in the twentieth century, then it would seem difficult to conclude that Schleiermacher belongs in a project such as this. Rather than allowing Christology to inform his anthropology in some meaningful way, the

---

17. Barth, *Protestant Theology in the Nineteenth Century*, 418.

18. Ibid., 450.

19. Ibid., 418.

20. Karl Barth, *The Theology of Schleiermacher*, ed. Dietrich Ritschl (Grand Rapids: Eerdmans, 1982), 55.

21. Barth, *Protestant Theology in the Nineteenth Century*, 457.

22. Barth thus describes Schleiermacher's Christology as a "heresy of gigantic proportions" (*Theology of Schleiermacher*, 104). H. R. Mackintosh similarly critiques Schleiermacher's "low" Christology and his failure to affirm the full deity of Jesus (Hugh Ross Mackintosh, *Types of Modern Theology: Schleiermacher to Barth* [London: SCM Press, 1990], 206–7). Similar assessments can be found in John S. Reist Jr., "Continuity, Christ, and Culture: A Study of F. Schleiermacher's Christology," *The Journal of Religious Thought* 26, no. 3 (1969): 24–27; Colin E. Gunton, *Yesterday and Today: A Study of Continuities in Christology* (Grand Rapids: Eerdmans, 1983), 89–99; Kathryn Tanner, *Jesus, Humanity and the Trinity: A Brief Systematic Theology* (Minneapolis: Fortress, 2001), 8.

direction of Schleiermacher's logic would move in precisely the opposite direction. Fortunately, we have some reasons for thinking that Barth's criticisms may not be entirely adequate. Although we will see in the next chapter that Barth articulated his christological anthropology in ways that are importantly different from Schleiermacher's, the latter nonetheless constructed his theology in such a way that Christology still plays a decisive role in defining what it means to be human.

First, it is important to remember that Schleiermacher's theology does not begin with an analysis of conscious experience *as such*. Rather than starting with a phenomenology of human experience in general, Schleiermacher begins with the specifically *Christian* experience of redemption, which means it is the experience of *having been redeemed by Christ*. Thus, to the extent that Schleiermacher's theology has an anthropological basis in the analysis of experience, it presupposes a more fundamental starting point in Christology. The only kind of experience that counts in Schleiermacher's theology is an experience that is always-already christological.[23] Thus, "there is no general God-consciousness which has not bound up with it a relation to Christ" (§62.3). Rather than thinking that propositions about God-consciousness can be derived from a kind of natural theology, Schleiermacher contends that these "propositions are in no sense the reflection of a meagre and purely monotheistic God-consciousness, but are abstracted from one which has issued from fellowship with the Redeemer" (ibid.). Thus, although the order in which Schleiermacher addresses his topics in *The Christian Faith*—beginning with a general account of God-consciousness and only subsequently moving into his account of the Redeemer—has often led people to assume that he constructs his argument around a kind of natural theology, his own explanation moves in a rather different direction. The experience of redemption is inherently christological, and it is only from this starting point that we can begin to analyze God-consciousness and its significance for the human person.[24]

---

23. Thus Mariña contends that Schleiermacher does not begin with "an anthropological analysis of self-consciousness that can be understood independently from the context of redemption" (Jacqueline Mariña, "Christology and Anthropology," in *The Cambridge Companion to Friedrich Schleiermacher*, ed. Jacqueline Mariña [New York: Cambridge University Press, 2005], 169).

24. This is such a fundamental starting point that Schleiermacher makes no attempt to defend the christological basis and orientation of the Christian experience of redemption. Any such endeavor would require that he ground theology in something other than the experience of our redemption in Christ, which he consistently refused to do. So although Barth may be correct in thinking that there are two foci in Schleiermacher's theological ellipse, we may want to reconsider which of the two exercises the stronger pull.

Second, Schleiermacher argues extensively for the absolute uniqueness of Jesus Christ even as he continues to affirm his commonality with the rest of us in virtue of his full humanity (§94). He thus contends that Christ's status as Redeemer depends on his "peculiar activity" and his "exclusive dignity" (§92). In other words, redemption depends on the absolute uniqueness of the Redeemer. Schleiermacher explicitly rejects the alternative possibility that Jesus might be merely "exemplary" (vorbildliche) of true humanity, as though Jesus was just a signpost pointing us toward a greater realization of the same potentiality inherent within us. For Schleiermacher, that entails an essentially Pelagian understanding of redemption, which he has already argued would fundamentally undermine the Christian experience of redemption in Christ (§93.2). A purely exemplary humanity can point toward self-realization, but it cannot redeem.

But might it not be the case that although Jesus was a merely exemplary human individual, he was one in whom a unique power was at work? In other words, could the uniqueness lie in the redemptive power at work in Christ rather than any particular characteristics of Jesus himself? Schleiermacher considers and rejects this understanding of Jesus as well. In this case, Jesus' uniqueness would be a mere happenstance of history; he would simply have been the first to receive the divine gift.[25] Schleiermacher offers two reasons for rejecting this conclusion. First, he argues that Jesus' God-consciousness is fundamentally different from that of all other humans because he alone is the one who has perfect God-consciousness intrinsically: "Of the Redeemer ... we must hold that the ground of His sinlessness was not external to Himself, but that it was a sinlessness essentially grounded in Himself" (§94.1). As Kevin Hector explains, Jesus alone is the one who perfectly receives and reproduces God's own activity in the world; consequently, he is God incarnate.[26]

---

25. Schleiermacher thus argues that Jesus is fundamentally different from the founders of all other religions. "For those other founders are represented as having been, as it were, arbitrarily elevated from the mass of similar or not very different men, and as receiving just as much for themselves as for other people whatever they do receive in the way of divine doctrine and precept" (§11.4).

26. Kevin W. Hector, "Actualism and Incarnation: The High Christology of Friedrich Schleiermacher," International Journal of Systematic Theology 8, no. 3 (2006): 307–22. Hector helpfully counters arguments against Schleiermacher's "low" Christology in which Jesus' uniqueness is either denied or inconsistently applied. He contends that a proper appreciation of Schleiermacher's "actualism" would help us see Jesus as the perfect actualization of God-consciousness and, consequently, as fully divine. While disagreeing with Hector that Schleiermacher thus offers a "high" Christology, Hunsinger agrees that it should not be considered a "low" Christology either. Thus, Hunsinger concludes that we need a third

Thus, it is not that Jesus just happened to be the human person on whom God decided to bestow the power of God-consciousness in a unique manner; instead, there is an intrinsic difference in the way in which Jesus expressed his perfect God-consciousness. "Otherwise it could only be explained as an arbitrary divine act that the restorative divine element made its appearance precisely in Jesus, and not in some other person" (§13.1). While remaining fully human, Jesus alone is the one in whom perfect God-consciousness arose as a natural and essential expression of his own being. He is distinct from all other humans "by the constant potency of His God-consciousness, which was a veritable existence of God in Him" (§94). The limited God-consciousness that we experienced before redemption should not be called the existence of God in humanity, even though it could be viewed as the condition for the possibility of such presence (§94.2). Instead, Jesus is the only one in whom "there is an existence of God in the proper sense" (§94.3).[27] Only in and through Jesus does God-consciousness become a reality in human nature such that "he alone mediates all existence of God in the world" (§94.2). Jesus thus differs even from a figure like Adam who would have experienced sinless perfection only as a result of his circumstances. Jesus alone has "a sinlessness essentially grounded in Himself" (§94.1), an "inner ground" that can only be "the union of the divine and the human in His Person" (§98.1).

Schleiermacher's second reason for emphasizing the uniqueness of Jesus and not simply the uniqueness of the power at work in Jesus is his understanding of the role that Jesus of Nazareth played in God's ordained plan for all of creation. According to Schleiermacher, Jesus of Nazareth was always intended to be the culmination of God's creative plans for humanity. He is "the one in Whom the creation of human nature, which up to this point had existed only in a provisional state, was perfected" (§92.1), the one in whom we see "the completion, only now accomplished,

---

category and that Schleiermacher's Christology is best viewed as a "middle" Christology that stands between the two extremes (George Hunsinger, "*Salvator Mundi*: Three Types of Christology," in *Christology, Ancient and Modern: Explorations in Constructive Dogmatics*, ed. Oliver D. Crisp and Fred Sanders [Grand Rapids: Zondervan, 2013], 42–59).

27. Thus, although Schleiermacher was sharply critical of the "two natures" language of Chalcedon (see esp. §96), he continued to maintain that God was uniquely incarnated in Christ. Nestlehutt contends that "Schleiermacher argued for a modification of the Chalcedonian definition rather than for its complete rejection. His alternative Christology is an attempt to preserve the quiddity or content of the formula, while rejecting the form and specific historic language" (Mark S. G. Nestlehutt, "Chalcedonian Christology: Modern Criticism and Contemporary Ecumenism," *Journal of Ecumenical Studies* 35, no. 2 [1998]: 184). Whether Schleiermacher was successful in this endeavor is, of course, an entirely separate question.

of the creation of human nature" (§89).[28] Even the preliminary and limited experiences of God-consciousness that we have before redemption are "no more than a mere approximation to that which exists in the Redeemer Himself" (§93.1). And he played this role specifically because in his eternal decree God determined that Jesus would be the one in and through whom perfect humanity would be realized (§89.3).[29] In this way, although Schleiermacher's understanding of election differs from Barth's in several important respects, they overlap in seeing Jesus as the historic outworking of God's eternal purposes for humanity.[30]

For these reasons, Schleiermacher argues that even though we can still regard Jesus as "exemplary" (*vorbildliche*) in that he does reveal to us the form of true humanity, we must also emphasize his "ideality" (*Urbildlichkeit*) (§93.1). An exemplar merely demonstrates the truth of something; the perfect ideal actualizes that truth in such a way that it becomes possible for others. Thus, Jesus not only *reveals* true humanity but he *realizes* it as the one God chose from eternity to be the culmination of his plan for all creation. By introducing his "powerful God-consciousness" into the world (§94.1) Jesus made true humanity possible for all other humans.

THE COMMUNITY OF THE REDEEMED: FORMING THE WORLD THROUGH GOD-SATURATED LIVING

We have been unpacking Schleiermacher's christological anthropology by following his account of redemption. Thus far we have seen that his dogmatic project revolves around the following two convictions:

1. Christians have in fact experienced redemption—i.e., the actualization of God-consciousness.

---

28. For more thorough discussions of the relationship between Christology and Schleiermacher's theology of creation, see Robert Sherman, *The Shift to Modernity: Christ and the Doctrine of Creation in the Theologies of Schleiermacher and Barth* (New York: T&T Clark, 2005) and Edwin Chr. van Driel, *Incarnation Anyway: Arguments for Supralapsarian Christology* (New York: Oxford University Press, 2008).

29. See esp. Schleiermacher's exegesis of the Christ-hymn in Colossians 1:15–20 (Friedrich Schleiermacher, "On Colossians 1:15–20 [1832]," trans. Esther D. Reed and Alan Braley, *Neues Athenaeum* 5[1998]: 48–80). Schleiermacher interprets the hymn as emphasizing Jesus as the consummation of creation, the fulfillment of its *telos*. For an excellent discussion of Schleiermacher's exegesis here, see Christine Helmer, "The Consummation of Reality: Soteriological Metaphysics in Schleiermacher's Interpretation of Colossians 1:15–20," in *Biblical Interpretation: History, Context, and Reality*, ed. Christine Helmer and Taylor G. Petrey, Society of Biblical Literature Symposium Series, no. 26 (Leiden: Brill, 2005), 113–31.

30. For more on the relationship between Barth and Schleiermacher on the doctrine of election, see Matthias Gockel, *Barth and Schleiermacher on the Doctrine of Election: A Systematic-Theological Comparison* (New York: Oxford University Press, 2006).

2. This redemption has taken place solely on the basis of the unique dignity and activity of Jesus of Nazareth.

Now we need to add two further elements to Schleiermacher's understanding of redemption:

3. Redemption must be mediated historically through the community of believers.
4. Redemption necessarily leads to Christian action.

According to Schleiermacher, we have not finished discussing the Christian experience of redemption until we account for precisely how the power of Christ's God-consciousness is mediated to other humans such that they are actually redeemed. As we have seen, Schleiermacher emphasized that Jesus is the one in whom God's eternal plan for humanity is actualized in history. Yet we are still left with the question of how the life experiences of a particular human individual who lived nearly two thousand years ago can have any real bearing on the existence of other humans. How does his God-consciousness come to have significance for us? This question will take us into the ecclesiological and ethical aspects of Schleiermacher's christological anthropology. Ecclesiology factors in here because Schleiermacher contends that it is only through the community of believers that the redemptive influence of Jesus has been passed on over the centuries. The ethical component, on the other hand, arises from the ecclesiological. Those who have experienced redemption through the fellowship of the redeemed will inevitably be shaped by that experience in ways that lead to the expression of God-consciousness in the world around them. Christian action in the church and in the world follows inevitably from the experience of redemption, extending the sphere of redemption and mediating Jesus' influence.

The Ecclesial Mediation of Redemption

Before we begin wrestling with the mediation of redemption from Jesus to the rest of humanity, it is important to understand that Schleiermacher viewed redemption as more than forgiveness. According to Schleiermacher, if we only need forgiveness, then perhaps we do not need any account of mediation. God could simply forgive us on the basis of Christ's actions, and the story would be done. But true redemption requires blessedness as well as forgiveness, the inner state of peace and wholeness in which our entire experience of the world is pervaded by

God-consciousness. This radical transformation of the inner life of the person, moving from the state of brokenness in sin to one of reconciliation and blessedness, is what raises the question of mediation.

Suppose it is true that person A has a feeling of absolute dependence that gives rise to God-consciousness in such a way that he arrives at blessedness. As Schleiermacher defined his terms, "feeling," "consciousness," and "blessedness" are entirely inward realities. They describe the inner life of a person. So how exactly does the inner state of person A come to influence person B such that the inner life of B is radically changed? According to Schleiermacher, failure to address this question is the fundamental problem of many standard theologies of redemption. On many accounts, there is no mediating connection between the inner life of A and the inner life of B. B is just miraculously transformed by A's experiences. For Schleiermacher, such a "magical" view of redemption is clearly inadequate (§100–101). As human creatures embedded in a creaturely world, we simply do not work that way. We must give some account for why it is that the inner life of A has had such a transformative impact on the inner life of B.[31]

For Schleiermacher, the answer begins with his concept of *communication*. In Schleiermacher's view, a "feeling" like the "feeling of absolute dependence" should not be understood as an entirely passive experience. Instead, "it is strongest in our most vivid moments, and either directly or indirectly lies at the root of every expression of our wills" (§3.5). In other words, although it is passively received from something beyond the self, once received it infuses everything the self does or thinks. The receptivity of the feeling gives rise to the activity of the self. Thus, the feeling does not exist exclusively for itself as some kind of purely "inner" reality, but it necessarily seeks to express itself "by means of facial expression, gesture, tones and (indirectly) words" (§6.2). The inward feeling inevitably seeks to communicate itself outwardly through action and speech. In this way, it "becomes to other people a revelation of the inward" (§6.2).

When Jesus entered the world with his perfect God-consciousness, then, it pervaded not only his experiences but his words and actions as well. Every aspect of his "self-presentation" exhibited the power and reality of his sinless perfection, "thereby attracting men to Himself and making them

---

31. For Schleiermacher, "The only miracle is that a person with a perfectly sinless God-consciousness, Jesus Christ, came to adulthood in the context of an overall life of sin, that is, without benefit of a community of faith" (§103.4).

one with Himself" (§101.4). The communication of God-consciousness has an evocative power that awakens God-consciousness in others and draws them together in fellowship. When the disciples saw God-consciousness at work in Jesus, they intuitively recognized it as an expression of their own deepest being. As we saw earlier, human persons were created for God-consciousness; thus, when they come into contact with it, they immediately recognize it as that which fulfills their own nature and purpose. This is the "vital human receptivity" on the basis of which the supernatural activity of God can become "a natural fact of history" (§88.4). The disciples thus experienced redemption as they came into direct contact with Jesus' God-consciousness through his life and words.[32]

Yet Schleiermacher also contends that "our Christianity ought to be the same as that of the Apostles," and, therefore, that "our Christianity too must be generated by the personal influences of Christ" (§127.2). But how can this be when we do not come into contact with Jesus in the same way that the disciples did? One option would be to appeal to the Bible itself as the means of connecting us with the words and deeds of Jesus. But although the Bible played a large role in Schleiermacher's theology of redemption, he rejects the conclusion that it alone is adequate for mediating redemption today (§100.3). The Bible is necessary for conveying an accurate picture of Jesus, but it cannot convey God-consciousness itself. If it could, then we might question whether the life of Jesus was truly necessary. God could have conveyed everything necessary in a set of written instructions, dispensing with the messy and difficult realities of a particular, historic life (§108.5). Indeed, one could argue that this would have been a more efficient approach since God-consciousness could have been spread far more rapidly throughout the world if all we needed was the dissemination of the correct instructions.

---

32. One of the key assumptions of Schleiermacher's theology of redemption is that "the death of Christ cannot play a decisive role in redemption, because if his death is necessary for redemption, then Christ's first followers could not have experienced redemption until he died or was resurrected" (Kelsey, *Thinking about Christ with Schleiermacher*, 65). Consequently, Jesus' redemptive influence must flow primarily from his life rather than his death. For similar reasons, although Schleiermacher affirms the resurrection, he does not think it has redemptive significance (see esp. §99). Hieb thus thinks that it would have been more consistent for Schleiermacher to reject the resurrection as having a place in Christian theology (Nathan D. Hieb, "The Precarious Status of Resurrection in Friedrich Schleiermacher's Glaubenslehre," *International Journal of Systematic Theology* 9, no. 4 [2007]: 398–414). Yet Rick Elgendy usefully argues that Schleiermacher could have developed a more constructive account of the resurrection by presenting it as the consummation of the incarnation, and, consequently, as the pinnacle of redemption (Rick Elgendy, "Reconsidering Resurrection, Incarnation and Nature in Schleiermacher's Glaubenslehre," *International Journal of Systematic Theology* 15, no. 3 [2013]: 301–23).

Instead, Schleiermacher contends that Jesus' God-consciousness is mediated historically by the very community that he initiated with the disciples. The attractive power of God-consciousness draws people together in communities of redemption that seek to extend the reach of God-consciousness even further by *communicating* God-consciousness through their own words and actions.[33] In this way, the fellowship of believers becomes, in a quite literal way, the mediator of redemption. We are not simply those who bring into the world a *message* about redemption that is received through some other means. The words and actions of the community are the very means of redemption such that "it is only out of this new corporate life that the communication of the divine grace comes to each individual" (§90.1). Thus, for Schleiermacher "salvation or blessedness is in the Church alone" (§113.3).[34]

As Richard R. Niebuhr explains, "There is no trace here of a Kierke-gaardian notion of timeless, direct contemporaneity with the God-man."[35] But neither is there the lack of any real connection like we find in a purely exemplary view of redemption. Instead, we have a real connection to Jesus, but our connection is mediated through the community.[36] Each succeeding generation of Christians serves as another link in the chain that connects us back to Jesus himself. According to Schleiermacher, "the truth is that the new life of each individual springs from that of the community, while the life of the community springs from no other individual life than that of the Redeemer" (§113.1).[37] Schleiermacher thus envisions a chain of redemption that begins with Jesus and extends to human persons today, but in which

---

33. According to Schleiermacher, this happens primarily in Christian preaching, which involves the re-presentation of Jesus that has "a directly rousing effect" on those who hear (§18.3).

34. Schleiermacher distinguishes his conception of ecclesial mediation from the Roman Catholic position that the church mediates salvation in the world by arguing that the Catholic view "deprives Christ of the honour due to Him, and puts Him in the background, and even in a measure subordinates Him to the Church" (§24.3). In other words, the Catholic view transfers the work of Christ to that of the church (§24.4).

35. Niebuhr, *Schleiermacher on Christ and Religion*, 44.

36. As Dawn DeVries explains, "The word of Christ, though proclaimed in the community, singles out the individual, and to the consciousness of someone in the grip of conversion all human instrumentality vanishes and Christ is immediately present" (Dawn DeVries and B. A. Gerrish, "Providence and Grace: Schleiermacher on Justification and Election," in *The Cambridge Companion to Friedrich Schleiermacher*, ed. Jacqueline Mariña [New York: Cambridge University Press, 2005], 199).

37. The community that Schleiermacher has in mind here is not coextensive with that of the institutional church. Instead, he has in mind any kind of "fellowship" in which regenerate persons gather (§113.1).

the middle links in the chain are the successive generations of regenerate persons through whom Jesus' historic influence is transmitted in their time. Today, when people experience redemption within the church, they are coming into direct contact with Jesus' own God-consciousness, not by some magical means, but through the historic mediation of his own people.[38]

This is the context in which Schleiermacher develops his theology of the Spirit. Although we do not have time here to unpack his view of the Spirit in any detail, his account of the mediation of redemption through the church would be incomplete without his pneumatology. Since Christians continue to experience redemption in the church, we must say that "the Being of God" remains in the church and that this is what continues "the communication of the perfection and blessedness of Christ" (§116.3). Schleiermacher argues that this continued experience of God's presence in the church is what we call the "Holy Spirit," and he argues that "there is no fellowship with Christ without an indwelling of the Holy Spirit" (§124).[39] But we should not understand this as a reference to some supernatural entity who exists independently of the church and only empowers it as an external force. Instead, "the expression 'Holy Spirit' must be understood to mean the vital unity of the Christian fellowship as a moral personality ... its *common spirit*" (§116.3). The Spirit is the "inward impulse" that all redeemed persons feel "to become more one in their common co-operative activity and reciprocal influence" (§121). He is what animates "the life in common of believers" (§123). The Spirit is coextensive, even identical, with the church's corporate experience of God-consciousness, the experience of redemption.[40] Thus "the life of Christ in us and the leading of the Holy Spirit in us" are virtually identical in Schleiermacher's theology (§124.2).

All of this means, though, that ecclesiology stands at the very center of Schleiermacher's understanding of the human person. We are all minimally human in that we have been created with the capacity for

---

38. "Our proposition, therefore, depends upon the assumption that this influence of the fellowship in producing a like faith is none other than the influence of the personal perfection of Jesus himself" (§88.2).

39. Kevin Hector explains the logic of Schleiermacher's argument in this way: "We are conscious, according to Schleiermacher, of the fact that our redemption depends wholly upon God's activity, and we are conscious that redemption is mediated to us through the community; from this, it follows that such mediation must *itself* be God's activity" (Kevin W. Hector, "The Mediation of Christ's Normative Spirit: A Constructive Reading of Schleiermacher's Pneumatology," *Modern Theology* 24, no. 1 [2008]: 3–4).

40. Francis Schüssler Fiorenza, "Schleiermacher's Understanding of God as Triune," in *The Cambridge Companion to Friedrich Schleiermacher*, ed. Jacqueline Mariña (New York: Cambridge University Press, 2005), 181.

God-consciousness, the ability to have an experience of the world that is pervasively guided by an intuitive awareness of our absolute dependence upon God himself. That basic capacity is an important part of the race-consciousness that allows us to recognize our fellow humans despite the vagaries of time, place, and culture (§6.2). Yet Schleiermacher's system entails the corresponding conclusion that we do not experience the fullness of humanity apart from fellowship. Since "Christian piety never arises independently and of itself in an individual, but only out of the communion and in the communion" (§24.4), and since God-consciousness is essential to true humanity, then it must be the case that true humanity itself arises only in and through Christian community. It is only by coming into contact with the community of the redeemed that we come into contact with Jesus' own God-consciousness and are transformed in such a way that our own capacity for God-consciousness is awakened and we come to realize our humanity in ways that would not have been possible otherwise. Indeed, as Schleiermacher argued, "institution of this new corporate life would have to be regarded as the completion, only now accomplished, of the creation of human nature" (§89). In a very real sense, we do not experience the world humanly until we enter the sphere of the church and begin to experience the world Jesus-ly.[41]

The Church and the Individual

Schleiermacher thus conceptualized the human person as a being who is only formed in community. As Niebuhr summarizes, the human person "never appears as, and is not conceivable as, a pure individual."[42] Not only does the human person receive his or her physical being from those who come before (i.e. parents) but human persons also depend on the community for their psychological constitution. "The sense of an inner unity of selfhood is aroused in each person through the recollections and descriptions of him given to him by other persons or Thou's standing over against him."[43] Schleiermacher was thus strongly criti-

---

41. This does not necessarily mean that he downplays the significance of humanity outside the church. Indeed, we have already seen that Schleiermacher thinks that God-consciousness can be realized, albeit to a very limited extent, before redemption. All human persons manifest this intrinsic characteristic of humanity to a greater or lesser degree. Thus, Schleiermacher appreciated the ways in which non-Christian religious communities can facilitate a partial increase in God-consciousness (§6-9).

42. Niebuhr, *Schleiermacher on Christ and Religion*, 116.

43. Ibid.

cal of the social contract tradition "according to which each individual has a unified nature prior to his entrance into society and the state."[44] Instead, Schleiermacher argued that human persons are formed by an essential "sociability" (*Geselligkeit*) in which a person develops as a person only through his or her relationships with others.[45] As Niebuhr explains, "All experience that presupposes a positing of the self involves a Thou. Schleiermacher discards the *nicht-Ich* of his contemporaries in favor of the *Du* as the designation of that which genuinely opposes the I. The *nicht-Ich* is simply a negation of the I."[46]

According to Schleiermacher, the communal grounding of the individual human person can also be traced back to the essential unity of the human race (§60.2). Schleiermacher contended that the only way to understand the Christian experience of redemption in Christ is by affirming the corporate nature of both sin and redemption. Original sin involves "the corporate act and the corporate guilt" of humanity, both of which establish "the universal need of redemption" (§71). Without this universal conception of sinfulness, Schleiermacher argued, we will inevitably lower our view of the redemption offered in Christ since his work would no longer appear necessary for the redemption of all people. Thus, "the denial of the corporate character of original sin and a lower estimate of the redemption wrought by Christ usually go hand in hand" (§73.3). Yet it is precisely the communal grounding of the human person that establishes the corporate character of humanity in both sin and redemption. Schleiermacher did not account for the unity of humanity by appealing to human "nature" as an abstract universal in which we all participate and which was cleansed or healed through the incarnation or the atonement. Instead, he presented humanity as an organic fellowship, one that necessarily precedes and includes all human persons, and one that constitutes the being of those so included. The universal sinfulness of humanity is thus explained by the fact that all human persons participate in the human community, broadly construed, that shapes their self-consciousness in sinful ways and hinders the development of God-consciousness. And this same interdependence is what grounds the efficacy of Jesus' own life and work. "It is just this interdependence of

---

44. Frederick C. Beiser, "Schleiermacher's Ethics," in *The Cambridge Companion to Friedrich Schleiermacher*, ed. Jacqueline Mariña (New York: Cambridge University Press, 2005), 61.

45. Ibid.

46. Niebuhr, *Schleiermacher on Christ and Religion*, 116, n. 79.

human beings on one another that makes it possible for the salvation of the whole race to be accomplished in the historical life of one person."[47]

With this conception of the human person, it stands to reason that any strong form of individualism would be viewed as a fundamental problem. Indeed, we have already seen that one of his fundamental religious insights is that the feeling of dependence lies at the heart of all human experiences. Even in our most mundane experiences of the world, we intuitively recognize that we are dependent beings who are limited and defined by the circumstances and the network of relationships into which we are thrown at birth. For Schleiermacher, then, one of the basic forms of sin is to fail to acknowledge this essential dependence and to pretend as though we are somehow autonomous and self-constituting. Or, in a form that is slightly less tragic, we might at least acknowledge this essential dependence and yet still fail to allow this awareness to shape our self-identity and self-conscious experience of the world.[48] Schleiermacher thus rejected all forms of "self-apotheosis," which Boyd defines as "the absolutizing of the significance and rights of a self or a collective self (society), and consequently the alienation of men and groups from each other and from the natural world of which they are part."[49] When we deny our essential mutuality, whether as individuals or as entire communities, we turn the "other" into a mere instrument of the self, thus subsuming the intrinsic significance of the other in the attempt to deify the self as the ultimate reality.

At the same time, though, this strong emphasis on the constitutive nature of the community does not entail a corresponding rejection of the individual in every sense. Thinking back to his conception of religious self-consciousness again, we must remember the *active* as well as the *passive* poles of conscious experience. Although there is a feeling of dependence in which we intuitively know ourselves to be constituted by others, we also have a feeling of freedom in which we are aware of ourselves as significant particulars capable of influencing others in turn and making a unique contribution to the constituting community. Indeed, according to Frederick Beiser, one of Schleiermacher's primary criticisms of Kantian ethics was "its failure to account for the intrinsic worth of

---

47. Mariña, "Christology and Anthropology," 165.

48. George N. Boyd, "Schleiermacher: On Relating Man and Nature," *Encounter* 36, no. 1 (1975): 15.

49. Ibid., 16.

individuality."[50] Niebuhr thus points out that Schleiermacher's anthropology entails two irreducible poles: "being-for-the-self" and "being-for-community."[51] Alongside the constitutive nature of the community, we must also posit an "inner and underivable selfhood" that constitutes the self as a unique particular and "underlies all the temporal moments of the self's existence."[52] Indeed, Schleiermacher defines the human person as "the continuous unity of self-consciousness" (§123.3), thus including a strongly individualistic aspect to his view of the human person, even while maintaining the corporate pole by arguing that this very self-consciousness is mediated in important ways by the surrounding community.[53] In the end, Schleiermacher contends that the individual and the community were inseparable in the kingdom of God: "in this Kingdom of God … the establishment and maintenance of the fellowship of each individual with God, and the maintenance and direction of the fellowship of all members with one another are not separate achievements but the same" (§102.2). Schleiermacher thus avoids any understanding of the human person that "relegates either term of the polarity to a secondary status."[54]

The Church and the Activity of Redemption

Schleiermacher's understanding of the person-forming nature of God-consciousness and the communal mediation of God-consciousness in the world leads directly into his view of ethics and the world-forming nature of Christian action. As Schleiermacher describes the transformative reality of redemption, all the activities of the individual are now "differently determined … and even differently received — which means that the personal self-consciousness, too, becomes different" (§100.2). This transformed person thus becomes an ever-increasing conduit of

---

50. Beiser, "Schleiermacher's Ethics," 60. Mariña concurs, arguing, "One of Schleiermacher's most original contributions to ethics lies in his analysis of the importance of individuality for ethical life" (Jacqueline Mariña, *Transformation of the Self in the Thought of Friedrich Schleiermacher* [New York: Oxford University Press, 2008], 7).

51. Niebuhr, *Schleiermacher on Christ and Religion*, 120.

52. Ibid., 121.

53. The "continuous unity" in this statement entails Schleiermacher's conviction that even our preredemptive experiences continue to shape our personal identities after redemption: "even if someone were actually to reach the point of having the new life diffuse itself over his entire essence, yet the portion of his life spent before his regeneration would still form part of his personality" (§123.3).

54. Niebuhr, *Schleiermacher on Christ and Religion*, 117.

God-consciousness in the world. In this way, the circle of redemption gets expanded wherever God "finds those in whom His activity does not merely remain, but from whom, moving on, it can work upon others through the revelation of His life" (§100.2).

In his theological ethics, Schleiermacher argues that Christian moral action is the process of re-establishing and expanding blessedness in the individual, in the Christian community, and throughout the world.[55] That is not only the vocation of the Christian, but it is "the continual realization of human nature itself."[56] According to Schleiermacher, as the God-consciousness develops in people, it necessarily leads to both a desire for knowledge and a desire to act (§3). Both of these inform Christian ethics as the theological discipline in which we strive to understand the nature of Christian action as an expression of Christian piety. This is what Schleiermacher has in mind when he defines Christianity as "a monotheistic faith, belonging to the *teleological* type of religion" (§11). Christianity is a teleological kind of piety because, as Boyd explains, "each moment of God-consciousness is oriented to express itself in activity which aims at shaping both self and world in the recognition of their fundamental and mutual givenness."[57] In other words, Christianity is teleological because the development of God-consciousness in individuals and communities necessarily seeks to express itself through the activity of those redeemed people in the world such that an ever-expanding circle of people comes to participate in redemption through the awakening of their God-consciousness. For Schleiermacher, this is the kingdom of God: the active and ever-expanding sphere of Jesus' redemptive influence through the work of his redeemed people.

Christian action thus seeks to expand Jesus' influence in three spheres: the individual, the church, and the world. In all three, Christian action seeks to overcome a lack of blessedness and work toward the realization of absolute blessedness.[58] In doing so, Christian action operates

---

55. For a good overview of Schleiermacher's writings on ethics, see esp. Hermann Peiter, *Christian Ethics according to Schleiermacher: Collected Essays and Reviews*, ed. Terrence N. Tice, trans. Edwina Lawler (Eugene, Ore: Pickwick, 2010).

56. Friedrich Schleiermacher, *Selections from Friedrich Schleiermacher's Christian Ethics*, trans. James M. Brandt (Louisville: Westminster John Knox, 2011), 148.

57. Boyd, "Schleiermacher," 15.

58. Schleiermacher has been criticized for paying insufficient attention to the formation of the individual in Christian ethics (John P. Crossley Jr., "Schleiermacher's Christian Ethics in Relation to His Philosophical Ethics," *Annual of the Society of Christian Ethics* 18 [1998]: 106). This probably stems from the fact that Schleiermacher pays relatively little

between the two poles of "pain" and "pleasure" (§5).[59] Pain refers to any state in which the sensuous consciousness continues to resist the influence of God-consciousness and to preclude the full experience of blessedness. Pleasure is the state in which the sensuous consciousness becomes a willing vehicle of God-consciousness and the expansion of the kingdom. Corresponding to this, Schleiermacher identifies two kinds of Christian action. "Corrective" action denotes activities that seek to mitigate the condition of pain by reestablishing the reign of the spirit over that of the flesh.[60] "Disseminating" action seeks to support the condition of pleasure by expanding the reach of redemption. That reach can be either intensive (increasing the experience of blessedness in the individual) or extensive (increasing the scope of blessedness in the world). Either way, the goal remains the same: working toward absolute blessedness.

In his account of Christian action we also encounter the same balance between the individual and the community that we addressed above. As we have seen, Schleiermacher views the experience of redemption as both an individual and a corporate reality. The experience is something that each person has individually, yet the experience is common to all Christians and is mediated only through the Christian community. Thus the common spirit of the church and the individual experience of the Christian are inseparable realities, each serving to shape and inform the other. We can say the same of Schleiermacher's account of Christian action. Each Christian is a particular manifestation of the common spirit of the community, individualized by the unique way in which that common spirit is actualized in that person. At the same time, though, it remains a function of the common spirit. Thus, the actions of the person simply are the actions of the community insofar as they manifest the common spirit of the community (§121). Although Schleiermacher has been critiqued at times for emphasizing the constitutive role of the community in such a way that there seems to be no room for the moral action

---

attention to issues like virtue and character in his dogmatic account of ethics, focusing instead on the power of God-consciousness working through the individual (ibid., 103). Nonetheless, as we have seen, Schleiermacher describes God-consciousness as inherently person-forming, perfecting that which is inherent in the individual human nature. Thus, individual formation must factor into his account of Christian action insofar as God-consciousness continues to shape and perfect the capacities of humanity.

59. Friedrich Schleiermacher, *Introduction to Christian Ethics* (Nashville: Abingdon, 1989), 73–74.

60. Ibid., 101–2.

of the individual or the prophetic critique of the community,[61] he does emphasize the reciprocal influence of community and individual in such a way that both are necessary and significant.[62]

In many ways, then, Schleiermacher's theology of Christian moral action is a theology of love. On Schleiermacher's account, as Christian individuals and communities are shaped by God-consciousness toward a deeper experience of blessedness, they shift from being-for-self and become persons shaped by being-for-others.[63] As the feelings of relative and absolute dependence come to shape human life and action, we are necessarily drawn toward community and both our speech and actions are oriented toward community (§121). As Jacqueline Mariña explains, "The love of Christ is a gift to each individual; once received the person is empowered to love others through the love of Christ. As such, the love of Christ for humanity founds the community of the kingdom of God ... It is this founding of the kingdom that is the principle [sic] work of Christ and the manner in which he redeems humanity."[64] In this way, the corporate nature of sin is overcome by the community of redemption.

It is also in Schleiermacher's understanding of Christian action that the idea of Jesus as the exemplar of humanity comes back into play. Although we have already seen that Schleiermacher rejects exemplarism as an adequate account of Christology in general, he nonetheless maintains its significance for informing Christian action. Indeed, the fundamental guideline that he establishes for guiding moral behavior is that one should "act such that your behavior always resembles the behavior of Christ."[65] Schleiermacher thus spent considerable time exploring the details of Christ's life,[66] and he is generally regarded as "one of the eminent New Testament scholars of his time."[67]

---

61. E.g., Niebuhr, *Schleiermacher on Christ and Religion*, 69.

62. For a more thorough discussion of this point, see Mariña, *Transformation of the Self in the Thought of Friedrich Schleiermacher*.

63. Eilert Herms, "Schleiermacher's *Christian Ethics*," in *The Cambridge Companion to Friedrich Schleiermacher*, ed. Jacqueline Mariña, trans. Jacqueline Mariña and Christine Helmer (New York: Cambridge University Press, 2005), 227.

64. Mariña, "Christology and Anthropology," 166.

65. Schleiermacher, *Introduction to Christian Ethics*, 91.

66. See esp. Schleiermacher, *The Life of Jesus*.

67. Helmer, "The Consummation of Reality," 115. See also Christine Helmer, "Schleiermacher's Exegetical Theology and the New Testament," in *The Cambridge Companion to Friedrich Schleiermacher*, ed. Jacqueline Mariña (New York: Cambridge University Press, 2005), 229–47.

CHRISTOLOGY AND ANTHROPOLOGY IN A NEW KEY

Schleiermacher's theology offers a glimpse into a kind of christological anthropology that we have not yet encountered. Although Schleiermacher agrees with our other theologians that Jesus is both the revelation and realization of true humanity, he offers a radically different explanation for why that is the case. This very uniqueness is what makes Schleiermacher a valuable dialogue partner in this project. As Martin Redeker claims, "Schleiermacher is 'different' and just for that reason he is relevant."[68]

Throughout his anthropology, Schleiermacher consistently demonstrates the importance of his Christology. Although he derives his understanding of the human person from the interplay of Christology, ecclesiology, soteriology, and ethics, his Christology drives his understanding of humanity in important ways. Only in Jesus' absolute blessedness and perfect God-consciousness do we see the fundamental truth of what it means to be human. And only through Jesus do we have the possibility of becoming truly human in the context of the fellowship of those who have been redeemed by Christ, empowered by the God-consciousness that was actualized by Christ, informed by the example of blessedness left by Christ, and engaged in the mission of extending the sphere of Christ's redemptive influence. For Schleiermacher, this is the essence of what it means to be fully human.

That leaves us with the question raised at the beginning of the chapter about whether Schleiermacher's theological anthropology qualifies as meaningfully *christological*. On the account of Schleiermacher's anthropology offered here, that would clearly appear to be the case. Despite questions that may remain about the adequacy of his Christology, Schleiermacher affirmed the uniqueness of Jesus' person and work, thus avoiding the critique that he offers the kind of "low" Christology in which it becomes difficult to understand why Jesus has unique explanatory value for humanity in general. On the basis of that Christology, Schleiermacher then made a number of important claims about what it means to be human, claims that he applied to a broad range of anthropological issues. On this account, then, Schleiermacher's anthropology seems to meet all the criteria for a christological anthropology.

Those who remain unconvinced by this account and remain concerned about the Barthian worry that the fundamental logic of

---

68. Martin Redeker, *Schleiermacher: Life and Thought*, trans. John Wallhausser (Philadelphia: Fortress, 1973), 2.

Schleiermacher's theology moves from anthropology to Christology will almost certainly arrive at a different conclusion regarding the extent to which he offers a truly christological anthropology. Instead, they will more likely contend that he presents an anthropological Christology. Since I have already given my reasons for thinking that Schleiermacher's account of God-consciousness is more thoroughly christological than this objection suggests, I will not revisit the question here. My purpose for noting the objection is simply to point out its significance for understanding both the nature of Schleiermacher's anthropological project and the criteria we have established for identifying christological anthropologies. Although there will be some level of reciprocity between anthropology and Christology in any theological system, it seems likely that most will view the relationship asymmetrically, with one or the other exerting a more basic influence on the resulting theological understanding. This objection highlights the fact that discerning the shape of this asymmetrical reciprocity impacts the corresponding assessment about the extent to which a theologian's understanding of humanity is christological.

CHAPTER 5

Embodied Souls

The Ontological Determination of the Human in Karl Barth's Anthropology

The ontological determination of humanity is grounded in the fact that one man among all others is the man Jesus ... Theological anthropology has no choice in this matter. It is not yet or no longer theological anthropology if it tries to pose and answer the question of the true being of man from any other angle.

Karl Barth, *Church Dogmatics*[1]

ALTHOUGH WE HAVE ALREADY EXPLORED ways in which several earlier figures related Christology to anthropology, few thinkers in the history of the church have pursued a christological anthropology with greater rigor than displayed in Karl Barth's *Church Dogmatics*, particularly in III/2 where he argues throughout that a properly theological view of the human person must be thoroughly grounded in Christology as its necessary starting point.[2] Not satisfied with abstract claims about the anthropological significance of Christology, Barth demonstrates how this christological orientation reshapes how we understand specific issues like relationality, ontology, and temporality. Barth thus aims for an

---

1. Karl Barth, *Church Dogmatics*, 13 vols., ed. G. W. Bromiley and T. F. Torrance (Edinburgh: T&T Clark, 1956–1975), III/2, 132 (hereafter *CD*). Many of the arguments for this chapter are taken in summary form from my *Embodied Souls, Ensouled Bodies: An Exercise in Christological Anthropology and Its Significance for the Mind/Body Debate*, T&T Clark Studies in Systematic Theology (London: T&T Clark, 2008).

2. T. F. Torrance considered it "in some ways the most arresting aspect of Barth's theology" (Thomas F. Torrance, *Karl Barth, Biblical and Evangelical Theologian* [Edinburgh: T&T Clark, 1990], 22.

anthropology that is "christologically determined" throughout,[3] firmly convinced that "the nature of the man Jesus alone is the key to the problem of human nature."[4]

In this chapter, we will consider the way Barth's christological anthropology shaped his approach to the mind/body relationship, a question that has received significant attention in the modern era among scientists, philosophers, biblical scholars, and theologians alike. Unlike most, however, Barth argued that even something as apparently esoteric as the interaction between "mind" and "body" can only be rightly understood from a christological perspective, ultimately grounding the issue in Christology, pneumatology, and the covenantal relationship between God and human persons. In the end we will see that although Barth's approach does not give us a definitive answer to whether we should understand the human person in terms of dualism or materialism, he offers a robustly christological framework within which to assess the theological adequacy of any particular proposal for human ontology.

THE ONTOLOGICAL DETERMINATION OF HUMANITY

Barth builds his understanding of the human person on the claim that a properly Christian anthropology is "grounded in the fact that one man among all others is the man Jesus." If we attempt to understand the human from any other vantage point, we will be limited to "the phenomena of the human," or those things about the human that can be known from nontheological perspectives.[5] Although studying such phenomena can helpfully illumine our understanding of humanity, we cannot learn about true humanity unless we view the human person through the lens provided by Jesus himself. As Barth boldly declares, "Theological anthropology has no choice in this matter. It is not yet or no longer theological anthropology if it tries to pose and answer the question of the true being of man from any other angle."[6] To see precisely why Barth thought that Jesus is the "Archimedean point" from which we can establish some knowledge of true humanity, we will need to understand what Barth said

---

3. *CD* I/2, 12.

4. *CD* III/2 136. Thus, according to Ray Anderson, "Karl Barth, more than any other theologian of the church, including the Reformers, has developed a comprehensive theological anthropology by beginning with the humanity of Jesus Christ as both crucified and resurrected" (*On Being Human: Essays in Theological Anthropology* [Grand Rapids: Eerdmans, 1982], 18).

5. Ibid.

6. *CD* III/2, 132.

about election, the sinlessness of Christ, and the idea that we have been summoned through Jesus into a particular relationship with God.

For Barth, the fact that Jesus alone is the "ontological determination of humanity" flows necessarily from the fact that in Jesus Christ alone God has eternally elected to be God-for-us. Thus, "the being of man as being with Jesus rests upon the election of God."[7] And this means we can only understand Barth's christological anthropology by wrestling with his doctrine of election, one of the most important and challenging dimensions of Barth's theology.[8]

For Barth, election is fundamentally about Jesus Christ, who is both the "object" and the "subject" of election. In other words, Jesus is the object of election in that he alone is the truly elect one; all others are only elect insofar as they are "united in Him and represented by Him."[9] But Jesus is also the subject of election in that Jesus Christ *is* the eternal act of election in which God determines to be God-for-us-in-Jesus.[10] That is who God is because that is who he has determined to be. Election, then, is the determination of both divine and human realities.[11] In Jesus, God determines who he will be *and* who we are.

---

7. *CD* III/2, 142.

8. For more comprehensive discussions of Barth's doctrine of election see F. Stuart Clarke, "Christocentric Developments in the Reformed Doctrine of Predestination," *Churchman* 98, no. 3 (1984): 229–45; John Colwell, *Actuality and Provisionality: Eternity and Election in the Theology of Karl Barth* (Edinburgh: Rutherford House, 1989); Mary Kathleen Cunningham, *What Is Theological Exegesis? Interpretation and Use of Scripture in Barth's Doctrine of Election* (Valley Forge, Pa.: Trinity Press International, 1995); Bruce L. McCormack, "The Sum of the Gospel: The Doctrine of Election in the Theologies of Alexander Schweizer and Karl Barth," in *Toward the Future of Reformed Theology*, ed. David Willis-Watkins, Michael Welker, and Mattias Gockel (Grand Rapids: Eerdmans, 1999), 470–93; Bruce L. McCormack, "Grace and Being: The Role of God's Gracious Election in Karl Barth's Theological Ontology," in *The Cambridge Companion to Karl Barth*, ed. John B. Webster (New York: Cambridge University Press, 2000), 92–110; John C. McDowell, "Learning Where to Place One's Hope: The Eschatological Significance of Election in Barth," *Scottish Journal of Theology* 53 (2003): 316–38; Michael O'Neill, "Karl Barth's Doctrine of Election," *Evangelical Quarterly* 76, no. 4 (2004): 311–26; Suzanne McDonald, "Barth's 'Other' Doctrine of Election in the Church Dogmatics," *International Journal of Systematic Theology* 9, no. 2 (2007): 134–47.

9. *CD* III/3, 105.

10. This entails the preexistence of the man Jesus (i.e., the *Logos incarnandus* and not just the *Logos asarkos*), which Barth defended primarily through his exegesis of John 1:1–2 (*CD* II/2, 95–99). For a good discussion of some of the objections that have been raised to Barth's understanding of the preexistence of the man Jesus, see John Thompson, "The Humanity of God in the Theology of Karl Barth," *Scottish Journal of Theology* 29 (1976): 261–64.

11. According to Eberhard Jüngel, this "primal decision constitutes the primal relationship of God to man and in this primal relationship there takes place the 'primal history' in which *God already has a relationship* to man *before* all creation" (Eberhard Jüngel, *God's Being Is in Becoming* [Grand Rapids: Eerdmans, 2001], 88–89; cf. *CD* II/2, 12–13).

Barth argues that both of these points are necessary for maintaining a proper understanding of the relationship between Christ's humanity and our own. Barth can claim that Jesus, as the subject of election, is the ontological determination of humanity specifically because "His election includes ours within itself and because ours is grounded in His."[12] But the security of this ontological determination is only established by the fact that Jesus is also "the One who elects us."[13] As he argues,

> Now without our first assertion we cannot maintain such a position. For where can Jesus Christ derive the authority and power to be Lord and Head of all others, and how can these others be elected "in Him," and how can they see their election in Him the first of the elect, and how can they find in His election the assurance of their own, if He is only the object of election and not Himself its Subject.[14]

The doctrine of election thus grounds Barth's christological anthropology in God's eternal decision to be God-for-us-in-Jesus. Jesus is the true human because in him we have both the eternally electing God and the eternally elect human.

Although Barth's christological anthropology is ultimately grounded eternally in the decree of election, Barth argues that it also finds a historical grounding in the sinless faithfulness of Jesus Christ. Postlapsarian humanity has fallen into "perversion and corruption," a state that shapes every aspect of human existence.[15] Such a state threatens the very existence of humanity as all human persons now stand in contradiction to their created essence. And the pervasive nature of sin means that in addition to the ontological discontinuity we face the problem of epistemological discontinuity. On our own, we simply have no epistemological access to humanity uncorrupted by the fall.

In the face of such ontological and epistemological discontinuity, it seems we must despair of *being* truly human, let alone *knowing* what it means to be truly human. For Barth, however, God's sovereign grace prevents such a pessimistic conclusion. God simply refuses to allow us to destroy ourselves and unmake that which he created for relationship with himself.[16] Although sin now shapes everything that we know and

---

12. *CD* II/2, 120.
13. *CD* II/2, 115.
14. *CD* II/2, 116.
15. *CD* III/2, 26.
16. *CD* III/1, 53.

experience about humanity, "we must not absolutize sin," and make it the primary category for understanding anthropology.[17] God's gracious love ensures that humanity remains even after it has fallen into the "self-contradiction" of sin.[18]

And it is precisely in Jesus Christ that this gracious faithfulness finds its ultimate expression. Human nature continues to exist despite its radical corruption because it is grounded in Jesus' faithfulness to the covenantal relationship for which he and all human persons have been eternally elected. Jesus alone refused to fall into the self-contradiction of sin and remains God's covenantal copartner.[19] Thus, "human nature in Jesus is the reason and the just foundation for the mercy in which God has turned to our human nature."[20] Jesus became the guarantor of humanity as the "archetypal man" who secures humanity from "non-being."[21]

As the ontological ground of true humanity, however, Jesus' humanity also has epistemological significance. In Jesus alone do we see true humanity. So, "true man, the true nature behind our corrupted nature, is not concealed but revealed in the person of Jesus, and in His nature we recognize our own, and that of every man."[22] To the extent that theological anthropology seeks to comprehend true humanity, then, it must find its starting point in the lived humanity of Jesus Christ and him alone.

Finally, the third piece of Barth's christological framework is that Jesus is not only the eternal and historical ground of theological anthropology, but he is also the one in whom God encounters all human persons and summons them to be his covenantal copartners. That God has entered the

---

17. *CD* III/2, 37.

18. *CD* III/2, 31.

19. Barth did not see Jesus' sinlessness as an ontological difference between his humanity and ours—such a difference would mean he was not human as we are—but rather affirmed that Jesus took on our human nature as it stands under the contradiction of sin (*CD* I/2, 151ff). Nevertheless, Jesus, as empowered by the Holy Spirit, lived a truly human life in relationship to God as his covenantal partner and so lived a sinless life, though standing in solidarity with the human race under God's judgment on sin (John Thompson, *Theology beyond Christendom: Essays on the Centenary of the Birth of Karl Barth* [Allison Park, Pa.: Pickwick, 1986], 89.) Von Balthasar noted that the sinlessness of Jesus thus "guarantees human nature an unbroken continuity" and ensures that man does not fall into irredeemable chaos (Hans Urs von Balthasar, *The Theology of Karl Barth*, trans. Edward T. Oakes [San Francisco: Communio, 1992], 116). It is, therefore, the continuity of human nature manifest in the covenantal faithfulness of Jesus Christ that ensures the continued availability of real human nature for theological consideration.

20. *CD* III/2, 48.

21. *CD* III/2, 144.

22. *CD* III/2, 43.

sphere of humanity in the incarnation means that all humans "are confronted by the divine Other" in Jesus Christ.[23] He is the "divine Counterpart of every man."[24] Thus, "to be a man is to be in the particular sphere of the created world in which the Word of God is spoken and sounded."[25]

In Jesus Christ, then, God summons and claims all humans. He is the sphere in which all humans encounter the divine Other and are addressed by him. A theological anthropology that takes seriously the reality of the incarnation, then, must understand the human person *first* as a creature summoned and addressed by God. Everything else we might learn about humanity must be shaped by that defining reality.

> Man *is* the being which is addressed in this way by God. He does not become this being. He does not first have a kind of nature in which he is then addressed by God. He does not have something different and earlier and more intrinsic, a deeper stratum or more original substance of being, in which he is without or prior to the Word of God. He is from the very outset, as we may now say, "in the Word of God."[26]

Humanity must, therefore, be defined as "the creaturely being which is addressed, called and summoned by God."[27] Barth did not mean, however, that true humanity is available only to Christians or others who have heard some specific address. The fact that the eternally Elect/Elector has entered into the sphere of human existence means that all humans have in fact been encountered by the divine Other. The summons is real for everyone; what awaits is the proper response on our part to this powerful address. For Barth, then, even though true humanity is grounded in eternity through the decree of election, it is not a static concept. Instead, true humanity comes into being as we respond to the summons that all humans have received in Christ. Even if we are not consciously aware of the summons, it is still one that grasps us as human persons who live in the sphere in which the God-man himself has come to us.

FROM THE ONE TO THE MANY

Barth thus has a clear theological explanation for his christological anthropology oriented around the conviction that Jesus is "the ontological

---

23. *CD* III/2, 133–34.

24. *CD* III/2, 134.

25. *CD* III/2, 149.

26. *CD* III/2, 149–50.

27. *CD* III/2, 149.

determination" of humanity as the eternal Elector/Elect, as God's faithful copartner, and as the one in whom all humans are confronted and summoned by the divine Other. Unlike many theologians, however, Barth does not leave us with just this theological framework. Instead, he presses on to consider some of the many methodological implications involved in seeking an understanding of humanity in general from his specifically christological starting point. And most importantly, Barth's methodology involves distinguishing between two anthropological moments: "In our exposition of the doctrine of man we must always look in the first instance at the nature of man as it confronts us in the person of Jesus, and only secondarily—asking and answering from this place of light—at the nature of man as that of every man and all other men."[28]

Unsurprisingly, then, Barth's methodology begins with Christology. Given the revelatory significance of Jesus' humanity, Barth contends that theological anthropology must begin with his unique existence. Anything incompatible with this christological starting point is *ipso facto* non-human."[29]

Nonetheless, Barth sees the inadequacy of stopping here, as though everything important about theological anthropology can be said in the key of Christology. Instead, he recognizes that in addition to affirming Jesus' commonality with all humans as the archetype of true humanity, we must also recognize some fundamental discontinuities. Most importantly, Jesus alone is the union of divine and human in a single person, and he alone is the perfect expression of sinless faithfulness. While neither of these detracts from his true humanity—indeed each establishes his true humanity more firmly by ensuring that he in fact is the one who truly lived as God's covenantal copartner—they do identify points of discontinuity between his perfect humanity and our own. Thus, there can be no direct move from Christology to anthropology.[30] Consequently, a christological anthropology must be an anthropology of inference. Instead of simplistically drawing general anthropological truths directly from what we observe about Jesus, we must "infer from His human nature the character of our own."[31] So, although Barth maintains that anthropology must begin with Jesus, we cannot move directly from those particularities of his lived humanity to truths about humanity in general.

---

28. *CD* III/2, 46.

29. *CD* III/2, 226.

30. *CD* III/2, 71.

31. *CD* III/2, 54.

With that distinction in mind, we can identify the four steps in Barth's anthropological methodology:

1. Study Jesus with an emphasis on his soteriological work.
2. Stipulate criteria necessary for understanding the christological material.
3. Draw general inferences for anthropology.
4. Develop specific anthropological proposals.

Barth thus begins every anthropological study with an analysis of Jesus' own life, paying particular attention to his primary identity as the Savior.[32] On that basis, he then identifies key fundamental assertions that we must affirm about Jesus in light of who he revealed himself to be. But even these christological criteria are still not assertions about humanity in general. Instead, these criteria serve as the *framework* for theological anthropology rather than providing its specific *content*. They are "the limits within which we shall always have to move in our search for a theological concept of man."[33]

We begin moving toward the content of anthropology with step three, where we transition from the christological moment to the anthropological one. The third step is possibly the most difficult to describe in Barth's methodology since he did not offer principles for moving from the christological criteria to assertions about humanity in general. For Barth the key is that the anthropological assertions cannot simply be identical to the christological criteria, since there can be no direct move from Christology to anthropology, but they must be necessitated in some way by the christological criteria.

Finally, having identified general anthropological principles required by the christological starting point, Barth moves to the specific anthropological conclusions, which will serve as the basis for engaging the specific loci of a theological anthropology (e.g., the mind/body relationship, free will, gender/sexuality). Without this final step, Barth argues, a christological anthropology would remain overly abstract, filled with general truths that fail to engage real issues. For Barth, though, Christology "gives rise to a definite anthropology" because it can and should address these material concerns as the final step in viewing the human person christologically.[34]

---

32. *CD* III/2, 58.

33. *CD* III/2, 74.

34. *CD* III/2, 552.

HOW MANY PIECES WOULD YOU LIKE? BARTH ON MIND AND BODY

Barth clearly offered a robust christological framework for understanding the human person. But can such a christological starting point really have much to say about something as esoteric and complex as the mind/body relationship? I think we will find that the answer is yes, provided we are clear about the precise question. Remember that Barth's methodology rejects a direct move from Christology to anthropology, blocking any naive attempt to answer difficult anthropological questions by appealing to Christology alone. So we should not be surprised to discover that Barth does not attempt to give a detailed account of the mind/body relationship.[35] Instead of answering the question *What is the ontological constitution of the human person?* Barth focuses on the question *What must we believe about the ontological constitution of the human person in light of who Jesus has revealed the human person to be?* And as we will see, although answering that question may not give a specific theory of human ontology, it will give us a christological framework within which specific proposals may be posited and evaluated.

The Archimedean Point: Starting with Jesus

Consistent with his methodology, Barth begins his study of human ontology by looking at who Jesus Christ revealed himself to be through his redemptive work. For the sake of space, though, we will not attempt to walk through all four steps of Barth's methodology independently. Instead, we will look at five criteria that Barth thought were fundamental for understanding human ontology and how each flows from his understanding of Jesus' humanity. With those criteria in mind, we will then be able to identify the implications that Barth's christological starting point has for specific proposals regarding the mind/body relationship.

1. The Unity of the Human Person

According to Barth, the first thing we must notice when considering the life and ministry of Jesus is the unity of his person in all that he does.

---

35. Barth sounded at times like he was offering a physicalist or materialist account of human ontology, stating that the human should be viewed as a "concrete monism" (*CD* III/2, 393). On the very next page, though, he affirmed "the concrete and Christian dualism of soul and body" (ibid., 394). So an adequate understanding of his anthropological ontology will require us to consider the ways in which he is trying to navigate between these two apparently exclusive positions.

Although the gospel narratives clearly portray Jesus as a physical being with a real "inner" life (e.g., affections, intellect, volition), we consistently see him as a single human person in whom there is no tension between these inner and outer aspects. Instead, the narratives emphasize the unity of Christ's person in all of his actions.[36] This unity becomes particularly clear in the radical transition involved in Jesus' death and resurrection. Even here we see no "division" between the body and the soul.[37] Instead, "as the same whole man, soul and body, He rises as He died, and sits at the right hand of God, and will come again."[38] After the resurrection, he remains a single body/soul entity who remains identical to the body/soul being who lived before the resurrection. Barth thus concludes that the christological data requires a holistic perspective on the body/soul relationship. Any form of dualism that simply divides the person of Jesus Christ into two discontinuous elements is inadequate to the christological data.[39] Instead, we must take the whole person and the unity of its aspects as our point of departure.

2. The Duality of the Human Person

The second criterion of a christological approach to the mind/body relationship, though, emphasizes the other side of the coin. Despite the holistic emphasis of the first criterion, we must also recognize the duality that we see in Jesus Christ. Barth contends that in Jesus the body and the soul are united but distinguishable, neither identical nor reducible to one another.[40]

For Barth, a person's *body* is her material body which as such is "visible, outward, earthly."[41] The body, therefore, represents the objective and empirical aspect of human nature. It is also what determines the "manner" and "nature" of a given being's existence.[42] But although all creatures are material bodies of some sort, they are not all *merely* material

---

36. *CD* III/2, 328. For Barth, the unity of Christ's inner/outer aspects is displayed particularly clearly in his atoning sacrifice (*CD* III/2, 328–40; IV/1, 225).

37. *CD* III/2, 328.

38. Ibid.

39. *CD* III/2, 327. Barth's arguments in this section are more summative than exegetical, focusing primarily on the overall impression of the texts than their specific details (see Joseph L. Mangina, *Karl Barth: Theologian of Christian Witness* [Aldershot: Ashgate, 2004], 43).

40. *CD* III/2, 367.

41. Ibid.

42. Ibid.

bodies. Some can become alive as they are "besouled," transcending mere materiality as "organic bodies."[43] *Soul*, then, denotes primarily the subjective life of a material organism.[44] It is the "independent life of a corporeal being," where *life* refers to "capacity for action, self-movement, self-activity, self-determination."[45]

Jesus thus comprises both soul and body. And here we must again emphasize the unity of these aspects. Indeed, body and soul are so closely joined in Barth's anthropology as to seem inseparable.[46] Barth even argues that soul and (organic) body are incoherent notions independent of one another.[47] Life cannot exist as an abstract principle apart from the body which it enlivens; neither can an organic body exist without the life that makes it more than a lump of inert matter. Every action and experience in Jesus' life thus manifests the unity of these two aspects.

Nonetheless, despite the fact that we see in Jesus that a person is "wholly and simultaneously" soul *and* body, the relationship between them is one in which there is still an "inner differentiation."[48] As we have seen, soul and body are interdependent and possibly even inseparable, but they remain distinct aspects of a human person. Looking at Jesus, "we are confronted by the remarkable fact that . . . we have to do with a whole, but with a whole in which there is antithesis, and therefore with a duality."[49] The holistic portrayal of Jesus in the gospel narratives does not preclude recognizing a real distinction between the inner and outer aspects of his being.

---

43. *CD* III/2, 377.

44. *CD* III/2, 364.

45. *CD* III/2, 374.

46. Barth's understanding of the state of the body/soul relationship after death is not entirely clear. At times he suggests that physical death entails the cessation of the human person, calling death "the end of all human and creaturely life and creativity and work" (*CD* IV/2, 295). He even says of Jesus that he "ceased to be" at the time of his physical death (IV/3.1, 312). In other places, though, he suggests some kind of continued existence, referring to a dead human person as "a bodiless soul and a soulless body" (III/2, 355). And elsewhere he emphasizes only the severe limitations of a disembodied soul (*CD* III/2, 425), suggesting that it does maintain some form of existence after the death of the body (cf. *CD* III/2, 370).

47. *CD* III/2, 331, 376. Some have suggested that this means the body/soul distinction for Barth is merely conceptual (e.g., Paul K. Jewett and Marguerite Shuster, *Who We Are: Our Dignity as Human* [Grand Rapids: Eerdmans, 1996], 41–42; Mangina, *Karl Barth: Theologian of Christian Witness*, 199). For Barth, however, although the soul cannot be considered independently of the body, it is, as we have seen, neither identical with nor reducible to the body. Thus, even if the soul is inseparable from the body, Barth presents it as having its own objective reality in distinction from the body.

48. *CD* III/2, 372.

49. *CD* III/2, 367.

3. An Ordered Ontology

Having established the unity and the duality that we see in Jesus Christ, Barth argues that we must also recognize the "indestructible order" manifested in the body/soul relationship. This is the third principle of his christological ontology. Barth argues that the gospel narratives consistently present Jesus as one in whom we see the priority of the soul as that which guides and directs the life of the body.[50] In Jesus we see someone who performed all of his deeds, particularly the atonement, knowingly, freely, and actively.[51] Consequently, we must acknowledge the priority of Jesus' subjective life over his bodily life, which is of "decisive importance … in the anthropology of Jesus."[52] For Barth, this means that we have to view the human person not as a "chaos," in which there is no discernable order, but a "cosmos," which Barth defines as a "formed and ordered totality" in which there is "a higher and a lower, a first and a second, a dominating and a dominated."[53] The soul is that which leads and commands while the body is that which follows and obeys.[54]

Barth emphasizes, however, that recognizing that the order in the body/ soul relationship does not dissolve the essential unity of the human person. We are still not dealing with any division or separation between the body and soul of Jesus, only a proper order in the interdependent relationship. And Barth also rejects the conclusion that such an anthropological hierarchy denotes any devaluating of the human body. Both body and soul are necessary and valued aspects of a human life.[55] Rather than downplaying the importance of the body, Barth argues that both body and soul find their unique significance and dignity through their relationship to the other.[56]

This ordered relationship is what Barth has in mind when he defines the human person as "a rational being."[57] The *ratio* of the human being refers not to intellectual capacities but to the "meaningful order" of soul

---

50. He specifically appealed to such examples as Jesus fasting in the desert (Matthew 4:1–2), his agony in Gethsemane (Matthew 26:39), and Jesus' affirmation of Mary's contemplation over Martha's bodily activity (Luke 10:38–42) (see *CD* III/2, 339).

51. See esp. Barth's summary of the doctrine of reconciliation (IV/1, 79–156).

52. *CD* III/2, 418.

53. *CD* III/2, 332.

54. *CD* III/2, 424.

55. *CD* III/2, 338.

56. *CD* III/2, 339.

57. *CD* III/2, 419.

and body.[58] In every human activity, then, we see an ordered unity that transcends "simple distribution" or even "cooperation,"[59] but in which we always have a "primacy of the soul."[60] Although Barth argues that this same ordered relationship exists in all human persons, the rational ordering of the two moments is hidden in the tensions and contradictions of human life.[61]

4. Spirit-ed Humanity

Fourth, no analysis of Jesus' life can ignore the "unique relation" he shared with the Holy Spirit.[62] Jesus thus demonstrates that a christologically adequate theological anthropology will also need to be robustly pneumatological. And this holds for our understanding of the body/soul relationship as well.

Barth identifies at least three ways in which we see the Spirit at work in human ontology. First, we see the Spirit at work in the *creation* of the human person. Jesus owes his very existence to the work of the Spirit.[63] This is true in virtue of the Spirit's involvement with Jesus' conception, but it also stems from how Barth understood the relationship between the soul as the principle of life and the body as the material object enlivened by the soul. Since the body is simply "a spatio-material system of relations," no merely material body possesses inherently its own principle of independent life.[64] Insofar as a body is to become a *living* body, and thus become the subject of a personal life, it must receive that life as "an event over whose occurrence he has no control."[65] In other words, life itself is a gift, the event in which the body becomes ensouled and alive. And for Barth, this event is an expressly pneumatological event. The Spirit is "the fundamental determination"[66] of human nature because the Spirit is "the principle which makes man into a subject."[67]

---

58. Ibid.

59. *CD* III/2, 400.

60. *CD* III/2, 418.

61. *CD* III/2, 331–32.

62. *CD* III/2, 332.

63. *CD* III/2, 333.

64. *CD* III/2, 377.

65. *CD* III/2, 353.

66. *CD* III/2, 363.

67. *CD* III/2, 364.

In addition to the work of creation, the Spirit is also at work in the *preservation* of the human person. In Jesus we see a human person who was continually dependent on the empowering work of the Spirit. Rather than merely receiving his life as a gift at the beginning and subsequently operating as an autonomous individual, Jesus manifested the pneumatological shape of human existence throughout his life. And again this coheres with Barth's presentation of the body/soul relationship. Just as the body is not able to initiate life on its own, neither is it able to sustain its own life. The Spirit is the "transcendent determination" of human life because the body/soul union is not a fixed possession but is something that must be continually established by God through the agency of the Spirit.[68] The human person is constituted by a pneumatological event that "must be continually repeated" for humans to remain human.[69]

Finally, we must also recognize the Spirit's work of *regeneration*. At first glance, it might seem odd to emphasize the regenerative work of the Holy Spirit in an anthropology that takes as its starting point the sinless life of Christ. For Barth, though, the human nature that Jesus assumed in the incarnation was not some kind of already purified prelapsarian humanity, but the very fallen and fleshly human nature that we struggle with every day. In the incarnation, Jesus took up this flesh and through the enlivening work of the Spirit transformed it into something "quickening and living and meaningful."[70]

For Barth, then, the pneumatological criterion establishes that the humanity of Christ has a pneumatological ground at every moment. Jesus only becomes human, remains human, and transforms humanity through the enlivening and empowering work of the Spirit.

5. Covenantal Humanity

The final criterion in Barth's christological analysis of the human person has already been hinted at in our discussion of Jesus as God's faithful

---

68. *CD* III/2, 348. Some worry that this might suggest an Apollinarian understanding of humanity in which human spirituality and subjectivity lose any real significance (Arnold Bruce Come, *An Introduction to Barth's "Dogmatics" for Preachers* [London: SCM Press, 1963], 152). Rather than vitiating the human dimension, though, Barth's approach seeks to emphasize that the human person is radically dependent on the Spirit at all times (cf. Stuart McLean, "Creation and Anthropology," in *Theology beyond Christendom: Essays on the Centenary of the Birth of Karl Barth*, ed. John Thompson [Allison Park, Pa.: Pickwick, 1986], 133–34).

69. *CD* III/2, 359.

70. *CD* III/2, 336.

covenant copartner. For Barth, this final piece is what gives explanatory power to everything that preceded. In Jesus we must recognize the unified human person, in whom distinct aspects work together in their proper order through the enlivening work of the Holy Spirit, specifically because this is the kind of being that God has constituted and called as his covenantal copartner. If the first four criteria offer the *what* of human ontology, the covenant provides the *why*. The pneumatological event, by which humans become human, is also the event in which human capacity for covenantal relationship is grounded: "Spirit in His fundamental significance is the element in virtue of which man is actively and passively introduced as a partner in the covenant of grace, in which he is installed in his position as God's partner in the particular stages and decisions of the history of this covenant and in which he is equipped for his function as such."[71] Human capacity for covenantal relationship stems from humanity's pneumatologically grounded dual constitution.[72] Thus, Barth's understanding of the body/soul relationship can be described as offering a *covenantal ontology*.[73]

MAKING THE ANTHROPOLOGICAL MOVE: SOME IMPLICATIONS OF A CHRISTOLOGICAL ONTOLOGY

As we discussed earlier, Barth did not stop at offering general christological criteria. As valuable as those might be, if we do not press on to consider their implications for specific anthropological issues, our theological anthropologies will remain overly abstract and removed from everyday concerns. Thus, Barth's anthropological methodology is not complete until we have moved from the christological to the anthropological. Although we began to do some of that in the previous section, we will do that more decisively here by considering precisely what implications Barth's christological analysis has for understanding the body/soul relationship in humans generally.

Moving from the second to the third step in Barth's methodology, we can identify some of the anthropological implications of Barth's

---

71. *CD* III/2, 347.

72. Cf. *CD* III/2, 399–416.

73. Recognizing the interrelationship between human ontology and covenantal relationality, John Webster asserts, "Without that substantial anthropology and its corresponding emphasis on the realization of selfhood through action, Barth's understanding of covenant, and his consistent stress on the moral character of human response to God, would be simply unthinkable" (John Webster, "Rescuing the Subject: Barth and Postmodern Anthropology," in *Karl Barth: A Future for Postmodern Theology?*, ed. Geoff Thompson and Christiaan Mostert [Hindmarsh: Australian Theological Forum, 2001], 56.

christological criteria. In other words, given what Barth has already said about the humanity of Jesus Christ, what must be true about human nature in general? And I think we can identify at least four things that must be true of humanity if Jesus has in fact revealed what it means to be truly human. While we could certainly identify other features of human existence required by this analysis, these seem to be the most fruitful for addressing the mind/body relationship today.

1. The body is integral to being human. Barth's clear emphasis on the incarnation and the importance of the body and its inseparability from the soul in all of Jesus' actions and experiences strongly suggests that any adequate understanding of the human person must include an equal emphasis on the body as an integral aspect of human existence. And when one includes the fact that Jesus remained embodied after the resurrection, the likeliest conclusion is that an adequate anthropology must include at least the hope of postmortem embodiment as part of its eschatological picture of the human person.

2. The human person should have a robust "inner" life as a conscious self. As John Webster states, Barth's anthropology clearly requires a "rather robust sense of human selfhood" given his emphasis on the subjective life of the human person and the leading work of the soul in all the activities of the body.[74] Though Barth never clearly defined the term *subject*, it at least involves seeing the person as a significant individual who can be identified with certain actions and experiences.[75] Thus, Barth's criteria seem to require viewing the human person as a *self*, which according to one contemporary definition can be understood as "a subject of consciousness, a being capable of thought and experience and able to engage in deliberative action."[76] Though Barth would differ from many modern definitions of selfhood by rejecting a tendency to *over*emphasize interiority and individuality, Barth's anthropology still requires a high view of the interior life of the human individual.[77]

---

74. Ibid.

75. See *CD* III/2, 335, 352, 371, 374.

76. E. J. Lowe, "Self," in *The Oxford Companion to Philosophy*, ed. Ted Honderich (New York: Oxford University Press, 1995), 517.

77. For good discussions on the modern emphasis on interiority and individuality, see Charles Taylor, *Sources of the Self* (New York: Cambridge University Press, 1989) and Stanley J. Grenz, *The Social God and the Relational Self: A Trinitarian Theology of the Imago Dei* (Louisville: Westminster John Knox, 2001). Barth's emphasis on both the external and internal dimensions of the human person thus presents a strong critique of the modern self (see Simon Fisher, *Revelatory Positivism? Barth's Earliest Theology and the Marburg School* [New York: Oxford University

Viewing the person as a self in this way, Barth's anthropology also requires the human person to have a real and vital subjective consciousness. Although "consciousness" can be used in a variety of ways, it refers most often to some kind of "phenomenal awareness," or the qualitative experiences of a given subject.[78] Barth clearly affirms that the human person is a self-conscious entity — human persons have first-person awareness of themselves.[79] And Barth's depiction of the vital "inner life" of Jesus, which he later affirms of humans in general, must be understood as involving a certain "feel" for the human subject.[80]

3. Humans are moral agents capable of directing their actions and being held responsible for them. Having presented the humanity of Jesus as involving a soul and body in an *ordered* relationship in which the soul leads and the body follows, Barth's view of humanity entails seeing human persons as moral agents capable of directing their own actions.[81] According to Barth, we must understand Jesus' actions, especially the atonement, as freely chosen and directed by him. Thus, for Barth, the very nature of human life involves the agential "capacity for action, self-movement, self-activity, self-determination."[82]

Closely related to this, Barth's ontology seems committed to some form of mental causation. As that which guides and directs the body, the soul must have some kind of causal influence on the body and its actions. Barth thus argues for the "downward" causal influence of the soul as it controls the body.[83]

Press, 1988], 192; Mangina, *Karl Barth: Theologian of Christian Witness*, 14; Fergus Kerr, "The Modern Philosophy of Self in Recent Theology," in *Neuroscience and the Person: Scientific Perspectives on Divine Action*, ed. Robert J. Russell et al. [Vatican City: Vatican Observatory, 2002], 27).

78. Consciousness is thus commonly understood as the what's-it-likeness (i.e. qualia) of a phenomenal experience made famous by Thomas Nagel, "What Is It Like to Be a Bat?" *Philosophical Review* 83 (1974): 435–56.

79. See *CD* III/2, 375.

80. See *CD* III/2, 329, 373. This becomes particularly clear in Barth's discussion of perceptual experience. According to Barth, the very notion of a covenantal relationship requires the capacity for a self-conscious experience whereby the human becomes aware of some other being (*CD* III/2, 399–401). Construing that experience such that it minimized or even eliminated the qualitative experience of the covenantal relationship would seem antithetical to Barth's covenantal ontology.

81. We can define *agent* loosely here as "the capacity for developing 'intentions' that are causally related to the production of actions" (cf. John R. Searle, *Intentionality: An Essay in the Philosophy of Mind* [New York: Cambridge University Press, 1983], 83–98).

82. *CD* III/2, 374.

83. *CD* III/2, 339, 368. Barth thus explicitly rejects any "epiphenomenal" understanding of mental causation (*CD* III/2, 382).

Finally, given that each human is an agent capable of directing its own actions through the causal relationship between mind and body, Barth emphasizes the "freedom" of the human person. As the obedient Son who lived freely and faithfully in his covenantal and redemptive work, Jesus exemplifies a humanity that is both free to live faithfully before God and capable of being held responsible for the right exercise of that freedom. Barth thus rejects the idea that human actions are fully determined by cultural or biological influences rather than being determined for covenantal freedom by God.[84] Indeed, for Barth, "The soul is itself the freedom of man."[85]

4. Human personhood is contingent but continuous. Finally, Barth's Christology offers a view of human personhood that emphasizes both its contingent status (i.e., we do not "possess" our personhood intrinsically) and the continuing identity of the human person so constituted (i.e., we remain the same human individuals despite the radical changes and transitions that a human person experiences). The contingency of personhood is seen most clearly in the pneumatological event that constitutes us as human persons. We become and remain human only insofar as the Spirit constitutes us as God's covenantal copartners. Barth, therefore, opposes any attempt to present some aspect of the human person as inherently immortal.[86]

At the same time, though, Barth resists any attempt to understand this contingent personhood in a way that would undermine the identity of the person in both its synchronic (identity at a given time) and diachronic (identity through time) forms.[87] The clear emphasis in the Gospels is on the continuous identity of Jesus Christ even as he depends moment by moment on the work of the Spirit to sustain his human existence as an ensouled body. Even after so radical a transition as Jesus' death, burial, and resurrection, Jesus remains the "same whole man, soul and body."[88] And continuous identity would also seem to be required given Barth's emphasis on the human person as a conscious self capable

---

84. See esp. III/4, 565–685; cf. also John B. Webster, *Barth's Ethics of Reconciliation* (Cambridge: Cambridge University Press, 1995); John B. Webster, *Barth's Moral Theology: Human Action in Barth's Thought* (Edinburgh: T&T Clark, 1998).

85. *CD* III/2, 418.

86. *CD* III/2 380, 392–93.

87. On the synchronic/diachronic distinction see Eric T. Olson, "Personal Identity," in *The Blackwell Guide to Philosophy of Mind*, ed. Stephen P. Stich and Ted A. Warfield (Oxford: Blackwell, 2003), 352–68.

88. *CD* III/2, 327.

of meaningful actions for which he or she can be held responsible.[89] Indeed, the very nature of Barth's covenantal ontology presupposes the relatively stable identities of the individuals involved. Thus, although the human receives personhood extrinsically through the work of the Spirit, Barth maintained the continuous identity of the person so constituted.

PARADIGMATIC HUMANITY: TOWARD A FRAMEWORK FOR HUMAN ONTOLOGY

The final step in Barth's methodology is to take the anthropological principles inferred from his christological criteria and apply them to material issues in theological anthropology. So before we can bring this study to a fitting conclusion, we need to ask about the specific implications these criteria have for how Barth addressed theories about the mind/body relationship. And the key for understanding this aspect of Barth's christological anthropology is to realize that he does not use these criteria to develop a specific ontological *theory* for describing the precise contours of the body/ soul relationship. Instead he uses them to develop a christological paradigm or framework within which any particular theory of humanity must function.[90] On that basis, Barth offered a number of criticisms of both dualism and physicalism, arguing that both fall short of an adequately christological view of the human person. Barth thus offered a way of *thinking* and *speaking* about the body/soul relationship that helps limit the range of legitimate options to those that might be viewed as christologically adequate but does not itself stipulate any particular theory.

Barth clearly thought that his anthropological principles preclude any form of substance dualism as an adequate approach to the mind/ body relationship. We can define substance dualism as maintaining that humans are comprised of both mental and physical substances, which are fundamentally different kinds of things and are at least conceivably separable. And Barth contended that we must view all such dualistic perspectives on the human person as inadequate because they undermine (at least) our first and fourth principles (embodiment and contingent personhood). Regarding the first, he argues,

---

89. Philosophers have long recognized the close relationship between continuous personal identity and concern for the future (cf. Amy Kind, "The Metaphysics of Personal Identity and Our Special Concern for the Future," *Metaphilosophy* 35.4 [2004]: 536–54).

90. For a discussion of the use of paradigm/model/theory language in theological language see Marc Cortez, "Context and Concept: Contextual Theology and the Nature of Theological Discourse," *Westminster Theological Journal* 67, no. 1 (2005): 85–102.

> In general, the character and result of this anthropology are marked by a separation of soul and body, an exaltation of the soul over the body, a humiliation of the body under the soul, in which both really become not merely abstractions but in fact two "co-existing" figments—a picture in which no real man ever recognized himself, and with which one cannot possibly do justice to the biblical view and concept of man.[91]

In other words, Barth thought that although substance dualism clearly recognizes the existence of both soul and body, it does so in a way that undermines the holistic unity of the body/soul relation and the value of embodiment as an essential aspect of being human. Barth also contended that at least some forms of substance dualism violate the fourth anthropological principle (contingent personhood) in that they view the person as an immortal soul.[92] And some might even argue that substance dualism runs afoul of the third principle despite its strong emphasis on the soul as leading and directing the activities of the body. Here we encounter the famous "mental causation" problem for substance dualism. Given the ontological discontinuity of soul and body, *how* exactly does the soul exercise causal control over the body?

Barth thus argued that a christological starting point renders substance dualism untenable as an account of the body/soul relationship. He does not address, though, whether one might be able to develop a modified form of substance dualism, one that maintains the existence of distinct substances in the human person, but with a strong emphasis on their interdependence and the intrinsic value of embodiment for human personhood.[93] Such accounts might well fare better with regard to Barth's criteria, suggesting that his blanket condemnation of substance dualism may have overreached his own christological paradigm. Rather than rejecting dualism outright, it might have been more consistent to point out that certain forms of dualism appear christologically inadequate.[94]

---

91. *CD* III/2, 382.

92. *CD* III/2, 380, 392–93.

93. See, for example, William Hasker, *The Emergent Self* (Ithaca: Cornell, 1999); John W. Cooper, *Body, Soul, and Life Everlasting* (Grand Rapids: Eerdmans, 2000); J. P. Moreland and Scott B. Rae, *Body & Soul: Human Nature and the Crisis in Ethics* (Downers Grove, Ill.: InterVarsity, 2000); Dean W. Zimmerman, "Christians Should Affirm Mind-Body Dualism," in *Contemporary Debates in Philosophy of Religion*, ed. Michael L. Peterson and Raymond J. VanArragon (Oxford: Blackwell, 2004), 315–26; Richard Swinburne, *Mind, Brain, and Free Will* (New York: Oxford University Press, 2013).

94. Barth himself was well aware that "substance dualism" encompasses a number of mind/body theories that share family resemblances but also important differences (*CD* III/2, 383–90).

A similar pattern manifests itself when we turn to Barth's critique of physicalist perspectives on the human person. According to physicalist theories, the human person is entirely comprised of physical entities and processes.[95] Although Barth appreciated the physicalist emphasis on the intrinsic importance of embodiment, he contended that a physicalist ontology runs into problems with (at least) our second and third principle (selfhood and agency).[96]

Many have argued that physicalist theories of the human person also struggle with respect to the continuity of identity aspect of the fourth principle. If the human person is simply identical to some bodily organism, then it seems to follow that the human person ceases to exist when the bodily organism dies. If that is the case, however, how do we know that the person resurrected later is in fact identical to the person who existed previously? Unlike the dualist, the physicalist cannot appeal to the soul as the principle of identity (i.e., the person's identity is constituted by the continuity of the soul from one body to another). However, although Barth did not himself raise this question in his discussion, it seems unlikely that he would have viewed it as a problem since he did not think that the continued identity of the human person is established primarily in the identity of either soul or body through time. Instead, Barth argued that personal identity is grounded primarily in God's covenantal faithfulness to the human person. I remain *me* even in death because God watches over me and remains faithful to me.[97] Just as personhood is contingent on the continual working of God, so personal identity is contingently established on God's covenantal faithfulness. Rather than being a threat to my continued personhood, though, grounding my identity in God's faithfulness is the surest possible way of establishing my continued identity. For Barth, then, continued personal identity is no more difficult to establish for the physicalist than it is for the dualist since both find their continued identity extrinsically in God's own covenantal faithfulness.

---

95. There is no commonly accepted definition of "physical," but one common approach is simply to argue that "physical" entities and processes are simply those things studied by the physical sciences (e.g., Andrew Melnyk, "How to Keep the 'Physical' in Physicalism," *Journal of Philosophy* 94, no. 12 [1997]: 622–38; Ralph Ellis, "Consciousness, Self-Organization, and the Process-Substratum Relation: Rethinking Nonreductive Physicalism," *Philosophical Quarterly* 13, no. 2 [2000]: 173–90).

96. See esp. *CD* III/2, 382–94.

97. *CD* III/2, 371. See also *CD* IV.2, 315–16.

CHRISTOLOGY AS A PARADIGMATIC FRAMEWORK FOR ANTHROPOLOGY

We could say more about how Barth's christological framework could be applied to these various debates regarding the mind/body relationship in the human person.[98] For the purposes of this study, though, we have seen enough to understand the logic of his christological anthropology. Many theologians begin their discussion of the mind/body issue by looking to scientific or philosophical sources. For Barth, although these are important voices that need to be included in the conversation, they cannot provide the necessary theological starting point. Instead, he looks first to the person and work of Jesus. He alone is the eternal, historical, and existential ground of true humanity. We cannot arrive at any real understanding of humanity, any insight capable of penetrating through the phenomena of the human and arrive at a knowledge of true humanity itself, apart from the Archimedean point available only in Jesus Christ.

This does not mean, though, that we can derive anthropological insights from any straightforward analysis of the gospel narratives. A disciplined christological anthropology will recognize the differences between Jesus and all other humans based on his deity, sinlessness, and particular humanness. Barth thus offered a nuanced methodology for moving from Christology to anthropology, one that refuses to collapse anthropology into Christology—as though everything important that we need to say about the human person can be derived directly from Christology—while retaining Christology as the necessary starting point of a truly *theological* anthropology.

A truly christological anthropology, then, will determine first what we *must* believe about humans in general on the basis of Christology, and only then will it draw conclusions about particular anthropological issues like the mind/body debate. This means that Christology serves as the paradigmatic framework within which we have to understand the human person. Christology does not answer all of our anthropological questions, but it does offer a way of thinking christologically about anthropology, one that even has implications for as complex an issue as the mind/body relationship.

---

98. For a more thorough discussion of this issue in relation to Barth's christological anthropology, see Cortez, *Embodied Souls, Ensouled Bodies*, 155–87.

CHAPTER 6

Personal Being

John Zizioulas and the Christological Grounding of Human Personhood

———•———

Christ does not simply stand vis-à-vis each man, but constitutes the ontological ground of every man.

John D. Zizioulas, *Communion and Otherness*[1]

FEW ANTHROPOLOGICAL CONCEPTS ARE USED more widely and with less clarity than that of the *person*. Across nearly every discipline — theology, philosophy, law, ethics, politics, many of the sciences, and more — we encounter ideas of the person, clearly establishing this as one of the more significant concepts in modern discourse about what it means to be human. Yet not only do we lack any commonly agreed-on definition of *person*; we do not even have a consensus about what factors would need to be included in any such definition. *Person* remains one of those concepts with broad intuitive appeal and little conceptual clarity.[2]

According to John Zizioulas, this confusion stems at least partly from a set of irreconcilable problems at the heart of modern concepts of the person: particularly those involving freedom, uniqueness, and community. Although modern society often claims these as important aspects of its vision of humanity, Zizioulas argues that its understanding of the person is ultimately too shallow and incoherent to support these ideas in any meaningful way. What we need is a new understanding of the person. Or

---

1. John D. Zizioulas, "Human Capacity and Human Incapacity: A Theological Exploration of Personhood," in *Communion and Otherness: Further Studies in Personhood and the Church* (New York: T&T Clark, 2006), 243.

2. For helpful discussions on this, see the essays in J. Wentzel van Huyssteen and Erik P. Wiebe, eds., *In Search of Self: Interdisciplinary Perspectives on Personhood* (Grand Rapids: Eerdmans, 2011).

actually, an old one. Thus, one of the primary arguments in Zizioulas's many writings has been that *person* is an inherently theological concept with historical roots in the Trinitarian theology of the early church. And only by rediscovering those roots will we rescue personhood from its captivity to modern ideas of the person with their inherent ambiguities and irresolvable tensions.

Zizioulas thus offers an understanding of the human person that revolves around the doctrine of the Trinity. We only understand rightly what it means to be a person by reflecting on the personhood of the Father, the Son, and the Spirit in their unity and distinctiveness. To be a person, on this account, is to be in community: to exist as a unique and free being who is constituted as such by meaningful relationships with other persons. As interesting as this Trinitarian account of personhood might be, though, this alone would not take us very far in our study of explicitly *christological* anthropologies. Fortunately, Zizioulas also offers a robustly christological framework for understanding what it means to talk about a *human* person. According to Zizioulas, Jesus is "the person *par excellence*" who both *reveals* and *realizes* true personhood in history.[3] Other humans only come to be persons as they are included in the personhood of Christ: "he is the person in whom all created persons may truly be persons."[4] Thus, although Zizioulas grounds his general account of personhood in the Trinity, his understanding of *human* personhood is thoroughly christological. Understanding what Zizioulas means by this will take us into the heart of his christological anthropology.

DIVINE PERSONHOOD AND AN ONTOLOGY OF LOVE

Zizioulas argues that there are two basic ways of trying to understand the nature of human personhood.[5] The first approaches personhood from a creaturely perspective, either through an introspective analysis of human experience or by establishing human uniqueness through a comparison with other creatures. As different as these might appear, both focus largely on the universal features of the human "nature." In other words, focusing on creaturely realities yields an understanding of *person* in terms of universal properties like consciousness or rationality. We then deter-

---

3. Edward Russell, "Reconsidering Relational Anthropology: A Critical Assessment of John Zizioulas's Theological Anthropology," *International Journal of Systematic Theology* 5, no. 2 (2003): 175. The emphasis in all quotations in this chapter is original unless otherwise noted.

4. John Zizioulas, *Lectures in Christian Dogmatics* (New York: T&T Clark, 2008), 5.

5. See esp. Zizioulas, "Human Capacity," in *Communion and Otherness*, 206–49.

mine whether something qualifies as a person on the basis of whether or not it is an individual who bears the relevant properties.

For reasons that will soon become clear, Zizioulas rejects this creaturely approach to personhood entirely. As he argues, "The observation of the world cannot lead to an ontology of the person, because the person as an ontological category cannot be extrapolated from experience."[6] Instead, Zizioulas contends that the only adequate way to approach personhood is by understanding the nature of divine personhood. Only in this way will we see that a person must *not* be viewed as an individual with the requisite properties. Instead, a person is *"a relational 'mode of being'"* in which the being is constituted as a personal being in relationship with some Other.[7]

For Zizioulas, then, the "fundamental question" to be addressed at the beginning of any inquiry into the nature of human personhood is the following: *"Are we as theologians to draw our concept of human personhood from the study of the human person or from God?"*[8] To this question, he responds unequivocally that we must begin with the personhood of God if we are to have any adequate understanding of personhood at all. And for him, approaching personhood through the lens of the Trinity establishes at least four vital principles. Persons are (1) ontologically fundamental, (2) constituted in community, (3) causally basic, and (4) absolutely unique. Let's consider each of those in turn.

Person Is the Ultimate Ontological Category

Zizioulas regularly frames his understanding of personhood in historical terms. On his account, the early theologians of the church, particularly figures like Athanasius and the Cappadocians, developed a radically new ontology in response to the "ontological monism" of ancient Greek thought.[9] The ancient Greeks, according to Zizioulas, emphasized the

---

6. John D. Zizioulas, "On Being a Person: Towards an Ontology of Personhood," in *Communion and Otherness: Further Studies in Personhood and the Church* (New York: T&T Clark, 2006), 103.

7. John D. Zizioulas, "The Trinity and Personhood: Appreciating the Cappadocian Contribution," in *Communion and Otherness: Further Studies in Personhood and the Church* (New York: T&T Clark, 2006), 176.

8. Ibid.

9. John D. Zizioulas, "Personhood and Being," in *Being as Communion: Studies in Personhood and the Church* (Crestwood, N.Y.: St. Vladimir's Seminary Press, 1985), 29. Zizioulas's interpretation of patristic theology has generated considerable debate in recent years. For the purposes of this chapter, our focus will be on Zizioulas's systematic formulations rather than

essential unity of being (*ousia*) over the particularity of individual existence. Greek thought thus "remained tied to the basic principle which it had set itself, the principle that being constitutes in the final analysis a unity in spite of the multiplicity of existent things because concrete existent things finally trace their being back to their necessary relationship and 'kinship' with the 'one' being."[10] In this framework, *ousia* is ontologically fundamental, and any particulars, including *persons*, must therefore be ontologically "derivative."[11] Such an emphasis on ontological oneness, according to Zizioulas, eradicates the possibility of true *otherness*. After all, to *whom* would someone relate if there are no true *others*?

In contrast, Zizioulas contends that patristic theologians developed a radically new cosmology that prioritized both particularity and communion, making *person* "the *ultimate* ontological category."[12] In his first published book, Zizioulas argued that the early church's theological reflections were shaped by its "eucharistic consciousness."[13] In the Eucharist, the church experienced the reality that it was the eschatological body

the validity of his historical interpretations. For some critical assessments of Zizioulas's patristic work, see esp. John Wilks, "The Trinitarian Ontology of John Zizioulas," *Vox Evangelica* 25 (1995): 63–88; Lucian Turcescu, " 'Person' versus 'Individual,' and Other Modern Misreadings of Gregory of Nyssa," *Modern Theology* 18, no. 4 (October 1, 2002): 527–39; Lewis Ayres, "On Not Three People: The Fundamental Themes of Gregory of Nyssa's Trinitarian Theology as Seen in 'To Ablabius: On Not Three Gods,' " in *Rethinking Gregory of Nyssa*, ed. Sarah Coakley (Oxford: Blackwell, 2003), 15–44; Nigel Rostock, "Two Different Gods or Two Types of Unity? A Critical Response to Zizioulas's Presentation of 'The Father as Cause' with Reference to the Cappadocian Fathers and Augustine," *New Blackfriars* 91, no. 1033 (2010): 321–34; Nicholas Loudovikos, "Person Instead of Grace and Dictated Otherness: John Zizioulas's Final Theological Position," *Heythrop Journal* 52, no. 4 (2011): 684–99. For more sympathetic discussions, see Aristotle Papanikolaou, "Is John Zizioulas an Existentialist in Disguise? Response to Lucian Turcescu," *Modern Theology* 20, no. 4 (2004): 601–8; Alan Brown, "On the Criticism of *Being as Communion* in Anglophone Orthodox Theology," in *The Theology of John Zizioulas: Personhood and the Church*, ed. Douglas H. Knight (Aldershot: Ashgate, 2007), 35–78; Aristotle Papanikolaou, "Personhood and Its Exponents in Twentieth-Century Orthodox Theology," in *Cambridge Companion to Orthodox Christian Theology* (Cambridge: Cambridge University Press, 2008), 232–45; Alexis Torrance, "Personhood and Patristics in Orthodox Theology: Reassessing the Debate," *Heythrop Journal* 52, no. 4 (2011): 700–707.

10. Zizioulas, "Personhood and Being," 29.

11. Zizioulas, "On Being a Person," 102.

12. Zizioulas, *Being as Communion*, 16. Zizioulas routinely uses the term *patristic* to describe the early theologians he interacts with, but he acknowledges that by this he primarily means the Cappadocian Fathers (Zizioulas, "On Being a Person," 105).

13. John Zizioulas, *Eucharist, Bishop, Church: The Unity of the Church in the Divine Eucharist and the Bishop during the First Three Centuries*, trans. Elizabeth Theokritoff (Brookline, Mass.: Holy Cross Orthodox Press, 2001). For a good summary of this, see Aristotle Papanikolaou, "Divine Energies or Divine Personhood: Vladimir Lossky and John Zizioulas on Conceiving the Transcendent and Immanent God," *Modern Theology* 19, no. 3 (2003): 357–85.

of Christ, united to him through the Spirit.[14] As they reflected on this "experience ... of *ecclesial being*,"[15] they realized that if God saved them *for* personal communion, he must himself *be* a God of personal communion. After all, he cannot offer what he does not have himself. If we see in the ecclesial community gathered around the Eucharist that "the being of God could be known only through personal relationship and personal love,"[16] then God himself must be a relational being. Indeed, "without the concept of communion it would not be possible to speak of the being of God."[17]

With this insight, patristic theologians began pushing toward "a philosophical landmark, a revolution in Greek philosophy,"[18] involving a relational ontology in which *person*, specifically the person of the Father, is the fundamental ontological reality in the universe. In God we do not see some naked *ousia* that is more fundamental than the three persons and from which the persons emanate through natural necessity.[19] "God is not first one and then three, but simultaneously one and three."[20] This means that the Trinity is "a *primordial* ontological concept and not a notion which is added to the divine substance or that which follows it."[21]

The search for an adequate language with which to speak of this new ontology led the patristic theologians to combine two key terms: *hypostasis* and *prosōpon*.[22] Before this, *hypostasis* had been largely synonymous with *ousia* and denoted the nature/essence side of being. *Prosōpon*, on the other hand, referred merely to the shifting roles someone might play in society

---

14. Although our focus in this chapter is on the christological aspects of Zizioulas's anthropology, it would be a mistake to downplay the importance of pneumatology as well. Indeed, for Zizioulas, there can be no Christology without pneumatology (see esp. John D. Zizioulas, "Christ, the Spirit and the Church," in *Being as Communion: Studies in Personhood and the Church* [Crestwood, N.Y.: St. Vladimir's Seminary Press, 1985], 123–42; John D. Zizioulas, "Pneumatology and the Importance of the Person: A Commentary on the Second Ecumenical Council," in *Communion and Otherness: Further Studies in Personhood and the Church* [New York: T&T Clark, 2006], 178–205).

15. Zizioulas, *Being as Communion*, 16.

16. Ibid.

17. Ibid., 17.

18. Zizioulas, "Personhood and Being," 36.

19. Ibid., 40.

20. John Zizioulas, "Introduction: Communion and Otherness," in *Communion and Otherness: Further Studies in Personhood and the Church* (New York: T&T Clark, 2006), 5.

21. Zizioulas, *Being as Communion*, 17.

22. See esp. Zizioulas, "Personhood and Being," 29–41; Zizioulas, "The Trinity and Personhood," 156–65.

or on a stage. Thus, although *prosōpon* carried a social notion that lent itself to the relational emphasis of this new ontology, it had no ontological depth. Mere roles were not enough to convey the ontologically fundamental reality of personhood. *Hypostasis*, though, struggled with the opposite problem. While it carried ontological weight through its association with *ousia*, it conveyed no sense of relationality. Their solution was to combine the two and create a new concept entirely, one in which relationality itself was ontologically fundamental.[23]

Thus, according to Zizioulas, patristic theologians broke from the ontological monism of ancient Greek thought and, based on their eucharistic experience of ecclesial being, developed a radically new cosmology in which *person* was the ontologically fundamental reality. Everything begins with the person.

Persons Are Constituted in Free Communion

In addition to establishing the ontological significance of personhood, Zizioulas also argues for its essentially relational nature. According to Zizioulas, patristic theologians interpreted the Johannine declaration "God is love" (1 John 4:16) as a statement about the relational nature of the divine being. "Love is not an emanation or 'property' of the *ousia* of God ... but is *constitutive* of his *ousia*; i.e. it is that which makes God what he is."[24] Thus, love is God's "mode of existence" such that love "hypostasizes" God and constitutes his being as *relational* being.[25] The three persons of the Trinity are *one* "because they are so united in an unbreakable communion (*koinōnia*) that none of them can be conceived apart from the rest."[26] The very names of the triune persons entail relationship, and the very otherness of each person entails relationship since "no Person can be different unless he is related."[27] Indeed, "the substance of God ... has no ontological content, no true being, apart from communion."[28]

---

23. Elizabeth Groppe points out that there is some ambiguity in how Zizioulas presents the relationship between *hypostasis* and *ousia*, sometimes presenting *hypostasis* as the "cause" of the *ousia*, but elsewhere suggesting that two "exist in a relation not of causality but of identity" (Elizabeth T. Groppe, "Creation Ex Nihilo and Ex Amore: Ontological Freedom in the Theologies of John Zizioulas and Catherine Mowry LaCugna," *Modern Theology* 21, no. 3 [2005]: 468). Either way, Zizioulas's emphasis on the ontologically fundamental nature of *hypostasis* remains.

24. Zizioulas, *Being as Communion*, 46.

25. Ibid.

26. Zizioulas, "The Trinity and Personhood," 159.

27. Zizioulas, "Introduction: Communion and Otherness," 5.

28. Zizioulas, *Being as Communion*, 17.

On this account, a person is something that can only emerge through relationship, "it is an 'I' that can exist only as long as it relates to a 'thou' which affirms its existence and its otherness."[29] Such a position has often been criticized for suggesting that persons are nothing but relations and that relations somehow exist *prior* to the persons constituted by them.[30] Yet, as Douglas Knight points out, Zizioulas recognizes that by itself a "relation" is merely an abstraction.[31] When he says that relations constitute the person, he is not suggesting that relations have some kind of autonomous existence apart from persons, only that persons do not exist *as persons* apart from the relationships that make them personal beings. In the second half of this chapter, we will see that Zizioulas thinks there is an important sense in which human beings do in fact exist prior to becoming persons. In the divine being, though, the eternality of the persons establishes the ontologically fundamental nature of personhood such that person and being coincide perfectly.[32]

If persons are inherently relational, though, Zizioulas contends that they must also be significantly *free*. The fact that a person can only exist in the relationship between an *I* and a *Thou* means that persons are constituted only in a particular kind of relationship, one in which a being recognizes another as truly Other and reaches out to that Other in love. Critiquing the introspective move in "I think, therefore I am," Zizioulas contends that a more adequately Trinitarian ontology would begin with "*I am loved*, therefore I am."[33] For such a relation to be a true expression of love, though, it must be free. Although we will say more in the next section about the relationship between nature, personhood, and freedom, we must note here that one of Zizioulas's primary concerns is

---

29. Zizioulas, *Communion and Otherness*, 9.

30. See esp. Harriet A. Harris, "Should We Say That Personhood Is Relational?" *Scottish Journal of Theology* 51, no. 2 (1998): 214–34.

31. Douglas H. Knight, "Introduction," in *The Theology of John Zizioulas: Personhood and the Church*, ed. Douglas H. Knight (Aldershot: Ashgate, 2007), 4.

32. Zizioulas does say that his relational ontology entails the conclusion that *to be* and *to be in relation* are "identical" ("Truth and Communion," in *Being as Communion*, 89). But he is simply affirming by such claims that persons are ontologically fundamental. In other words, for anything to exist, it must be in relation to at least one person because everything that exists comes from, and therefore stands in relation to, God himself. And in the next section, we will see that Zizioulas specifically means that everything comes from the person of the Father. In this sense, to exist *is* to be in relation.

33. John D. Zizioulas, "On Being Other: Towards an Ontology of Otherness," in *Communion and Otherness: Further Studies in Personhood and the Church* (New York: T&T Clark, 2006), 89.

to establish that God is not a Trinity of persons because of some necessity of the divine nature, as though the *ousia* of God somehow precedes the *hypostases* such that the three *hypostases* are a mere consequence, the necessary result of having that kind of nature.[34] If that were the case, the persons would have their being in necessity rather than freedom. That cannot be the case for a God who *is* love.

The freedom that Zizioulas has in mind, though, should not be understood in terms of mere "choice." In that kind of freedom, the individual takes precedence, standing apart from the Other and deciding whether to engage in meaningful relationship. Indeed, that kind of freedom requires significant ontological space between the two beings in order for them each to make their own free choices relative to the Other. Starting again from the doctrine of the Trinity, though, Zizioulas challenges any such notion of freedom. The Father, the Son, and the Spirit do not stand back from each other and merely choose to relate to one another. Their freedom is the freedom to love and be loved. Indeed, in the Trinity "freedom becomes identical with *love*."[35] Thus, the freedom of personal being is "not freedom *from* the other but freedom *for* the other."[36]

This kind of freedom entails that persons are always "going outside and beyond the boundaries of the 'self' ... in a movement of *affirmation of the other*."[37] This is what Zizioulas refers to as the *ecstatic* aspect of personhood. We see this most clearly in the Trinity where the Father constitutes the personal nature of the divine *ousia* by bringing forth the Spirit and the Son—the focus of our next section—who in turn love and affirm each other and the Father, establishing the Trinity as a relationship of mutual affirmation. But we also see this in the move to creation, in which God expresses his personal freedom by creating something other than himself. Here again we would misconstrue the nature of personal freedom if we thought of this as a mere "choice," as though God simply weighed the options of creating or not creating. "God's ontological freedom is ... freedom as ecstasis, freedom as the transcendence of all boundaries, freedom as unlimitable and uncircumscribable love."[38]

---

34. Zizioulas routinely uses *ousia* and "nature" in largely synonymous ways.

35. Zizioulas, "Introduction: Communion and Otherness," 9.

36. Ibid.

37. Zizioulas, *Communion and Otherness*, 10.

38. Groppe, "Creation Ex Nihilo and Ex Amore," 472.

Persons Only Come from Persons

For Zizioulas, then, personhood is ontologically fundamental and essentially relational. Yet, the specific nature of triune personhood presses us toward a further conclusion: It is specifically the *person of the Father* who is causally, and thus ontologically, fundamental, not some generic divine *ousia*. Zizioulas again frames this as a patristic response to the challenges of ancient Greek thought, a system that Zizioulas contends not only precluded true otherness, but also real freedom.[39] In their closed ontological system in which everything is contained in and constrained by *ousia*, all particulars, including even God himself, are bound by "ontological necessity."[40] Their existence is determined by this more fundamental ontological reality. If God creates others and enters into relationship with them, he does so only as the direct and necessary consequence of having the kind of nature that he does. Such a system has no room for the free expression of love that constitutes true personhood.

Patristic theologians, particularly Athanasius, broke the closed ontology of the Greeks with the doctrine of creation *ex nihilo*.[41] By establishing a sharp created/uncreated distinction and identifying God alone as the uncreated one who freely creates all that exists, they were able to separate God from the ontological system of the world more clearly and create space for real otherness and freedom.[42] Thus, the *ex nihilo* doctrine introduced "a radical difference into ontology," allowing them to make the world "*a product of freedom.*"[43]

This move would not have been entirely successful, though, if they separated God from the *ousia* of the world, only to leave him bound by the necessity of his own *ousia*. For God to experience in himself the freedom that he offers to his people in salvation, his personal existence cannot be a mere extension of his own being either. In other words, if God created as a necessary expression of his *ousia*, indeed if his own relationality was merely a necessary consequence of having the kind of nature that

---

39. Zizioulas, "Personhood and Being," 29.

40. Ibid.

41. See esp. Zizioulas, "Pneumatology and the Importance of the Person," 180–82; and John D. Zizioulas, " 'Created' and 'Uncreated': The Existential Significance of Chalcedonian Christology," in *Communion and Otherness: Further Studies in Personhood and the Church* (New York: T&T Clark, 2006), 250–85.

42. Zizioulas, "On Being Other," 18–19.

43. Zizioulas, *Communion and Otherness*, 15.

he does, then we remain locked in an ontology that makes the person derivative and disallows true freedom.[44]

Here Zizioulas draws explicitly on the theology of the Cappadocians to argue that the pivotal move in patristic theology is to identify the *hypostasis* of the Father *rather than* the generic divine *ousia* as the ontologically and causally fundamental reality. Unlike Western theologians who appeal to the *ousia* as the principle of unity in God, thus suggesting that the *ousia* is the more fundamental ontological reality in the divine being, Zizioulas contends that "the unity of God, the one God, and the ontological 'principle' or 'cause' of the being and life of God does not consist in the one substance of God but in the *hypostasis*, that is *the person of the Father*."[45] Indeed, as we have already observed, Zizioulas maintains that "there is no bare essence, no nature-as-such."[46] Thus, the divine *ousia* has always-already been instantiated as *person*, as Father.

This means, for Zizioulas, that it is specifically the person of the Father who is the "cause" of both the Son and the Spirit.[47] The Trinity involves a *"movement* from the one to the three" such that the Father *"caused* the other two persons to be distinct hypostases."[48] Zizioulas derives some confirmation of this from the fact that "God is love." He contends that in this context "God" refers not to the divine *ousia* in abstraction, or even the three-in-relation, but specifically to the *Father*, who is "that person which 'hypostasizes' God, which makes God to be three persons."[49] In other words, Jesus here declares that the Father is the one who constitutes the divine being in love by causing the personal existence of the Son and the Spirit. The ontology of love finds its source and origin in the person of the Father, who constitutes God as triune "not because the divine *nature* is ecstatic but because the Father as a *person* freely wills this

---

44. And according to Zizioulas, this is precisely the view of Western theology. Thus, despite emphasizing God's essential relationality, Western theology fails to escape the orbit of ontological monism, and cannot arrive at an adequate concept of the person (Zizioulas, "Personhood and Being," 40).

45. Ibid.

46. Zizioulas, *Lectures in Christian Dogmatics*, 52.

47. Zizioulas, "Personhood and Being," 41. This, according to Zizioulas, is why both the biblical authors and the early creeds consistently associated God with the Father (Zizioulas, "The Father as Cause," in *Communication and Otherness*, 113–17). This also follows from the patristic emphasis on the *monarchia* of the Father, which was quickly extended from its original reference to rulership or authority to include ontological source (ibid., 119).

48. Zizioulas, "The Father as Cause," 119.

49. Zizioulas, "Personhood and Being," 46, n. 41.

communion."[50] Since the Father does this eternally, the triune persons are coeternal. There never was a time when the Father existed apart from the Son and the Spirit. Indeed, it is not even conceivable that the Father could have existed without the other persons of the Trinity since "'Father' has no meaning outside a relationship with the Son and the Spirit, for he is the Father of someone."[51]

Zizioulas argues that if we establish our understanding of personhood on the basis of the divine persons, we must draw the conclusion that to say that personhood is ontologically fundamental is also to say that personhood is causally fundamental. Personhood does not come into being as a natural necessity but only as it is brought into being by another person. Indeed, Zizioulas contends that the Cappadocians rejected the very notion of substantial causation; substances do not cause things, only persons do.

Persons Are Irreplaceably Other

A Trinitarian understanding of personhood requires one final aspect. Although much of Zizioulas's argument relates to the necessity of relationality and community for true personhood, he maintains an equally firm conviction that true personhood requires a parallel commitment to the fact that "otherness is *absolute*."[52] Between the Father, the Son, and the Spirit, there is absolute uniqueness such that none of the three can be confused with the other.[53] Although they mutually shape each other's identities, they are all unique and unrepeatable particulars. "Ultimately,

---

50. Ibid., 44.

51. Zizioulas, *Lectures in Christian Dogmatics*, 53. Despite this emphasis on the interdependence of the triune persons, Zizioulas maintains the primacy of the Father in a way that establishes a hierarchy of relations in the Trinity. Some have criticized him on precisely this point, contending that it essentializes hierarchy in the Trinity (e.g., the hierarchy is not merely a functional arrangement), which in turn motivates various kinds of hierarchicalism in the church and the world (see esp. Miroslav Volf, *Exclusion and Embrace: A Theological Exploration of Identity, Otherness, and Reconciliation* (Nashville: Abingdon, 1996); Alan J. Torrance, *Persons in Communion: An Essay on Trinitarian Description and Human Participation* (Edinburgh: T&T Clark, 1996); Russell, "Reconsidering Relational Anthropology"). However, although Zizioulas explicitly embraces both sets of hierarchy as a direct implication of his theology, it is not entirely clear that this must be the case. Causal relations do not necessarily entail organizational or authoritative relations. Even if he is correct in affirming the causal primacy of the Father, we cannot merely assume this leads to the kinds of hierarchical implications he derives from them.

52. Zizioulas, "Introduction: Communion and Otherness," 5.

53. According to Zizioulas, "otherness" is a more absolute distinction than mere "difference." "Difference is a natural or moral category; uniqueness belongs to the level of personhood" (Zizioulas, "On Being Other," 69).

therefore, a particular being is 'itself'—and not another one—because of its uniqueness which is established in communion and which renders a particular being unrepeatable as it forms part of a relational existence in which it is indispensable and irreplaceable."[54]

Zizioulas contends that this offers a view of personhood that is importantly different from modern conceptions. We commonly think of personhood as a set of properties (e.g., rationality or consciousness) that a particular entity may or may not instantiate. We thus speak of someone as "having" personhood, by which we mean that they have the requisite properties to qualify as a personal being. As universal properties that can be instantiated by multiple individuals, they are properties of the human "nature." And we go on to individuate humans by noting the different ways in which they instantiate these and other universally human properties (e.g., size and location). On this view, then, human persons are different from each other in how they manifest these common properties.

If we begin with the divine persons, though, this *cannot* be the right way to understand personhood. Despite his contention that the unity of the divine being is maintained by the *hypostasis* of the Father rather than the divine *ousia*, he also affirms the classic Trinitarian notion that the *hypostases* of the Father, Son, and Spirit can be "distinguished only by their relations of ontological origination."[55] All three equally and simultaneously instantiate *all* the properties of the divine nature. Thus, what distinguishes the divine persons is not mere *difference* (i.e., varying ways of instantiating universal properties) but real *otherness*. Difference involves mere "*variety* or *diversity*."[56] True otherness, on the other hand, requires absolute *uniqueness*. And this cannot be established by any appeal to universal properties, however well differentiated particular instantiations might be, but only by recognizing the other as an absolute Other. "The only otherness we can speak of in the case of the Trinity is personal otherness. It is an otherness that involves uniqueness and radical alterity stemming not from natural or moral qualities, or from a combination of such qualities, but from unique relations."[57] The nature of this uniqueness must remain somewhat obscure because, as we see in the Trinity, we cannot appeal to anything more fundamental than

---

54. Zizioulas, "Human Capacity," 214.

55. Zizioulas, "The Trinity and Personhood," 173.

56. Zizioulas, "On Being Other," 69.

57. Ibid., 70.

the absolute otherness of the three persons themselves. Any such move would immediately make the persons derivative on that more fundamental reality and undermine the relational ontology itself. Thus, "the particular is raised to the level of ontological primacy; it emerges *as being itself* without depending for its identity on qualities borrowed from nature and thus applicable also to other beings, but solely on a relationship in which it constitutes an indispensable ontological ingredient."[58]

This is what Zizioulas means when he contends that both *ekstasis* and *hypostasis* are fundamental to personhood and, consequently, to being itself.[59] Real personhood requires both the fundamental otherness of the particular (*hypostasis*) as well as the continual movement toward the Other in which both the particular and the Other are constituted as real persons (*ekstasis*).

The Shape of Personhood in a Relational Ontology

All of this explains Zizioulas's oft-repeated contention that personhood "is not moral or psychological but *ontological*."[60] In other words, as important as it might be to understand the moral and/or psychological implications of personhood, we cannot offer an adequately Trinitarian understanding of personhood on those terms. Any such attempt would immediately degenerate into the kind of ontological monism and individualism that Zizioulas finds so problematic in the modern world. Instead, we need to recognize personhood as an ontological category; indeed, it is *the* ontological category. Without person, there would be no being, no existence.

Ultimately, Zizioulas contends that only by starting with the divine persons can we arrive at a proper understanding of personhood itself:

If we draw it from the observation of humanity, we shall inevitably arrive at an identification of personhood with individuality, collection of qualities, centre of consciousness, and all the rest ... If, on the other hand, we derive personhood from the holy Trinity, the result will be different. For divine personhood, being defined *solely* and *exclusively* in terms of a *relational 'mode of being,'* admits of no individualism in the sense of an entity conceivable in itself, subject to addition and combination, a centre of consciousness and a concurrence of natural and moral properties.[61]

---

58. Zizioulas, "On Being a Person," 107.

59. Zizioulas, "Human Capacity," 213.

60. Zizioulas, "Introduction: Communion and Otherness," 5.

61. Zizioulas, "The Trinity and Personhood," 176.

Only on the basis of his understanding of divine personhood, then, can we properly understand the specifically anthropological aspects of personhood in Zizioulas's theology.

DIVINE PERSONHOOD IN HUMAN PERSONS

Zizioulas thus understands a *person* to be an ontologically fundamental reality in the world, one that involves both absolute uniqueness and essential relationality, in which entities are constituted as persons in free community. Given the ontologically fundamental nature of personhood, we should not be surprised to discover that Zizioulas thinks this personal ontology has implications for all of creation. Indeed, "nothing in existence is conceivable in itself, as an individual ... since even God exists thanks to an event of communion."[62] The task of this section, then, is to see how Zizioulas applies his theology of divine personhood to his theology of creation in general and, more importantly for our purposes, to his theology of the human person.

At this point in the chapter, though, questions arise as to whether Zizioulas's approach qualifies as *christocentric* in any meaningful way. After all, everything we have said to this point has been robustly Trinitarian. If anything, Zizioulas's emphasis has been on the significance and priority of the Father in establishing the ontological significance of personhood. From this perspective, maybe Zizioulas might be considered a *patrocentric* theologian.[63]

Regardless of whether such a label would be adequate for describing Zizioulas's approach to the Trinity, a very different picture presents itself when we move into the specifically anthropological aspect of Zizioulas's

---

62. Zizioulas, *Being as Communion*, 17. Zizioulas makes this even more clear in another place: "In this way, creation becomes mainly an act not of divine power (omnipotence) but of divine communion, that is, of an involvement of created existence in the Father-Son (and Spirit) relationship (Zizioulas, "The Father as Cause," 116).

63. E.g., Najeeb G. Awad, "Between Subordination and Koinonia: Toward a New Reading of the Cappadocian Theology," *Modern Theology* 23, no. 2 (2007): 181–204. Indeed, Zizioulas has been critiqued for being *too* rigorous in applying a specifically Trinitarian methodology (Richard M. Fermer, "The Limits of Trinitarian Theology as a Methodological Paradigm: 'Between the Trinity and Hell There Lies No Other Choice' [Vladimir Lossky]," *Neue Zeitschrift für Systematische Theologie und Religionsphilosophie* 41, no. 2 [1999]: 158–86). I am not suggesting this as an adequate label or attempting to imply that Zizioulas unnecessarily denigrates the Son or the Spirit in his theology (any more than I think the label *christocentric* has any of the same implications for someone's view of the Father and the Spirit). I'm merely using this to ask whether Zizioulas's emphasis on the Father in his doctrine of the Trinity raises challenges for locating him in a project focused on specifically *christological* approaches to anthropology.

theology. Here we see that "the mystery of man reveals itself fully only in the light of Christ."[64] In other words, although Zizioulas begins with the Trinitarian persons as a revelation of true personhood, Christology constitutes the necessary starting point for understanding the shape and origin of personhood in human persons.

The Human as a Biological Being

To begin, Zizioulas makes an important distinction between the *"hypostasis of biological existence"* and the *"hypostasis of ecclesial existence."*[65] With this distinction, we will see that Zizioulas understands the biological realities of human life as a necessary but ultimately insufficient condition for human personhood. For real personhood to become a part of human existence, something more is needed.

According to Zizioulas, the biological *hypostasis* refers to the human as a created being, born as a physical entity in a finite world. Although we will see that he does not view this creational state as negative in itself, he does argue that it leaves humans susceptible to two "passions."[66] On the one hand, unlike the divine persons, our particular *hypostases* are preceded both temporally and ontologically by the more fundamental human *ousia*. Thus, we are bound by the very "ontological necessity" that the patristics sought to avoid for God's own being.[67] Second, because we exist as particular instances of a more universal nature, separated from one another both spatially and temporally, we fall prey to the problem of "individualism."[68] In other words, in its created state the human person is "an entity independent ontologically from other human beings."[69] This is most easily seen in the fact that each human is bound by a particular body that "behaves like a fortress of an ego," preventing us from realizing the relationality that constitutes true personhood. Although the body is a necessary part of the human being, the physical means through which we interact with the world around us,[70] it is also that which "leads finally

---

64. Zizioulas, "Human Capacity," 237.

65. Zizioulas, "Personhood and Being," 50.

66. Ibid.

67. Ibid. "In human existence, nature precedes the person ... they, therefore, represent and embody only part of the human nature" (Zizioulas, "The Trinity and Personhood," 158).

68. Zizioulas, "Personhood and Being," 51.

69. Zizioulas, "The Trinity and Personhood," 159.

70. For Zizioulas, "The body is ontologically constitutive for the human being and so essential for its identity and particularity" (Zizioulas, "On Being Other," 62). And although

to the individual," which Zizioulas sees as the opposing counterpart to the truly personal.[71] Together, the ontological necessity and individualism of our finite realities lead to the inevitable outcome of death as "the cession of 'space' and 'time' to other individual hypostases, the sealing of hypostasis as individuality.'"[72]

As a purely natural/biological being, the human is not a *person*—a unique and unrepeatable entity constituted by relationship and living freely for the Other. Instead, the human as a biological *hypostasis* is a "tragic figure."[73] Although he is born as a result of *ekstatic* action (i.e., the relationship between a father and a mother) into a world created by a personal being, his biological state inclines toward necessity, individualism, and death. It would thus seem that the biological realities of human existence preclude the very possibility of the human being achieving true personhood.

The Human as a Christological Being

For Zizioulas, then, only the divine persons are the kinds of eternally unique and absolutely free beings who constitute true personhood. If there is to be any kind of creaturely personhood that corresponds to this divine reality, it will only be as creaturely realities come to participate in the reality of divine personhood.[74] As Robert Turner concludes, "There is no true human personhood which is not constituted by a union with the divine persons."[75]

Establishing the union between the divine and the human that makes real personhood possible in the created world is where Christology comes into play. And since Zizioulas presents the challenge of human

---

the body has problematic aspects in that it inclines us toward individualism, it is also that by which we engage others in meaningful relationship. Thus, the body "is paradoxically the vehicle of otherness and communion at the same time" (ibid). It is "an *inseparable aspect of the human person*" (Zizioulas, "Human Capacity," 227). Russell rightly notes, though, that despite these occasional affirmations of the importance of embodiment, the overall weight of his presentation tends to downplay the body for understanding human personhood (Russell, "Reconsidering Relational Anthropology," 184).

71. Zizioulas, "Personhood and Being," 51.

72. Ibid.

73. Ibid., 52.

74. Norman Russell rightly notes the close relationship between personhood and participation in Zizioulas's theology, arguing that the former is just "a way of re-expressing what the Fathers meant by 'participation'" (Norman Russell, *The Doctrine of Deification in the Greek Patristic Tradition*, The Oxford Early Christian Studies [Oxford: Oxford University Press, 2004], 318).

75. Robert Turner, "Eschatology and Truth," in *The Theology of John Zizioulas: Personhood and the Church*, ed. Douglas H. Knight (Aldershot: Ashgate, 2007), 20.

personhood as a creational reality and not simply a consequence of the fall, he concludes that Christology is not purely soteriological. Christology extends beyond redemption to include the theological completion of God's creative purposes for humanity, which was "to effect the ultimate koinonetic union of creation with itself and with God in love" so that all creation comes to participate in the personal reality of God and become *hypostasized*.[76] This is the ecstatic movement of divine personhood directed toward creation. In creation, we see this initially when Adam received the "divine call" in which he was constituted as an Other and called into personhood.[77] By creating Adam in his image and summoning him into personal relationship, God invited Adam into a hypostatic state that would not have been available to him as a purely biological being, thus making human personhood possible.

Adam's role, however, was not limited to his own personhood alone. Consistent with the rejection of substantial causation, Zizioulas contends that human beings do not have their cause in some underlying substance. Instead, what causes all other human beings to exist is Adam as "*a particular being*."[78] As the Father is the personal cause of the Trinity, so Adam is the personal cause of humanity. Thus, the hypostasization of Adam was to have been "the constitutive event of humanity" in which all human beings become human persons.[79]

The story of creaturely personhood, though, extends even further. According to Zizioulas, human persons were to play a mediatorial role in extending this personhood to the rest of creation. "All creatures possess a *hypostasis*, a mode of being. Yet not all creatures are gifted with the freedom to relate this *hypostasis* to the divine 'mode of being' which is not subject to death."[80] Thus, although other creatures are particular beings that humans can engage as significant others, only humans are made in the image of God and have been "*endowed with the freedom to reflect divine personhood in creation*."[81] Thus, having received the gift of becoming persons through the divine summons into relationship, human persons were

---

76. Brown, "On the Criticism of *Being as Communion* in Anglophone Orthodox Theology," 59.

77. Zizioulas, "On Being Other," 41.

78. Zizioulas, "On Being a Person," 104–5.

79. Zizioulas, "On Being Other," 41.

80. Ibid., 95.

81. Ibid. "This means that, if the particular beings that make up the world are called 'hypostases'…, they are so called in view of their survival in the human hypostasis, which again is called by this name because it is an image of the truly hypostatic God" (ibid., 67).

to extend the gift of personhood by bringing all of creation into communion with God. This is the *"priestly character of humanity."*[82]

However, the "'chain' of hypostatic existence" is still not complete.[83] Given the creaturely limitations of Adam's biological *hypostasis*, Zizioulas contends that Adam alone could not have provided the bridge between the uncreated divine being and the particular being of all created entities. "If Adam as a particular being and not as a human nature is the primary cause of human being, he must be in a *constant relationship* with all the rest of human beings, not via human nature—for this would make nature acquire again the decisive priority—but *directly*, that is, as a particular being carrying in himself the *totality* of human nature, and not part of it."[84] Yet as a finite creature, this is precisely what Adam *cannot* do. Without some further explanation, then, it would seem that "Humanity ... *per se* cannot be a candidate for a personal ontology."[85]

It is only in the incarnation that we see the true ground of human personhood. Christ is the one who bridges the "gulf of otherness" by joining created and uncreated in a single person,[86] thus allowing created realities to participate in the very same relation (*schesis*) in which he is constituted as Son in relation to the Father and the Spirit.[87] "One must see in Christ a person in whom the division of 'natures' is changed into an otherness through communion."[88] Even more, though, Christ is a "catholic" or "corporate" person who establishes the personhood of all human persons by allowing them to participate in his own eternal sonship.[89] Thus, Christ is both *one* and *many*: "Christ is 'one' in his own hypostasis, that is, as he relates eternally to the Father, but he is also at the same time 'many' in that the same *schesis* becomes now the constitutive elements—the *hypostases*—of all those whose particularity and uniqueness and therefore ultimate being are constituted throughout the same filial relationship which constitutes Christ's being."[90] In this

---

82. Zizioulas, "Human Capacity," 238.

83. Zizioulas, "On Being Other," 67.

84. Zizioulas, "On Being a Person," 106.

85. Ibid., 107.

86. Zizioulas, "On Being Other," 19.

87. Zizioulas, "Human Capacity," 238–40.

88. Zizioulas, "Truth and Communion," 109.

89. See esp. Zizioulas, "Human Capacity," 241–43.

90. Ibid., 241.

sense, Christ is "the ontological ground of every man."[91] He comes as Savior not simply because he reveals true personhood, but because he is the one who "realizes in history *the very reality of the person* and makes it the basis and 'hypostasis' of the person for every man."[92]

In the incarnation, then, we see the truth of creation itself: "*The incarnate Christ is so identical to the ultimate will of God's love, that the meaning of created being and the purpose of history are simply the incarnate Christ.*"[93] Thus, God always intended for the incarnation to occur, without which creation could never achieve God's creational purposes. Even if humanity had not fallen, human beings would still have needed to be "transformed incrementally into Christ, that is, *man-with-God.*"[94] In other words, the incarnation is not just about restoring humanity back to its created state, as though creation was a state of perfection beyond which humanity could grow no further. Instead, Christology reveals that the *telos* of creation lies beyond itself.

In its purely biological *hypostasis*, then, human nature cannot attain true personhood. Personhood must always be received as a gift in relation with other persons, and that is what God made possible by joining divine and human in the person of the Son and summoning all humans to participate in the personal life of the Son. Hypostasized in the Son, human persons were then to extend that personal life by entering into meaningful life with the rest of creation. Tragically, of course, Adam refused the summons, which leads us into Zizioulas's understanding of sin, redemption, and the church: the ecclesial *hypostasis* of the human being.

The Human as an Ecclesial Being

Zizioulas has been criticized at times for not having an adequate theology of sin, focusing so much attention on the limitations of the biological *hypostasis* and the necessity of the incarnation, that it begins to sound

---

91. Ibid., 243.

92. Zizioulas, "Personhood and Being," 54. Zizioulas thus critiques the idea that Christology offers a mere *imitatio Christi*, as though the real solution to the human dilemma could come through mere example of true humanity. But he also rejects the notion that Christ provided the solution primarily through an act of substitutionary atonement, an act that would provide forgiveness but "would not affect man's being ontologically" ("Human Capacity," 244). Instead, we need a solution that would "de-individualize" humans and restore personhood to creation.

93. Zizioulas, "Personhood and Being," 97.

94. Zizioulas, *Lectures in Christian Dogmatics*, xvi. Thus, "*irrespective of the fall of man, the incarnation would have occurred*" (Zizioulas, "Personhood and Being," 97).

as though sin and redemption are relatively minor aspects of his overall theology.[95] And that is true in the sense that creation and incarnation are more fundamental realities for Zizioulas than sin and redemption. Nonetheless, the latter theological categories play a prominent role in human personhood *as we actually experience it*. Thus, for Zizioulas, no understanding of *human* personhood can possibly be complete without addressing how sin has impacted personhood and how personhood is restored christologically, which means at the same time pneumatologically and ecclesiologically.

By summoning Adam into personal being, God simultaneously established Adam as a being with ontological freedom, the freedom necessary for Adam to respond to the call and extend personal life to the rest of creation. And this freedom comes with the corresponding possibility that the call might be rejected.[96] And that, of course, is precisely what Adam did. By rejecting the divine summons into personal being, he simultaneously rejected *otherness* itself, lapsing into the biological *hypostasis* and its self-focused individualism, and breaking the hypostatic chain in creation.

Zizioulas's critique of individualism thus extends from his understanding of sin. According to Zizioulas, Western culture has been held captive by a conception of the human person that focuses largely on the isolated human:

> Our Western philosophy and culture have formed a concept of man out of a combination of two basic components: rational individuality on the one hand and psychological experience and consciousness on the other. It was on the basis of this combination that Western thought arrived at the conception of the person as an individual and/or a personality, that is, a unit endowed with intellectual, psychological and moral qualities centered on the axis of consciousness. Man's distinctive characteristic became in this way identical with his ability to be conscious of himself and of others and thus to be an autonomous self who intends, thinks, decides, acts and produces results.[97]

Of course, any such definition runs contrary to Zizioulas's principle that true personhood, as revealed in the divine persons, "cannot be conceived in itself as a static entity, but only as it *relates to*."[98] That is why he

---

95. E.g., Russell, "Reconsidering Relational Anthropology."

96. Zizioulas, "On Being Other," 43.

97. Zizioulas, "Human Capacity," 211.

98. Ibid., 212.

contends that it is simply impossible to find even an analogy of true personhood "within our experience of individualized existence."[99] The Western notion of personhood, then, is an apt description of sinful humanity, locked into individualism by the rejection of the divine call to personhood. This means that the problem of individualism is not primarily epistemological (we need to become more aware of how important relationships are for human existence) or ethical (we need to treat people as significant *others* and not mere *objects*), as though we could solve the problem of individualism through educational or moral efforts. Individualism is an *ontological* problem stemming from both creation *and* the fall. Consequently, the solution must be similarly ontological. We need a fundamental transformation of human life in which "the *constitutional make-up of the hypostasis* should be changed."[100] This means that true personhood must never be viewed as "a potentiality existing in man's nature which enables him to become something better and more perfect than that which he is now."[101] The intrinsic potentiality of the human can only lead to the biological *hypostasis*, never the realization of true personhood. Thus, "there is no question of the ecclesial hypostasis, the authentic person, emerging as a result of an evolution of the human race, whether biological or historical."[102] The ecclesial *hypostasis* comes only through Christ, who offers not just a *revelation* but the *realization* of true personhood in the world, and thus the possibility of *participation* in Christ's own hypostatic existence.[103]

For Zizioulas, though, the fact that human personhood is christological means it is at the same time ecclesiological and pneumatological. Hypostasization occurs as people are incorporated into Christ through the work of the Spirit such that they come to share, by adoption, in the very *hypostasis* of the Son. Although the Spirit maintains our particularity in this union, ensuring that we remain distinct *others*-in-relation, we also constitute a fundamental unity through our participation in the single *hypostasis* of the Son. The hypostasization of human persons creates the

---

99. Zizioulas, "Truth and Communion," 108.

100. Zizioulas, "Personhood and Being," 53.

101. Ibid., 59.

102. Ibid. Nonetheless, Zizioulas also wants to emphasize that this process involves the *transformation* rather than the *destruction* of the biological *hypostasis* (ibid., 53.) Although humanity's biological condition becomes problematic when it is divorced from the life-giving (and person-creating) power of the Spirit, it is not an evil in itself. Indeed, without the biological realities of the human person, we would not be able to play the priestly role of mediating personhood to the rest of creation.

103. Zizioulas, "Personhood and Being," 54.

very same unity-in-diversity that we see among the triune persons.[104] In this way, the Church is, in a rather literal sense, the "body" of Christ— i.e., the biological *hypostasis* in which the *hypostasis* of the eternal Son is realized and expressed in creation.[105]

In this context, Zizioulas emphasizes the fundamental importance of both baptism and the Eucharist in establishing and maintaining the hypostatic existence of the church and the Christian life.

> Given the fact that otherness is ontologically constituted by the birth of a particular being and terminated by death, the only way for a particular being ontologically to be truly Other is to be born again, this time not from nature but from the Spirit, and to overcome death through the "medicine of immortality." What Baptism initiates, therefore, the Eucharist fulfills. Otherness as the emergence of a new particular being through Baptism is granted eternal being through communion in the Eucharist. Thus the Church is communion and otherness at the same time.[106]

On the one hand, the "essence of baptism" is the "adoption of man by God, the identification of his hypostasis with the hypostasis of the Son of God."[107] If biological birth initiates an existence in which humans are ontologically dependent on nature, then we need a new birth if we are to experience the freedom of personal existence. "This 'new birth,' which is the essence of baptism, is nothing but the acquisition of an identity not dependent on the qualities of nature but freely raising nature to a hypostatic existence identical with that which emerges from the Father-

---

104. Russell expresses the concern that Zizioulas's anthropology "dissolves the individual person into corporate existence in the body of Christ" (Russell, "Reconsidering Relational Anthropology," 182), arguing that Zizioulas lacks an adequate pneumatology and that it is precisely the role of the Spirit to maintain the particular identity of human persons in Christ. In his "On Being Other," published a few years after Russell's critique, Zizioulas makes precisely that point: "The Spirit offers the particularizing force which guarantees that hypostasization in Christ will not end up in an absorption of the many into the one, in the loss of otherness" (Zizioulas, "On Being Other," 76). Yet it seems that the difficulty remains given Zizioulas's emphasis on humans being constituted as persons by participation *in the very same hypostasis* as the Son. It is not clear to me that merely positing the Spirit's ability to maintain human *otherness* is sufficient given Zizioulas's relational ontology. If all humans are constituted as persons by the very same personal relationship, and if personal relations are what constitute the very being of the particulars so related, it becomes difficult to find resources for continuing to talk about the continued particularity of human identity without appealing to the differences inherent in the biological *hypostasis*, differences that fall short of the absolute *otherness* Zizioulas requires.

105. Zizioulas, "Human Capacity," 241. Thus, "The Church exists as the hypostasization of all particular beings in the unique hypostasis of Christ" (ibid.).

106. Zizioulas, "On Being Other," 80.

107. Zizioulas, "Personhood and Being," 56.

Son relationship."[108] In the death and resurrection of baptism, we are reconstituted as personal beings as we are drawn into the personal life of the Son.[109] Eucharist, on the other hand, continues and sustains this personal existence as its concrete realization. As the sacrament that constitutes the church as the body of Christ, it is in the Eucharist that "this love of God the Father is offered to humanity as the unique *hypostasis* in which all human beings can freely obtain otherness and uniqueness."[110] Thus, the Eucharist is "the ontological affirmation of otherness and particularity through the assurance and foretaste of immortality."[111] At the same time the Eucharist is the "manifestation of the eschatological existence of man" as well as "a movement or progression towards this realization."[112] In baptism and Eucharist, then, we see and experience the eschatological hypostasization of humanity here and now.

This is the point at which Zizioulas thinks it appropriate to introduce the ethical dimensions of personhood. Although we have already seen that he rejects the possibility that personhood might be a merely ethical possibility, something we grow into through our own moral efforts, he consistently argues that personhood has ethical implications as we seek to express personal being in the church and the world. And we can only do this by modeling the personal life that we see in God himself.[113] Living purely out of the biological *hypostasis* always creates conflict and tension with others as we each seek to find space for living out our freedom as individuals. Thus, "there is a pathology built into the very roots of our existence, inherited through our birth, and that is the *fear of the other*."[114] In the context of such fear, we can only view difference as a threat and seek to eliminate it to whatever extent we can.[115] In the ecclesial *hypostasis*, on the other hand, we transcend mere difference and embrace radical *otherness* as a true and necessary good. This allows us to cherish the Other as an absolutely unique person and enter into real communion together,

---

108. Zizioulas, "On Being a Person," 109.

109. "As death and resurrection in Christ, baptism signifies the decisive passing of our existence from the 'truth' of individualized being into the truth of personal being" (Zizioulas, "Truth and Communion," 113).

110. Zizioulas, "On Being Other," 79.

111. Ibid.

112. Russell, "Reconsidering Relational Anthropology," 176.

113. Zizioulas, "Introduction: Communion and Otherness," 4–5.

114. Zizioulas, *Communion and Otherness*, 1.

115. Ibid., 2.

a communion in which the Spirit maintains both our particular unique-ness and our fundamental unity in Christ.

If true personhood is only realized through the sacramental action of the Spirit in the church, however, what implications does this have for understanding the humanity of those outside the church? Would this not suggest that such humans are not truly persons? Although this isn't an issue Zizioulas addresses directly, Jonathan Ciraulo argues that we can specu-late on an answer by drawing on a similar situation that Zizioulas has dis-cussed—namely, the *salvation* of those outside the church.[116] According to Zizioulas, although Christ and the sacraments are the ordinary means of salvation, we should exercise epistemological humility with respect to those outside the church.[117] It would thus seem likely that he would offer similar advice for dealing with the personhood of those outside the church.[118]

The Human as a Eucharistic Being

The last feature of Zizioulas's christologically shaped understanding of human personhood has to do with the reality of living in the tension created by the eschatological nature of the ecclesial *hypostasis*. As Zizioulas writes, "The truth and the ontology of the person belong to the future."[119] Although

---

116. Jonathan Martin Ciraulo, "Sacraments and Personhood: John Zizioulas's Impasse and A Way Forward," *Heythrop Journal* 53, no. 6 (2012): 995.

117. See esp. John Zizioulas, *The One and the Many: Studies on God, Man, the Church and the World Today* (Alhambra, Calif.: Sebastian Press, 2010), 396–97.

118. Jonathan Ciraulo explores several other possibilities for addressing this question in Zizioulas's theology, rightly dismissing them all as inadequate ("Sacraments and Person-hood," 995–97). The first, and least satisfying, would require us to say that what is truly important for personhood is living out the characteristics of the baptized life rather than the sacrament of baptism itself. Outside the church, then, humans are persons insofar as they reject individualism and love the other. According to Zizioulas, though, such an approach would constitute an ethical response to an ontological problem. Those outside the church might be able to imitate the baptized life, but they will still be missing out on the ontologi-cal transformation necessary for true personhood. A second approach might suggest that baptism is only the normative way of achieving personhood, leaving open the possibility of an extra-sacramental route to personhood. Since Zizioulas never addresses such a possibil-ity, however, any such suggestion is necessarily speculative. This would also run counter to Zizioulas's strong claims regarding the fundamental importance of baptism in the restora-tion of personhood. Thus, Jonathan Ciraulo suggests a third possibility, one that posits vary-ing *degrees* of personhood. On this approach, Zizioulas could still reserve full personhood for those baptized into Christ, while affirming limited personhood for all other humans. Such a quantitative approach to personhood, though, suggests that personhood is at least partly an intrinsic capacity of the biological *hypostasis*, something Zizioulas explicitly rejects.

119. Zizioulas, "Personhood and Being," 62.

the ecclesial *hypostasis* finds its historical realization in the Eucharist,[120] the Eucharist itself is a fundamentally eschatological event, the historical expression of ultimately eschatological realities.[121] Thus, the ecclesial *hypostasis* is realized historically in the Eucharist, which points toward the ultimate hypostasization of humanity that awaits in the eschaton.

What can we say, then, about the shape of human existence beyond the Eucharist? Zizioulas does not want to suggest we simply lapse back into our biological condition, since that would undermine the radical transformation that takes place in baptism. Yet he also wants to maintain the ultimately eschatological nature of the ecclesial *hypostasis*. Thus, he argues, "we really need a new ontological category," one that can account for life between the already and the not yet of human participation in divine personhood.[122] Zizioulas refers to this new category as the *eucharistic hypostasis*, the mode of existence in which human life is already being shaped by the reality of the *ecclesial hypostasis*, but in which it has not yet been truly freed from the necessity and individualism of the *biological hypostasis*.

In this *in-between* state, we are called to express through our historical existence the eschatological truth of personal being. Thus, "man is called to an effort to free himself from the necessity of his nature and behave in all respects as if the person were free from the laws of nature. In practical terms, this is what the Fathers saw in the *ascetic* effort which they regarded as essential to all human existence, regardless of whether one was a monk or lived in the world."[123] Unfortunately, Zizioulas says relatively little about the specific details of this ascetic effort, quite possibly because this is a relatively well developed area of study in Orthodox theology, and Zizioulas intends for this other literature to inform ascetic practice in the eucharistic *hypostasis*.[124]

Instead, Zizioulas describes what he calls the "eucharistic ethos,"

---

120. Ibid., 60–61.

121. See esp. John Zizioulas, "The Eucharist and the Kingdom of God," in *The Eucharistic Communion and the World* (London: T&T Clark, 2011), 39–82.

122. Zizioulas, "Personhood and Being," 59.

123. Zizioulas, "The Trinity and Personhood," 166; see Zizioulas, "Personhood and Being," 62–63, n. 66.

124. Thus, although Nicholas Loudovikos may be correct when he argues that Zizioulas has relatively little to say about the active nature of living out personal existence today, he surely goes too far when he suggests that this is lacking in Zizioulas's theology as a whole ("Person Instead of Grace, 692–93). Zizioulas clearly affirms that the summons into personhood requires a continuously free response, which constitutes the historic dimension of personhood ("On Being Other," 43).

which lives in light of the Eucharist and the realities enacted there—most importantly, the truth that "Being is a *gift*."[125] Thus, we are called to express a particular ethos—which he defines as "an *attitude*, an *orientation*, and *a way of relating* with whatever exists"[126]—in which "the only thing that *ultimately* matters ... is the *existence* of the Other."[127] We prioritize the Other over ourselves, sacrificing on behalf of the Other and reaching out to the Other in nonexclusive communion. This includes not only human Others, but all of creation. Living out our vocation of extending personal existence to all of creation, the human person acts as the "priest of creation."[128] Zizioulas thus places great emphasis on creativity and the arts, as well as ecological responsibility, as ways of extending otherness to non-human realities, while still maintaining the uniqueness of human personhood in the world.

MEDIATORS OF PERSONHOOD

Zizioulas offers an understanding of human personhood that is at the same time Trinitarian, christological, pneumatological, and ecclesiological. In many ways, his conception of humanity begins with ecclesiology, and specifically with the Eucharist. That is where we see and experience the eschatological reality of personhood, and, consequently, the nature and character of the God who created us for that destiny. That leads directly into Zizioulas's Trinitarian framework for personhood, drawing the fundamental principles of personhood from his understanding of the Trinity as grounded in the person of the Father and constituted through love (i.e., free communion). What makes Zizioulas's theological anthropology robustly christological, though, is that Christ alone is the revelation and ground of human personhood. He is the one who unites divine and human, realizing personhood in creation and revealing the fact that human beings can only become persons as they are hypostasized in Christ through the work of the Spirit.

From this christological starting point, Zizioulas develops an ecstatic view of personhood which involves a free movement toward the other, an "other" that includes all created beings. In this ecstatic movement

---

125. Zizioulas, "On Being Other," 88–98.

126. Ibid., 90.

127. Ibid., 91.

128. Ibid., 93. On this point, see esp. John Zizioulas, "Proprietors or Priests of Creation?" in *The Eucharistic Communion and the World*, 133–42; John Zizioulas, "Preserving God's Creation," in *The Eucharistic Communion and the World*, 143–76.

toward the other, the person extends personal existence by drawing other created beings into "the ultimate koinonetic union of creation with itself and with God in love."[129] In this way, Zizioulas defines humanity in such a way that being truly human includes humanity's relationship to the rest of creation. We are most fully human not only when we are drawn into Jesus' hypostatic existence, but also when we consequently turn to the other so that all creation comes to participate in this personal existence.

Zizioulas thus offers a robustly christological account of human personhood. For Zizioulas, we only know what it most fundamentally means to be human as we see humanity in the light of Jesus Christ. Some will still have questions about certain aspects of Zizioulas's theology of personhood. Debates will continue about the adequacy of his interpretation of the patristic sources, the hierarchical nature of the Trinity, and what precisely it means to say that relations are ontological. But his bold proposal offers a powerful lens for viewing the human person from an explicitly christological perspective.

---

129. Brown, "On the Criticism of *Being as Communion* in Anglophone Orthodox Theology," 59.

CHAPTER 7

The Black Messiah

Race, Liberation, and the Actualization of Humanity in James Cone's Christological Anthropology

We must not allow an abstract word of God to usurp God's word as Spirit who empowers persons to be who they are— fully human in search of the highest beauty, love, and joy.

James H. Cone, *For My People*[1]

THE THEOLOGIANS WE HAVE CONSIDERED so far all agree that knowledge of true humanity begins in some important way with Christology. They differ in the details of the content and method of a christological anthropology, of course, but they share the fundamental intuition that Christology offers a distinctive perspective without which we cannot understand human persons adequately. This entails the corollary that any mistakes we make in understanding who and what *Jesus* is will have correspondingly devastating implications for how we understand what it means to be *human*. If Christology informs anthropology, it can also eviscerate it.

According to James Cone, that is precisely the problem with most Christian anthropologies. Often described as "the father of contemporary black theology of liberation,"[2] Cone argues that Western theologians

---

1. James H. Cone, *For My People: Black Theology and the Black Church* (Maryknoll, N.Y.: Orbis, 1984), 152.

2. Dwight N. Hopkins, "General Introduction," in *The Cambridge Companion to Black Theology,* ed. Dwight N. Hopkins and Edward P. Antonio (New York: Cambridge University Press, 2012), 14; cf. also Gayraud S. Wilmore, *Black Religion and Black Radicalism* (Garden City, N.Y.: Doubleday, 1972), 216; Rufus Burrow, *James H. Cone and Black Liberation Theology* (Jefferson, N.C.: McFarland, 1994), 1; Carlyle F. Stewart, "The Method of Correlation in the Theology of James H. Cone," *Journal of Religious Thought* 40, no. 2 (1984): 27. It is important to recognize that Cone's theology is neither normative for nor determinative of black theology in general. Although Cone offers a distinctive voice, and one that represents a number of important emphases within black theology as a whole, we should not reduce all of black theology to his perspective alone.

have consistently misconstrued who Jesus was and what he came to do.[3] As a consequence of that christological failure, their anthropologies are similarly flawed. As we will see, Cone contends that we only understand the human person rightly when we see humanity as revealed in Jesus' liberating activity in and for oppressed people. Only then do we truly see human persons as those created for *freedom*—a freedom that not only releases the individual from bondage, but one that empowers entire communities to seek the freedom and well-being of all those in society. Thus, even if other theological perspectives claim that freedom is an important aspect of their vision of humanity, Cone will argue that their framework, and thus their understanding of what constitutes *true* human freedom, fails insofar as it neglects the fundamental importance of oppression and liberation in defining what it means to be human.

Understanding the relationship between Christology and anthropology in Cone's theology will thus require us to explore the relationship between the humanity revealed in Jesus Christ and the humanity that we see and experience in the context of oppression today. Only by allowing both of these to serve as sources of truth about the nature of humanity, informing each other in dialectical relation, will we understand Cone's vision of human persons as beings created for freedom. Thus, we will first summarize Cone's Christology and what it means to say that Jesus is the "Black Messiah." Only then will we turn our attention to the anthropological implications of Cone's Christology in the second half of the chapter. By the end, we will see that Cone offers a unique voice in this study of christological approaches to theological anthropology.

THE BLACK MESSIAH AND THE REVELATION OF THE LIBERATING GOD

In his seminal *A Black Theology of Liberation*, Cone begins by defining theology in a way that makes the task of theology inseparable from that of liberation as revealed in Jesus Christ:

> Christian theology is a theology of liberation. It is a rational study of the being of God in the world in light of the existential situation of an oppressed community, relating the forces of liberation to the essence of the gospel, which is Jesus Christ. This means that its sole reason for existence is to put into ordered speech the meaning of God's activity in

---

3. See esp. early works like James H. Cone, *Black Theology and Black Power* (New York: Seabury, 1969) and James H. Cone, *A Black Theology of Liberation* (Philadelphia: Lippincott, 1970). For the rest of the chapter, all page references to *A Black Theology of Liberation* will be to the reprint edition published by Orbis in 2012.

the world, so that the community of the oppressed will recognize that its inner thrust for liberation is not only consistent with the gospel but is the gospel of Jesus Christ.[4]

In other words, according to Cone, if we understand how God has revealed himself in Jesus, we will see that liberation is essential to the gospel itself. Thus, "to speak of the Christian gospel is to speak of Jesus Christ who is the content of its message and without whom Christianity ceases to be."[5]

However, Cone also contends that God's self-revelation is only properly understood when viewed "in light of the existential situation of an oppressed community." For Cone, we cannot understand Jesus apart from interpreting his action in the past (who Jesus *was*) in light of how Jesus continues to act for the liberation of humanity today (who Jesus *is*). As we turn to the specific details of Cone's Christology, then, we will need to wrestle with the interaction between two sources in Cone's theology: the biblical witness to Jesus' liberating activity in the past and our own experiences of his liberating activity in the present. As we do, we will discover that Cone sees Jesus as neither a mere theological concept nor a purely historical figure. Instead, he is "a liberating presence in the lives of the poor in their fight for dignity and worth."[6] Both of these perspectives are necessary for understanding Jesus Christ. As important as these are, though, Cone contends that we need yet a third perspective. In addition to understanding who he *was*, and who he *is*, we must also engage who he *will be*. Only then will we be prepared to understand and participate in the full reality of what it means to be human.

JESUS IS WHO HE WAS

For Cone, any adequate Christology must begin with the historical Jesus. "We want to know who Jesus *was* because we believe that that is the only way to assess who he *is*."[7] Although we will see that Cone thinks Christology must move beyond this historical starting point and consider who Jesus is for us today, he maintains that "there is no knowledge of Jesus Christ today that contradicts who he was yesterday."[8] Thus, the historical

---

4. Cone, *A Black Theology of Liberation*, 1. Emphases are original unless otherwise noted.

5. Ibid., 116.

6. James H. Cone, *God of the Oppressed* (Maryknoll, N.Y.: Orbis, 2014), xiii.

7. Cone, *A Black Theology of Liberation*, 118.

8. Cone, *God of the Oppressed*, 106.

Christ provides the "indispensable foundation of Christology."[9] Without this historical foundation, it would be too easy to create a Jesus in our own image.

However, to understand Jesus and what he reveals about humanity, we must recognize the importance of God's self-revelation in the Old Testament. As Cone says, "Historically, the story began with the Exodus,"[10] which stands as "the decisive event in Israel's history" because this was the event in which "Yahweh was revealed as the Savior of an oppressed people."[11] In this event, God elected Israel to be his people and demonstrated his opposition to all forms of oppression and enslavement. Consequently, if God's liberating activity on behalf of the oppressed is fundamental to the very nature of God, we cannot know God apart from knowing him "through God's political activity on behalf of the weak and helpless of the land."[12] At the same time that God elected Israel *from* enslavement, however, he also elected Israel *for* liberation. God's liberating activity both frees Israel and summons them to participate in the redemptive task.[13] Cone finds both of these themes—electing Israel *from* oppression and *for* freedom—throughout the Old Testament: "It is a fact: in almost every scene of the Old Testament drama of salvation, the poor are defended against the rich, the weak against the strong. Yahweh is the God of the oppressed whose revelation is identical with their liberation from bondage."[14] Thus, "there is no truth about Yahweh unless it is

---

9. Cone, *A Black Theology of Liberation*, 126.

10. Cone, *God of the Oppressed*, 58.

11. Ibid.

12. Ibid., 59.

13. Ibid.

14. Ibid., 64. Yet as he summarizes in the preface to the latest edition of *God of the Oppressed*, some critics have challenged his reading of the Old Testament. Pointing to the "texts of terror" in the Bible—e.g., the story of Hagar, the Conquest narratives, and laws condemning homosexuality—these critics challenge the claim that the Bible always reveals God as opposed to oppression in any form (ibid., xi-xii). Indeed, viewed from the perspective of the Canaanites, the Exodus is a paradigmatic story of oppression, not liberation! Cone responds to this challenge with his doctrine of Scripture. Like many modern theologians, Cone does not view the biblical texts themselves as divine revelation, instead contending that Scripture is "the witness to God's self-disclosure" (ibid., 29). By emphasizing their status as human witnesses, Cone concludes that the biblical texts provide reliable but still fallible information about God's self-revelation (ibid., 102). Thus we must assess even the biblical texts critically, never assuming that "the Bible is above criticism or that it serves as an absolute judge in faith and practice" (ibid., xii).

the truth of freedom as that event is revealed in the oppressed people's struggle for justice in this world."[15]

Despite this emphasis of the Old Testament, though, Cone contends that "Israel's story does not end with the Old Testament."[16] For God to be faithful to the promises of liberation that he gave to Israel, we must recognize that "the Old Testament pushes beyond itself to an expected future event which Christians say happened in Jesus Christ."[17] Jesus himself serves as the fulfillment of the redemptive story begun in the Old Testament; consequently, the "historical kernel" of Christology must be the fact that Jesus came as "the Oppressed One" who brings liberation to humanity.[18] Cone is well aware that it would be reductionistic to suggest that liberation is the *only* important theme in Christ's life. Nonetheless, he contends that this is the center that illuminates everything else that Christ does. Any attempt to explicate other christological themes apart from viewing them in light of the "sole reason" for which he exists, would necessarily result in a tragic distortion of that theme.[19]

Cone thus devotes considerable attention to studying the life of Christ as the historic culmination of God's liberating activity, arguing that any adequate Christology must build on "a critical, historical evaluation of the New Testament Jesus."[20] On this basis, Cone contends that we can trace the themes of oppression and liberation throughout Christ's life.[21] In the details of the birth narratives—e.g., the visit of the shepherds, Herod's killing of the babies, and the economic insignificance of Joseph and Mary—we see the social status that Jesus assumed at his birth, the truth "that he is one of the humiliated and the abused, even in his birth."[22] His

---

15. Cone, *God of the Oppressed*, 57.

16. Ibid., 66.

17. Ibid.

18. Cone, *A Black Theology of Liberation*, 119.

19. Ibid.

20. Ibid., 126. Jeffrey Siker rightly points out, however, that Cone has "what might be termed a minimalist approach to the historical Jesus" (Jeffrey S. Siker, "Historicizing a Racialized Jesus: Case Studies in the 'Black Christ,' the 'Mestizo Christ,' and White Critique," *Biblical Interpretation* 15, no. 1 [2007]: 33). In other words, he is concerned that by failing to engage the academic literature on the life of Jesus, Cone ends up with a rather superficial sketch of Jesus' life that struggles to ground Cone's christological claims in Jesus' concrete existence.

21. For a useful summary, see Michael Joseph Brown, "Black Theology and the Bible," in *The Cambridge Companion to Black Theology*, ed. Edward P. Antonio and Dwight N. Hopkins (New York: Cambridge University Press, 2012), 170–71.

22. Cone, *A Black Theology of Liberation*, 121.

baptism similarly "defines his existence as one with sinners and conveys the meaning of the coming kingdom."[23] The temptation scene declares Jesus' "refusal to identify himself with any of the available modes of oppressive or self-glorifying power."[24]

By the time we get to Jesus' public ministry, Jesus has already demonstrated himself to be one who has come to align himself with the poor and marginalized. His public ministry must be understood as an outworking of the decision already expressed in these earlier events. Jesus came as "the *inaugurator* of the Kingdom," which is inseparable from "his identification with the poor."[25] Cone draws regularly on Luke's gospel and its emphasis on the "poor" as those who are physically and economically poor, rejecting the suggestion that the Gospel focuses primarily on those who are merely poor *spiritually.*[26] Jesus consistently aligned himself with those who were physically and economically poor, the outcasts of society, and he demands that those who follow him similarly dedicate themselves to that cause. The life and ministry of Jesus thus stands in significant continuity with that of the Old Testament: God is a liberating God who calls people to stand with him against oppression and injustice.

At the same time, though, Cone contends that we must recognize the discontinuity stemming from the fact that "the cross and the resurrection stand at the center of the New Testament story."[27] Although Cone questions the legitimacy of interpreting the cross in a way that makes suffering a part of the atonement, an approach that he thinks has served to validate human oppression and suffering, he still contends that the cross is central to God's self-revelation as an unmistakable declaration of God's commitment to the freedom and full humanity of his people.[28] Consequently, all of Jesus' actions, which culminate in his life-giving sacrifice on the cross, "represent God's will not to let his creation be destroyed by non-creative powers."[29] Thus, "God in Christ becomes poor and weak

---

23. Ibid.

24. Ibid., 122.

25. Cone, *God of the Oppressed*, 68.

26. As Cone argues, "It is this kind of false interpretation that leads to the oppression of the poor. As long as oppressors can be sure that the gospel does not threaten their social, economic, and political security, they can enslave others in the name of Jesus Christ" (Cone, *A Black Theology of Liberation*, 123).

27. Cone, *God of the Oppressed*, 73.

28. Ibid., xv.

29. Cone, *A Black Theology of Liberation*, 74.

in order that the oppressed might become liberated from poverty and powerlessness."[30] In this way, Jesus does not simply repeat a message already given. Instead, he offers a "new element" in which the freedom that is disclosed "is more than the freedom made possible in history."[31]

Finally, having argued that freedom from oppression is the center of Jesus' life and ministry throughout, Cone concludes that his resurrection culminates this theme by declaring that God is present in and sovereign over all forms of oppression, even death itself. "Faith in the resurrection means that the historical Jesus, in his liberating words and deeds for the poor, was God's way of breaking into human history, redeeming humanity from injustice and violence, and bestowing power upon little ones in their struggle for freedom."[32] This in-breaking of divine power "is the disclosure that God is not defeated by oppression but transforms it into the possibility of freedom."[33] As a result, we have been freed from the oppressive fear of death that shapes so much of human existence.

Throughout his analysis of the historic Christ, Cone invests relatively little effort in engaging some of the questions of divinity and humanity that occupied much of the earlier christological anthropologies we have considered. Cone contends that theology has traditionally overemphasized the deity of Christ, commenting on his humanity only for the purpose of establishing that he is actually divine;[34] and consequently, "little is said about the significance of his ministry to the poor as a definition of his person."[35] However, when we do this "Christology is removed from history, and salvation comes only peripherally related to this world."[36] This does not mean that Cone rejects classical christological frameworks entirely; he simply thinks they miss the point of Christology. By debating endlessly about the relationship of "natures" and "persons," we have missed the reality that "Jesus is the Oppressed One whose work is that of liberating humanity from inhumanity."[37]

---

30. Ibid., 73.

31. Ibid.

32. Cone, *God of the Oppressed*, 110.

33. Cone, *A Black Theology of Liberation*, 125.

34. Cone, *God of the Oppressed*, 107.

35. Ibid.

36. Ibid.

37. Cone, *A Black Theology of Liberation*, 124.

JESUS IS WHO HE IS

This leads to the second move in Cone's Christology: the turn to the present. One of the great weaknesses in white theology, according to Cone, is its failure to move beyond the historical Jesus and recognize the importance of the resurrection.[38] The resurrection means that Jesus "transcends the limitations of history by making himself present in our contemporary existence."[39] Thus, although Cone continues to affirm that the *"wasness"* of Jesus is the necessary starting point for Christology, we must also affirm the necessity of his *"isness"* as that which "relates his past history to his present involvement in our struggle."[40] Otherwise, as important as his past might be, it would have little relevance to our present conditions. Cone thus contends that we must hold these realities "in dialectical relation."[41] Rather than approaching Christology either "from below" or "from above," we must do both at the same time, allowing each to inform the other.

For Cone, then, there is an important sense in which our understanding of Jesus himself flows from how we experience him at work in the world today. However, as Cone himself points out, this requires an act of discernment as we attempt to identify *where* and *how* Jesus is at work in our experience today. Thus Cone asks, "Is his presence synonymous with the work of the oppressed or the oppressors, blacks or whites? Is he to be found among the wretched or among the rich?"[42] For Cone, though, this

---

38. Ibid., 31.

39. Cone, *God of the Oppressed*, 115. This is also where Cone develops his understanding of the Spirit. For Cone, the Spirit is "the power of God at work in the world effecting in the life of his people his intended purposes" (Cone, *Black Theology and Black Power*, 57). The Spirit simply is "the power of Christ himself at work in the life of the believer" (ibid., 58). According to Garth Baker-Fletcher, Cone was among the first black theologians to develop a constructive account of the Spirit ("Black Theology and the Holy Spirit," in *The Cambridge Companion to Black Theology*, ed. Edward P. Antonio and Dwight N. Hopkins [New York: Cambridge University Press, 2012], 112).

40. Cone, *God of the Oppressed*, 110.

41. Ibid., 111. In his hermeneutics, Cone argues for a complex interaction between the Bible and black experience as sources of God's self-revelation. On the one hand, Cone affirms that the Bible is "an indispensable witness to God's revelation and is thus a primary source for Christian thinking about God" (Cone, *A Black Theology of Liberation*, 32). Yet he also contends that it is not possible to interpret the Bible apart from how we experience God in the present (e.g., Cone, *God of the Oppressed*, 75). Cone thus appeals to a "dialectic" between these two sources in which he cannot ultimately "justify" his appeal to black experience, as though there were some higher norm on which he could ground such an appeal, but must simply take the "risk" of affirming that the black experience of oppression is a more adequate starting point for understanding God's self-revelation than the white experience of oppressing (Cone, *A Black Theology of Liberation*, 32).

42. Cone, *A Black Theology of Liberation*, 127.

barely qualifies as a legitimate question.[43] If the Jesus that we experience today is the same as the Jesus that we see in the Gospels, then he surely stands with the oppressed and not with the oppressors.[44]

To understand the presence of Jesus today, we must look for him among the oppressed, seeking to understand what he is doing today in light of the ways in which people experience his redeeming power in the context of oppression. "We know who he is when our own lives are placed in a situation of oppression, and we thus have to make a decision for or against our condition. To say no to oppression and yes to liberation is to encounter the existential significance of the Resurrected One."[45] This is why Cone contends that we can only receive God's self-revelation in the context of oppression. If God is the liberating God who frees people from bondage, then we only see him truly when we see him through that lens. "There is no revelation of God without a condition of oppression which develops into a situation of liberation."[46] Consequently, *revelation is a black event.*"[47]

This last statement leads to the question of what Cone means by terms like *black* and *blackness*, how they relate to other forms of oppression, and how they describe the context for God's self-revelation through the liberating work of Jesus. Cone uses these terms in two distinct ways. On the one hand, blackness refers to phenotypical characteristics (skin color), racial ancestry (whether you have any black ancestors), and cultural conceptions (i.e., whether you are perceived in a given society as being black). On the other hand, Cone contends that being "black in America has very little to do with skin color. To be black means that your heart, your soul, your mind, and your body are where the dispossessed are."[48] Thus, Cone routinely uses blackness in a more metaphorical sense to signify "oppression and liberation in any society."[49] "Blackness ... stands for all victims of oppression who realize that the survival of their humanity is bound up with liberation from whiteness."[50] In this sense, *blackness* is

---

43. Elsewhere, he responds to a similar question with a curt "I think not" (Cone, *God of the Oppressed*, 82).

44. Cone, *A Black Theology of Liberation*, 127.

45. Ibid., 126.

46. Ibid., 48.

47. Ibid., 31.

48. Cone, *Black Theology and Black Power*, 151.

49. Cone, *A Black Theology of Liberation*, 5.

50. Ibid., 8.

an abstract term that refers to the realities of oppression and dehumanization experienced by a wide range of people groups.[51]

At the same time, though, he emphasizes the importance of black experience as describing the experience of particular people groups, those whose understanding of God's self-revelation is distinguished by the particular form of their oppression and of Jesus' liberating activity in their lives. This includes the negative experience that "blacks feel when they try to carve out an existence in dehumanized white society,"[52] "a life of humiliation and suffering"[53] in which white society tells black people that they are not really persons.[54] This could be done explicitly through various forms of enslavement and the commodification of black bodies, but also through implicit forms of dehumanization in which white perspectives on what constitutes true humanity and true human flourishing are established as normative for all humans. Either way, the black experience is marked by the oppressive message that black people are somehow less than fully human.

Yet black experience goes beyond just "encountering white insanity."[55] It also involves the positive acts in which the black community considers its own history, makes decisions about its own identity, and creatively expresses its self-understanding through its own unique culture. In this more comprehensive sense, "the black experience is the atmosphere in which blacks live. It is the totality of black existence."[56] Cone thus draws on a wide range of data when studying black experience, including black history, culture, music, literature, prayers, and more.[57]

Running throughout black experience is the liberating power of God in Christ. For Cone, we must believe Jesus to be active in black experience or we simply cannot account for the power and courage of the black

---

51. For Cone's autobiographical reflections on experiences as a black person, see esp. James H. Cone, *My Soul Looks Back* (Nashville: Abingdon, 1982); James H. Cone, *The Cross and the Lynching Tree* (Maryknoll, N.Y.: Orbis, 2011).

52. Cone, *A Black Theology of Liberation*, 28.

53. Ibid., 24.

54. Ibid., 105.

55. Ibid., 26.

56. Ibid., 25.

57. See esp. Cone's extended discussions of black experience as sources of theological reflection in *The Spirituals and the Blues: An Interpretation* (New York: Seabury, 1972) and *The Cross and the Lynching Tree*). As Victor Anderson has pointed out, though, one of the weaknesses of Cone's definition of blackness is that in both its positive and negative senses it requires a concept of whiteness against which to define itself (Victor Anderson, *Beyond Ontological Blackness: An Essay on African American Religious and Cultural Criticism* [New York: Continuum, 1995]).

church in its struggle against its oppressors. "What is it that keeps the community together when there are so many scares and hurts? What is it that gives them the will and the courage to struggle in hope when so much in their environment says that fighting is a waste of time? I think that the only 'reasonable' and 'objective' explanation is to say that the people are right when they proclaim the presence of the divine power, wholly different from themselves."[58] We must affirm that Jesus is present and active in black experience because that is the only way to make sense of "the witness of the black Church tradition and the contemporary testimonies of black people."[59] Like Schleiermacher, Cone takes the experience of redemption as the necessary starting point for theology. Yet he associates this specifically with the *black* experience of redemption.

From one perspective, then, Cone argues that there is something unique about the black experience of Jesus' liberating activity that makes it irreplaceable in understanding God's self-revelation. But Cone also recognizes that blacks are not the only ones who have experienced either oppression or Jesus' liberating activity. Although his earlier writings have been critiqued for overemphasizing the black, and specifically the black male, perspective, Cone later affirmed the legitimacy, even the necessity, of recognizing the perspective of other oppressed groups.[60]

In the Jesus who *is*, we see Jesus continuing the work of redemption by empowering people and communities for liberation. "The Lordship of Christ emphasizes his present rule in the lives of the people, helping them to struggle for the maintenance of humanity in a situation of oppression."[61] This is the context in which Cone affirms that "Jesus is the black Christ!"[62] By this, he does not necessarily intend to make a statement about Jesus' racial or ethnic background. He does think that "the particularity of Jesus'

---

58. Cone, *God of the Oppressed*, 112.

59. Ibid., 111.

60. Cone, *A Black Theology of Liberation*, xx. See esp. Jacquelyn Grant, "Black Theology and the Black Woman," in *Black Theology: A Documentary History*, ed. Gayraud S. Wilmore and James H. Cone (Maryknoll, N.Y.: Orbis, 1979), 320–36; James Evans Jr., "Black Theology and Black Feminism," *Journal of Religious Thought* 38, no. 2 (1981): 43–53; and Delores Williams, *Sisters in the Wilderness: The Challenge of Womanist God-Talk* (Maryknoll, N.Y.: Orbis, 1993).

61. Cone, *God of the Oppressed*, 115.

62. Cone, *A Black Theology of Liberation*, 127. Cone thus differs from Albert Cleage, who called for a literally black Messiah (Albert B. Cleage, *The Black Messiah* [New York: Sheed and Ward, 1968]). As Siker argues, then, "one could say … that Cone does not so much *historicize* a racialized Jesus as he *racializes* the Christ of Faith. Namely, he does not retroject a racial identity onto Jesus, rather he projects the historical Jesus onto a racial identity" (Siker, "Historicizing a Racialized Jesus," 32).

person as disclosed in his Jewishness is indispensable for christological analysis."[63] But he also says, "It seems to me that the *literal* color of Jesus is irrelevant, as are the different shades of blackness in America."[64] The point is not whether Jesus is phenotypically black, but whether he is fully and irrevocably committed to the needs of the oppressed. And to that, Cone can only respond with an unqualified yes!

The challenge for Christology, according to Cone, is that so much of our theology is governed by a hegemonic white perspective that uses Jesus as "an instrument of oppression."[65] The white perspective gives us a Jesus who focuses almost exclusively on addressing spiritual problems, ignoring the concrete realities of social oppression. Such images "are completely alien to the liberation of the black community,"[66] with their implicit suggestion that black experiences of enslavement, oppression, and racism are somehow less significant to Christ's liberating work than the existential feelings of guilt and anxiety experienced by a middle-class white person. Any so-called Jesus who remains silent about these brutal realities, necessarily belongs on the side of the oppressors. Any such Jesus needs to be destroyed as an enemy of God's own liberating activity.[67]

Jesus' work today continues to reveal God as the great Liberator who seeks the full human flourishing of all human persons. This is where Cone emphasizes the importance of the kingdom of God, which he defines as "a *black* happening."[68] By this, Cone means both that liberation is essential to the kingdom (black) and that the kingdom focuses primarily on a mode of living rather than a static condition (happening). Although we will see in the next section that Cone's eschatology includes the idea of God bringing about the consummation of his eschatological kingdom and the full and final realization of God's purposes for humanity, his primary emphasis during this age is the kingdom as an active state of living in opposition to all forms of dehumanization and oppression. "The event of the kingdom

---

63. Cone, *God of the Oppressed*, 109. Despite the fact that Cone makes this affirmation, it is not clear that Jesus' racial identity plays any significant role in Cone's work. At most, the fact that Jesus has a racial identity seems to validate experiencing humanity in racial categories today. Yet it is not clear how the specifically Jewish nature of Christ's identity serves to shape Cone's theological account of race.

64. Cone, *A Black Theology of Liberation*, 130.

65. Ibid., 117.

66. Ibid.

67. Ibid., 40.

68. Ibid., 131.

today is the liberation struggle in the black community. It is where persons are suffering and dying for want of human dignity. It is thus incumbent upon all to see the event for what it is—God's kingdom."[69] The kingdom is about participating in and aligning oneself with Jesus' liberating activity. Only in this way can we understand fully and truly who Jesus is and what he reveals about both God and ourselves.

WHO JESUS WILL BE

The third aspect of Cone's Christology has to do with the fact that Jesus "is not only the crucified and risen One but also the Lord of the future who is coming again to fully consummate the liberation already happening in our present."[70] With this emphasis, we come into contact with Cone's eschatology and its significance for Christology.

According to Cone, "the vision of the future and of Jesus as the Coming Lord is the central theme of black religion."[71] This is because the eventual return of Jesus is the fundamental ground of the hope that drives liberating action today. Christ's future return establishes that our ultimate liberation must come from outside history; true redemption requires the arrival of the eschatological kingdom and the consummation of God's plans for his people. This provides ground for hope specifically in the fact that "the oppressed have a future not made with human hands but grounded in the liberating promises of God."[72] Eschatological hope is ultimately founded on the sovereignty of God and his "will to liberate the oppressed," not our own frail and limited efforts.[73]

When viewed in light of his return and the establishment of his eschatological kingdom, Jesus Christ becomes for the oppressed "the One who stands at the center of their view of reality, enabling slaves to look beyond the present to the future, the time when black suffering will be ended."[74] This is a "vision of Christ's future that breaks into their slave existence," radically altering how they view their current circumstances.[75] The "will be" of Christ's future kingdom challenges the "is" of our present reality.

---

69. Ibid., 132.

70. Cone, *God of the Oppressed*, 116.

71. Ibid., 119.

72. Ibid., 145.

73. Ibid.

74. Ibid., 121.

75. Ibid., 120.

Cone recognizes his dependence here on modern theologies of hope, expressing appreciation for their emphasis on eschatology as more than simply "longing for the next world."[76] Instead, these theologies ground eschatological hope in "the actual presence of Jesus, breaking into their broken existence, and bestowing upon them a foretaste of God's promised freedom."[77] At the same time, though, he criticizes these theologies of hope for paying inadequate attention to questions of oppression and liberation. "How can Christian theology truly speak of the hope of Jesus Christ, unless that hope begins and ends with the liberation of the poor in the social existence in which theology takes shape?"[78]

According to Cone, without hope in the return of Christ, we will ultimately lapse into the kind of despair that undermines liberating action now. But he specifically rejects the suggestion that this is the kind of hope that is so overly focused on the future that it enables a form of quietism in the present (e.g., Marx's "opiate of the masses"). For Cone, "an eschatological perspective that does not challenge the present order is faulty."[79] Rather than pacifying the people and motivating them to be content within their oppressed states, Cone argues that truly *eschatological* hope more often leads to precisely the opposite result. He is worth quoting at length on this point:

> But in reality, the opposite happened more often than not. For many black slaves, Jesus became the decisive Other in their lives who provided for them a knowledge of themselves, not derived from the value system of slave masters. How could black slaves know that they were human beings when they were treated like cattle? How could they know that they were somebody when everything in their environment said that they were nobody? How could they know that they had a value that could not be defined by dollars and cents, when the symbol of the auction block was an ever present reality? Only because they knew that Christ was present with them and that his presence included the divine promise to come again and to take them to the "New Jerusalem." Heaven, therefore, in black religion was inseparably connected with Jesus' promise to liberate the oppressed from slavery. It was black people's vision of a new identity for themselves which was in sharp contradiction to their present status as slaves.[80]

---

76. Ibid., 116.

77. Ibid., 117.

78. Cone, *A Black Theology of Liberation*, 150.

79. Ibid., 145.

80. Cone, *God of the Oppressed*, 119–20.

Several aspects of this quote stand out as significant for our purposes. First, although this eschatological hope focuses on a future happening, it grounds a present reality. In eschatological hope, Jesus becomes "the decisive Other" who is present in the world today as the one who will eventually establish the kingdom, bring about justice, and end oppression. Jesus' *presence* includes his *promise*. Thus, we experience him now as the one whose presence includes the eschatological realities that transcend the broken condition of a world in which people can be "defined by dollars and cents."

This eschatological hope not only grounds Christian action, but it also reorients our own self-definitions. It is the coming Christ who "provided for them a knowledge of themselves" that could not be derived from the sinful structures of his broken world. Rather than defining themselves in the commodified terms of their enslavement, eschatological hope reveals to oppressed people that they have actually been created for freedom and are now being called to participate in and actualize that freedom even in the midst of their oppressed realities. The vision of "New Jerusalem" provides a "new identity."

Cone's eschatological framework thus draws together the ideas of Jesus' presence, the liberating action that his presence both accomplishes and motivates, and the new identity that arises for oppressed people in light of that liberating activity. All three of these will play important roles as we transition into the latter half of the chapter and explore the implications of Cone's Christology for understanding what it really means to be human.

HUMAN BEING AS THE EVENT OF FREEDOM

We can now move on to consider the anthropological implications of Cone's Christology and its emphasis on Jesus as the Liberator. On this basis, Cone offers a highly actualistic definition of humanity. To be human is to align oneself with other human persons and to work toward the full and free flourishing of all humanity. Human "essence" is something that must be shaped through human action. Consequently, true human *being* arises from right human *living*.

Yet this raises the question of whether Cone understands the relationship between Christology and anthropology in entirely exemplaristic terms. Does Jesus merely give us a model to follow, a guide for moral/ ethical conduct? As important as this might be, we stipulated in the introduction that we were looking for christological anthropologies that extend their insights beyond such moralistic inquiries. In the conclusion to this chapter, then, once we have considered in greater detail the precise shape of Cone's anthropology, we will return to this question and discuss the extent to which Cone offers the kind of christological anthropology that we are pursuing.

The Concrete Reality of Human Existence

Cone finds most traditional anthropologies frustrating for their tendency to focus on a knowledge of "ideal" or "true" humanity that is inadequate to the concrete realities of both God's self-revelation in Jesus and the human life that we see and experience in the world today. Any such approach is necessarily abstract, inadequate, and ultimately non-christological. Instead of identifying "true" humanity, such anthropologies actually serve as ideologies in the guise of Christian theology. Lacking an adequate ground in God's self-revelation as the Liberator, they fail to identify that which is most important about human existence. Instead, they fill the concept "human" with cultural conceptions that serve primarily to reinforce the power dynamics already at play in that context. Failing to realize this, theologians pretend that their socially located theological statements about humanity are somehow universally normative. At that point, anthropology becomes ideology.[81] Appealing to *true* humanity, they are merely baptizing the concept of humanity preferred by the ruling elite, and, at the same time, they are marginalizing and even oppressing any understanding of humanity that fails to correspond to this cultural ideal. Thus, "black theology is suspicious of those who appeal to a universal, ideal humanity. Oppressors are ardent lovers of humanity. They can love all persons in general, even black persons, because intellectually they can put blacks in the category called Humanity ... But when it comes to dealing with particular blacks ... they are at a loss. They remind us of Dostoevski's doctor, who said, 'I love humanity, but I wonder at myself. The more I love humanity in general, the less I love man in particular.' "[82]

In contrast, Cone contends that a properly christological approach to anthropology begins not with humanity in general but with "the concrete human being."[83] By this he means both the concreteness of Jesus' own historical existence, but also the concrete social situations in which we see and experience humanity today. Just as an adequate Christology requires the interplay of the historic Jesus presented in the Bible and

---

81. Cone, *For My People*, 29.

82. Cone, *A Black Theology of Liberation*, 90.

83. Ibid., 89.

our present experiences of the risen Christ, so our understanding of the human person requires us to navigate the dialectical tension between the humanity that we see in Jesus' historical life and the humanity that we experience around us every day.

This has a number of important consequences for the shape of theological anthropology. First, Cone argues that beginning with concrete reality means we must drop any thought of achieving knowledge of ideal humanity untainted by sin. Since "there is no way to get behind the human condition as we know it to be,"[84] our only knowledge of humanity must always be knowledge of humanity in the condition of sin. Although all of the theologians in this study would agree that sin problematizes our knowledge of humanity, Cone differs from most in suggesting that not even Jesus reveals the true humanity that lies behind the taint of sin. Instead, Jesus manifests what it means to be and live as a human person in the midst of a broken and suffering world. When we look at Jesus, we see the reality that "we are not what we ought to be" and have instead "taken a course completely alien to our being."[85] Yet Jesus reveals this precisely in the midst of brokenness, sin, and oppression. In his faithful humanity we do not see some kind of ideal, transcendent humanity that remains untouched by sin; instead, we see the revelation of true humanity in its proper mode of standing against oppression and for the liberation of all human persons.

Second, Cone argues that if we allow the concrete realities of particular human persons to drive our anthropologies, we will necessarily prioritize historical actions over abstract ontologies. This is true of Jesus as much as it is for other human persons. In Christology, we must always understand *who he is* in light of *what he does*.[86] And since *what he does* is something that continues to unfold in our present and in the eschatological future, we cannot "define Jesus Christ's essence once and for all time."[87] All we can offer are our best attempts at articulating our current

---

84. Ibid., 75.

85. Ibid., 112.

86. Cone, *God of the Oppressed*, 81.

87. Thus, Cone would not be troubled by questions about whether the social changes that have taken place in the decades since he wrote his earliest christological works might require new christological formulations (e.g., Chigor Chike, "Black Christology for the Twenty-First Century," *Black Theology* 8, no. 3 [2010]: 357–78). Since Jesus is "not a proposition" but "an event of liberation," we must always be willing to revisit our theological formulations in light of what he continues to do (Cone, *God of the Oppressed*, 32). Cone even concedes that there may come a time when *blackness* itself "may not be appropriate in the distant future" (ibid., 135).

understanding of Jesus' identity in light of his activity. The same holds for Cone's understanding of humanity in general. Cone thus affirms Sartre's view of the human person in which "there is no essence or universal humanity independent of persons in the concreteness of their involvement in the world."[88] Instead, "all persons define their own essence by participating in the world, making decisions that involve themselves and others."[89] Anthropology requires constant phenomenological analysis of concrete human existence because that is all we have. When we attempt to move beyond human existence and speculate about human essence, that is precisely when we lose sight of real humanity and begin again the slide toward ideology.

A third consequence of Cone's emphasis on concrete existence is that knowledge of true humanity only arises in the context of oppression. This arises christologically because this is the very context in which Jesus himself revealed the nature of human existence. "The basic mistake of our white opponents is their failure to see that God did not become a universal human being but an oppressed Jew, thereby disclosing to us that both human nature and divine nature are inseparable from oppression and liberation. To know who the human person *is* is to focus on the Oppressed One and what he does for an oppressed community as it liberates itself from slavery."[90] If we try to understand humanity apart from the realities of oppression, it necessarily means we are trying to understand humanity apart from Jesus. Consequently, "only the oppressed know what human personhood is."[91]

Cone's emphasis on approaching anthropology from the perspective of concrete human existence has at times been interpreted as entailing the corresponding conclusion that we cannot say anything about the human person that has universal validity. Yet Cone explicitly rejects this as a viable option for a Christian anthropology.[92] Indeed, such a

---

88. Cone, *A Black Theology of Liberation*, 89.

89. Ibid.

90. Ibid., 91.

91. Ibid., 92.

92. In this context Cone contrasts the existential philosophies of Jean-Paul Sartre and Albert Camus, contending that although the former offers an important insight in emphasizing that we need to analyze the concrete existence of human persons rather than speculate on some abstract "essence," the latter importantly retains the idea that there are universal truths about the human person that we must not jettison. Camus "appeals to a common value among human beings, a value capable of recognition by all and responsible for revolt against human oppression" (ibid., 89).

conclusion would deal a crushing blow to his confident assertions about God as the Liberator who works for the freedom of the oppressed and the corresponding insights that we can glean about the proper shape of human living in the world today. Similarly, it would seem to entail a kind of cultural incommensurability in which theological statements are radically limited to their cultural contexts. In contrast, Cone contends that his theology has always retained a role for the universal despite his strong emphasis on "locatedness."[93] Although revelation comes *through* such concrete particularities, truth is not limited *to* them.[94]

Freed to Be Human and to Be for Humanity

According to Cone, the most basic definition of the human person is this: "To be human is to be free, and to be free is to be human."[95] In light of the liberating activity of the Jesus who is and will be, we must see freedom as constituting the core of any adequately Christian anthropology. Freedom thus sits at "the very heart of the theological concept of the 'image of God.'"[96] Consequently, liberation is central to the Christian view of humanity: "If the image of God includes freedom, as is definitely implied in the divine-human encounter, then it must also include *liberation*,"[97] which entails "revolting against everything that is opposed to humanity."[98] The essence of Cone's christological anthropology, then, resides in his understanding of anthropological freedom and liberation.

Cone is well aware, though, that both of these concepts require careful unpacking; otherwise false notions of freedom and liberation will

---

93. Cone, *God of the Oppressed*, xiii. Lincoln makes an important distinction when he says that Cone's theology is "situational" but not "parochial" (C. Eric Lincoln, "Perspective on James H. Cone's Black Theology," *Union Seminary Quarterly Review* 31, no. 1 [1975]: 16). It is situational in that God's revelation only meets us in particular contexts, and our response to his revelation must be conditioned by those contexts. But it is not parochially "bound" by those local contexts because of the overlapping nature of our contexts and because the implications of God's self-revelation always transcend the local.

94. "Whatever else we may say about the gospel, it is not an expression of truth enclosed within, and thus limited to, one culture. Indeed to think of the gospel as if any one people had a monopoly on its truth and meaning would be to distort it. God is more than what any one people can elaborate and express" (Cone, *For My People*, 173).

95. Cone, *A Black Theology of Liberation*, 92.

96. Cone, *God of the Oppressed*, 133.

97. Cone, *A Black Theology of Liberation*, 98.

98. Ibid., 99. "The image of God is not merely a personal relationship with God, but is also that constituent of humanity which makes all people struggle against captivity" (Cone, *God of the Oppressed*, 134; see Cone, *A Black Theology of Liberation*, 99–100).

invade our anthropologies and twist our vision of the human person. It is essential that we reject any attempt to view liberation in purely spiritual terms, missing the social and political nature of the liberation that we see in Jesus' life and ministry. Although Cone recognizes the importance of our bondage to sin in general and the ways in which oppression harms the oppressors as well as the oppressed, he nonetheless rejects such spiritualizations as attempts to avoid the concrete, material significance of Jesus' redemption.[99] Since Jesus' identity is grounded in the fact that he is "a human being for oppressed persons," we must ensure that our definitions of what constitutes true humanity are themselves "limited to what it means to be liberated from human oppression."[100]

This means, however, that true humanity can only be realized in the context of oppression. Only there do we see the true threat to human existence in the dehumanization that necessarily results from oppression, and only in the context of oppression do we have opportunity to participate in Jesus' liberating activity by working for the liberation of our fellow humans. This is what Cone has in mind when he says, "Only the oppressed are truly free!"[101] According to Cone, the oppressed are the only ones who experience Jesus' liberating activity in the midst of sinful oppression, seeing both God's amazing power at work for the well-being of human persons and the depersonalizing reality of sin in its most destructive form. Thus, only the oppressed see both God and humanity for what they truly are.

Cone also rejects the false kind of freedom that emphasizes the autonomous individuality that characterizes so much of the Western tradition. Although Cone thinks that tradition was right to stress the importance of freedom, he contends that it misunderstood its nature. "Freedom is not a rational decision about possible alternatives; it is a participation of the whole person in the liberation struggle."[102] In other words, for Cone there is no such thing as individual freedom. In Christ, we see that true freedom is *freedom for humanity*. Consequently, freedom entails

---

99. Cone thus notes the danger of thinking that whites also are oppressed: "Black theology rejects this technique as the work of the white Christ whose basic purpose is to soothe the guilt feelings of white overlords" (ibid., 109). And later he contends, "White theologians and ethicists simply ignore black people by suggesting that the problem of racism and oppression is only one social expression of a larger ethical concern" (Cone, *God of the Oppressed*, 184).

100. Cone, *A Black Theology of Liberation*, 91.

101. Ibid., 93.

102. Ibid., 98.

responsibility, specifically the free responsibility of living for the well-being of humanity by seeking the liberation of all human persons. True freedom is not a choice that we need to make between aligning ourselves with the oppressed or the oppressors. Indeed, there is a sense in which the existence of the choice itself is a ramification of sin. Otherwise, how could we possibly think that aligning ourselves with the oppressors could be a legitimate option for those made in the image of the Liberator? Freedom is not the abstract capacity to wrestle with the possibility of choosing against humanity. Instead, true freedom is a human life lived for the sake of the other and for human flourishing in general.

Cone thus presents individualism as the essence of sin. At its core, sin is "living according to one's private interests and not according to the goals of the community."[103] That is largely because Cone thinks that "living according to one's private interests" is at the root of many, if not most, forms of oppression. With an exclusive focus on my own desires, I will necessarily view those around me as either commodities or obstacles. As commodities, I instrumentalize people and turn them into means for meeting my own desires. As obstacles, I view them as dangers to be controlled and oppressed. Either way, I fail to view other human persons as beings with intrinsic value, persons with whom I stand in solidarity and community.[104] Sin is "a condition of human existence in which we deny the essence of God's liberating activity as revealed in Jesus Christ," specifically by failing to work for the freedom and well-being of other human persons.[105] In that condition, "we cease to be fully human" because we have denied the very freedom that constitutes true humanity.[106]

Finally, Cone rejects any kind of freedom that focuses exclusively on material prosperity. Although Cone refuses to define freedom in abstraction from real oppression, which typically corresponds to economic

---

103. Ibid., 110.

104. "To be free means that human beings are not an object, and they will not let others treat them as an 'it.' They refuse to let limits be put on their being. They are at once a part of nature (subject to laws of the universe) and are independent of nature" (Cone, *A Black Theology of Liberation*, 95).

105. Ibid., 112.

106. Ibid. Thus, although Stephen Murray points out that Cone tends to describe the sins of the black community in terms of "a loss of identity, a desire to be white, an acceptance of the absurdity of a world in which white values define black existence," all of these would still fit Cone's definition of sin in that they undermine the full and free human flourishing of black persons (Stephen Butler Murray, "The Dimensions of Sin and Fallenness in the Theological Anthropology of Black and Womanist Theologies," *Journal of Religion* 84, no. 1 [2004]: 28).

disadvantage, he also criticizes any attempt to associate freedom in the present as the achievement of material success or security. "The kingdom is not an attainment of material security, nor is it mystical communion with the divine. It has to do with the *quality* of one's existence in which a person realizes that *persons* are more important than property."[107] His concern here is that if we define the kingdom in terms of material success, the oppressed will simply become the oppressors as they attempt to secure their own material well-being against the threat of the other. Instead, Cone argues that the true humanity that we see revealed in Christ is "inevitably associated with suffering,"[108] not because there is some intrinsic value in suffering but because asserting one's freedom for the sake of the other requires real sacrifice as we combat "the economic and social structures of oppression."[109] In Cone's thought, "freedom for Jesus" corresponds not to material prosperity but to "freedom for the oppressed."[110]

Cone thus defines the human person in terms of a specific notion of freedom, one that sees true humanity as living a life aligned with Jesus' own liberating activity on behalf of the oppressed. Yet this kind of freedom transcends moral/ethical behavior. Since our actions determine our being, defining humanity in terms of liberating action means that freedom constitutes the true "essence" of humanity in a rather robust sense. Properly defined, the term "human" describes a mode or way of life more than it does some kind of abstract essence. We are human insofar as we participate in Jesus' liberating activity for the well-being of the communities in which we find ourselves. "If the content of the gospel is liberation, human existence must be explained as 'being in freedom,' which means rebellion against every form of slavery, the suppression of everything creative."[111] In Cone's anthropology, then, the moral/ethical and the essential/ontological flow together. Exercising freedom for the sake of the other *is* the essence of humanity: "Human beings are made for each other, and no people can realize their full humanity except as they participate in its realization for others."[112]

---

107. Cone, *A Black Theology of Liberation*, 131.

108. Ibid., 103.

109. Ibid.

110. Ibid., 107.

111. Ibid., 92.

112. Cone, *God of the Oppressed*, xiii.

CONVERTING TO TRUE HUMANITY

If true humanity in its fullest sense is only revealed and realized in the context of oppression, though, what about the rest of us? At first glance, it would seem that Cone's christological anthropology runs the risk of suggesting that the oppressors are not only living subhumanly, but they are actually excluded from the possibility of realizing their full humanity simply because they are not among the oppressed. Indeed, we might even think that the oppressors are the ones who have the greatest need since they are excluded from the communities in which full humanity is both revealed and realized. However, such a conclusion would seem to repristinate the spiritualized notions of liberation and redemption that Cone rejected earlier.

Cone avoids this conundrum by drawing on the traditional language of conversion, though defined in ways that cohere with the anthropological centrality of freedom and liberation. Oppressors can convert by aligning themselves with the oppressed. On this account of conversion, *faith* has little to do with affirming specific truths, even those focused on the person and work of Jesus. Instead, faith involves "saying yes to God and no to oppressors."[113] In faith, we recognize God's liberating activity in the world and cast our lot with his kingdom purposes.[114] Similarly, "repentance has nothing to do with morality or religious piety in the white sense."[115] By this he means the notion of repentance is entirely about acknowledging the individual sins that separate the human person from God. Instead, Cone contends that repentance involves letting go of the power and privilege that comes from being among the oppressors and embracing the condition of the oppressed. Finally, corresponding to these notions of faith and repentance, conversion involves "a radical reorientation of one's existence in the world"[116] in which we align ourselves with the oppressed and "become black" with Jesus.[117]

As with "freedom," though, talk about "conversion" requires careful explanation lest we again incorporate notions that undermine a proper view of human existence. Cone thus critiques several false views of conversion. First, he critiques the notion that this conversion involves a simple declaration that you now stand on the side of the oppressed. From one perspec-

---

113. Cone, *A Black Theology of Liberation*, 50.

114. Ibid., 131.

115. Ibid.

116. Ibid., 103.

117. Ibid., 130.

tive, Cone recognizes the importance of such a declaration, especially since everyone knows that "blacks are those who say they are black, regardless of skin color."[118] Yet he contends that true conversion involves something deeper, something that ultimately is "the work of God, not a human work."[119] True conversion involves a declaration of blackness that corresponds to a deeper change in which you have been freed to align yourself with God's work of freedom, which is a kind of freedom that only the divine Liberator can produce.

Second, Cone rejects the notion that this kind of conversion can be an entirely inner, mental event in which the oppressors come to understand the dignity and value of the oppressed, committing themselves to living more charitably in the world. This kind of superficial "conversion" has more to do with easing the conscience of the oppressor than truly aligning oneself with the oppressed. True conversion requires the kind of freedom that only "becomes a reality when they throw in their lot with an oppressed community."[120] Freedom involves making decisions within the context of a community of persons who share similar goals and are seeking the same liberation. Freedom means taking sides in a crisis situation.[121]

Finally, Cone contends that we must be constantly on guard against the kind of false conversion in which white privilege continues to shape the narrative by imposing its own norms and perspectives on the new community.[122] In other words, it would be all too easy for the newly "converted" oppressors to continue exercising their privilege in the community, assuming that they already know what it means to be human and how to resist the dehumanizing forces of oppression. In this situation, no real conversion has taken place. The oppressors have simply adopted a new form of oppression.[123] Real conversion requires the oppressors to *join* the community and sacrifice "their precious white identity" by abandoning power and privilege.[124]

---

118. Ibid., 69.

119. Ibid.

120. Ibid., 100.

121. Ibid.

122. Cone, *God of the Oppressed*, 222.

123. Some of Cone's early critics challenged his strong rhetoric against the white oppressors, calling for more language of forgiveness and reconciliation (e.g., Major J. Jones, *Christian Ethics for Black Theology* [Nashville: Abingdon, 1974]). But Cone criticizes calls for "reconciliation" in which the oppressed are supposed to forgive the oppressors "without changing the balance of power" (ibid., 207). For Cone, real reconciliation occurs when people encounter God's liberating activity in the world such that the oppressors take the side of the oppressed and actually become oppressed (ibid., 209).

124. Cone, *A Black Theology of Liberation*, 69.

If Cone's theology of conversion requires that we align ourselves with oppressed communities in which we really join those communities as members, it also involves participating in the community's efforts to bring about the destruction of oppression, that is, the destruction of anything that hinders the realization of full humanity. As Cone says, *"No one is free until all are free."*[125] Since freedom is the definition of humanity, though, this entails the corresponding claim that no one is truly *human* until all are free. As long as oppression remains a reality for even a single human person, we do not yet experience humanity as divinely intended and as revealed in Jesus. From this perspective, true humanity is an eschatological state of being in which all persons are freed from oppression and for human flourishing. At the same time, though, as important as this eschatological perspective might be, Cone also talks about a form of full humanity that can be a present reality as well. "To be (fully) human," from this perspective, "is to be involved, participating in societal structures for human liberation."[126] The essence of human existence this side of the eschaton, then, is "being against evil by joining sides with those who are victims of evil."[127] Being human in the present is about striving to "achieve meaning in a dehumanized world"[128] specifically by working for the liberation of humanity from all forms of social oppression.

This means that, although Cone's anthropology should not be reduced to moral/ethical action, neither should the moral/ethical dimensions of true humanity be ignored altogether. If "humanity" really describes a mode of living, then humanity is a necessarily ethical concept. Cone thus devotes considerable attention to reflecting on the precise shape of human living in light of his christological description of human existence. Unfortunately, summarizing Cone's thoughts on how we should actualize our commitment to the full humanity of all human persons in specific actions is somewhat challenging because he rejects the possibility that we can articulate any "abstract principles" that might guide our efforts toward human flourishing.[129] Instead, ethical behavior must be "defined in and by the oppressed community."[130] Here as well Cone emphasizes the

---

125. Ibid., 93.

126. Ibid., 94.

127. Ibid., 88.

128. Cone, *For My People*, 28.

129. Cone, *God of the Oppressed*, 195.

130. Ibid., 189. "What we are to do, therefore, is not decided by abstract principles but is defined by Jesus' liberating presence in our community. The oppressed community is the place

concreteness of human living by arguing that we cannot decide in advance what might be appropriate or inappropriate ways of striving for full human flourishing in the world. He does reject the possibility that our efforts in this direction should involve "the destruction of humanity, even among oppressors."[131] But he refuses to eliminate the possibility of violent action entirely.[132] The key is that any action must be guided by a vision of true humanity in which we strive for the free flourishing of all human persons. "Our intention is not to make the oppressors the slaves but to transform humanity ... The ethic of liberation arises out of love, for ourselves and for humanity. This is an essential ingredient of liberation without which the struggle turns into a denial of what divine liberation means."[133]

The true form of humanity is both revealed and actualized in the context of oppression specifically because that is where we find Jesus' liberating activity in the world. Although this privileges the situation of the oppressed in the pursuit of full humanity, it does not leave the oppressors in an impossible bind. But it does mean that the oppressors will have to abandon the power and privilege of their white status and join with oppressed communities in their own liberating work. For such conversions to be true conversions, though, they must be initiated by God himself, who alone can transform the oppressors and grant the freedom necessary for real change.

BECOMING HUMAN THROUGH LIBERATING ACTION

In Cone's theological anthropology, humanity is defined as a particular mode of living in which humans align themselves *with* Jesus' liberating action *for* the full human flourishing of all people. Cone thus offers an anthropology in which Jesus Christ both reveals and actualizes the proper shape of human existence in a broken world that seems bent on destruction and dehumanization. Cone does not offer speculative insight into the nature of human "essences" or "natures," focusing instead on the ways human being is constituted by human action. In short, true human being arises from right human acting.

---

where we are called to hammer out the meaning of Jesus' presence for Christian behavior. This is a risk of faith, because there are no universal guarantees that our decision will be ethically consistent with our freedom in Christ. Therefore we must be in constant dialogue with each other about what we should and should not do in the struggle" (ibid., 195).

131. Cone, *God of the Oppressed*, 199.

132. E.g., Cone, *A Black Theology of Liberation*, 130.

133. Cone, *God of the Oppressed*, 199.

As we begin to look at the anthropological implications of Cone's Christology, it would be easy to explain the relationship between Christology and anthropology in his theology in entirely exemplarist terms. In Jesus' liberating activity, he left us an example of a human life well lived. Our task, then, is to model our own lives after his as we attempt to live as humanly as possible in the midst of our own sinfully broken circumstances.

Yet it would be a mistake to reduce the Christology/anthropology relationship in Cone's theology to that of example alone. At the very least, we need to recognize the important differences in Cone's Christology between Jesus Christ and the rest of humanity. Jesus alone is "the complete self-giving of God in Christ"[134] and "the event of God, telling us who God is."[135] Consequently, "Jesus was not simply a nice fellow who happened to like the poor. Rather his actions have their origin in God's eternal being."[136] Thus, despite the significant continuity between Jesus and the rest of humanity that creates the possibility for him to serve as a meaningful example of human living, we must also recognize significant discontinuity. If that is the case, then, we need to be aware that Cone may have in mind a deeper connection between Christology and anthropology than that of mere example.[137]

We can strengthen this conclusion further by noting the role that Jesus plays in introducing anthropological freedom into the world. For

---

134. Cone, *A Black Theology of Liberation*, 75.

135. Ibid., 31.

136. Cone, *God of the Oppressed*, 74.

137. Some might wonder, though, if this is an accurate reading of Cone's theology in light of later statements that he makes about the relationship between Jesus and God's revelation. According to him, dialogue with theologians from other perspectives convinced him that he could no longer view Jesus as "God's sole revelation" (ibid., xiv). Instead, Jesus was "an important revelatory event among many" (ibid.). Although this might seem to put Jesus on equal footing among other potential sources of revelation, Cone continues to maintain the central significance of Christ as a revelation of both God and humanity. Even if God reveals himself in other ways, no fresh revelation of God will contradict who he has revealed himself to be in Christ. "There is no knowledge of Jesus Christ today that contradicts who he was yesterday" (ibid., 106). Even in his later theology, he says, "I continue to focus on Jesus Christ as the starting point for Christian thinking about God" (ibid., xiii). Although this might be interpreted as denoting a mere preference—i.e., Cone continues to focus on the centrality of Jesus but some other Christian theologian might legitimately prefer some other starting point—he goes on to state that Jesus "defines Christian identity in faith and practice" (ibid., 4.). And he concludes with the explanation that his theological reflections begin with Jesus Christ "because I am a Christian" (ibid.). Thus, Cone seems to be arguing that Christology is central to Christian theology because Jesus is essential to Christian identity, faith, and practice. Even as he denies that Jesus is the sole source of revelation, then, he affirms that Jesus is the necessary center of Christian theology.

Cone, Jesus does not merely demonstrate what it looks like for human beings to live and act freely, offering a model of human freedom for us to follow. Instead, he contends that Jesus is "the eternal event of liberation in the divine person who makes freedom a constituent of human existence."[138] In other words, apart from Jesus, human persons have no real freedom. In this sense, Jesus not only reveals true humanity, he constitutes it.

Cone's christological anthropology thus unfolds through the complex interplay between Jesus as the exemplar of right human living and Jesus as the one who constitutes true humanity in freedom. Although he emphasizes "act" over "being" in ways that may sound purely exemplarist at times, we should not lose sight of the constitutive significance of Jesus Christ for humanity. Both strands are necessary for grasping how Cone views the role of Christology in understanding what it means to be human.

However, it would be all too easy to unpack such a theological anthropology in relatively abstract ways that remain distanced from the material concerns of poverty, racism, and other forms of oppression in this broken world. For Cone, no such approach could possibly be adequate to the form of humanity that we see in Jesus Christ. In Jesus' past, present, and future work, we see the truth that God is the great Liberator who works against oppression and for the full freedom of all human persons. This means that in contexts characterized by oppression, which describes all contexts in this broken world, we can only see and experience true humanity when we align ourselves with the oppressed and against the oppressors. That alone is where we see the brutal reality of dehumanization that prevents full human flourishing, and that is where we experience Jesus' liberating activity as that which reveals and actualizes the freedom that constitutes humanity as divinely intended. This is the kingdom of God at work in the world, and when we experience God's liberating presence, we have the opportunity through faith and repentance to align ourselves with God's kingdom work by joining the oppressed and working for the liberation of all humans. In Cone's terms, that simply *is* what it means to be human.

---

138. Cone, *God of the Oppressed*, 32.

CHAPTER 8

Developing Christological Visions of the Human Person

A cow is always simply a cow. It does not ask, "What is a cow? Who am I?" Only man asks such questions, and indeed clearly has to ask them about himself and his being. This is his question. His question follows him in hundreds of forms.[1]

Jürgen Moltmann, *Man*

We began this study with a simple question: What is a *christological* anthropology? In one sense, that is a relatively easy question to answer. If a christological anthropology is any anthropology that seeks to understand humanity in general from the person and work of Jesus Christ, then most Christian anthropologies would qualify as christological in at least some sense. Even "What would Jesus do?" fits this broad definition, with its assumption that Jesus is the normative ethical standard that should guide human behavior in general. As I explained in the introduction, though, the various studies in this book sought to press further. Is there a deeper sense in which Christology informs our understanding of humanity across a broad range of anthropological issues? If so, how have people done this and what lessons might we glean for developing christological anthropologies today?

As we bring this study to a conclusion, it will be helpful if we take a look back over the ground we have covered and make some observations about the various case studies, noting areas of similarity and dissimilarity, not for the purposes of developing a taxonomic framework for categorizing all christological anthropologies, but to highlight important

---

1. Jürgen Moltmann, *Man: Christian Anthropology in the Conflicts of the Present* (London: SPCK, 1974), 1.

issues that might be worth addressing in our own attempts to understand humanity. Along the way we will revisit the tentative definition of christological anthropology I offered in the introduction. Although we will see that this definition still applies in a general sense, the various case studies in this book will press us to clarify and strengthen that definition in several important ways.

THROUGH CHRIST-SHAPED LENSES

We should note first the disparate christological starting points utilized by our various authors. Although nearly all of them address the *imago Dei* and how Christ informs this vital aspect of a Christian anthropology, the real springboard for their anthropological reflections came from some other aspect of their Christologies. Thus, we have seen anthropologies that focus on the incarnation (Nyssa), God's love displayed on the cross (Julian), the righteousness of Christ that becomes ours through faith (Luther), Jesus' unique God-consciousness (Schleiermacher), the doctrine of election (Barth), the mediation of true personhood (Zizioulas), and Jesus' liberating activity on behalf of the oppressed (Cone). Each of those starting points shaped their respective anthropologies in distinct ways, demonstrating the significance of one's Christology for shaping the understanding of humanity that results.[2]

This does not necessarily mean, however, that we should try to trace all the differences between these various anthropologies back to differences in their Christologies. In the next section we will discuss the relationship between christological and non-christological sources of information about humanity. Here we can simply note the important role played by a variety of additional factors (e.g., other doctrines, information provided by nontheological disciplines, and the disparate cultural and historical locations of each theologian) in shaping their eventual anthropologies. Clearly, then, Christology is not the only factor influencing their anthropological conclusions, and we should exercise caution when identifying any particular anthropological variance as resulting directly from their disparate Christologies.

At the same time, however, we cannot avoid the conclusion that these starting points have real and necessary consequences for the resulting

2. We need to be careful, though, about thinking that these christological starting points encompass the entirety of any of these theologians' Christologies. Each study focuses on the particular aspect of that theologian's Christology that has the greatest impact on his or her anthropology, rather than trying to engage his or her Christology in its totality.

anthropologies. Adopting Gregory's transformative vision of human nature, for example, will generate importantly different anthropological conclusions than Cone's emphasis on Jesus' liberating praxis. This means that a christological anthropology would be well advised to invest considerable attention in its explicitly *christological* aspect. This kind of robust christological thinking is precisely what we see in our various studies; yet it is also what is lacking in at least some modern theological anthropologies. It is striking that even theological anthropologies that affirm the basic contention of a christological anthropology often have relatively little to say about the Jesus who apparently informs (in some way) what it means to be human. Of course, if we required theologians to articulate entire Christologies before they could say anything about anthropology, few would ever arrive at the latter task. Thus, unless we want to reduce anthropology to Christology — more on that in a moment — we cannot set the bar too high. Nonetheless, for the basic contention of christological anthropology to carry much weight, our theological anthropologies must be informed by Christologies that are sufficiently well developed to generate the requisite anthropological insights.

We might also ask how these various christological lenses relate to one another. Presumably, nothing prevents us from combining two or more of these perspectives so long as this can be done coherently. It might be difficult to envision how we would combine Gregory's incarnational emphasis with Schleiermacher's God-consciousness in a way that is both coherent and does justice to the respective christological emphases of each. Yet other combinations seem far more likely (e.g., Gregory and Zizioulas or Barth and Cone), and some might create interesting anthropological possibilities (e.g., Luther and Cone or Julian and Zizioulas). One of the benefits of comparative studies like this is the opportunity for new approaches and insights to develop from the interaction between otherwise disparate figures.

CHRISTOLOGICAL BUT NOT CHRISTOMONISTIC

However, despite the importance of these christological lenses for understanding the human person, none of our representative theologians evidences any interest in reducing anthropology to Christology. At the very least, none of them attempted to reduce all true statements about humanity in general to true statements about Jesus Christ. As important as Christology might be for informing theological anthropology, these two areas of inquiry remain distinct theological loci. Indeed, in the next section we will wrestle briefly with the difficult question of how christological claims relate to anthropological claims in these case studies. Here, though, we can note that this question flows directly from the insistence that these two fields of inquiry are importantly related yet remain distinct.

Additionally, although I was not able to address this question extensively in the various studies, several of our theologians explicitly utilize nontheological perspectives in developing their understanding of the human person. Gregory was not only familiar with the medical and scientific data on the human person available in his day, but he often interacted with it as he developed his theological anthropology. Similarly, Schleiermacher interacted extensively with both philosophical and psychological resources as he sought to understand the nature of religious experience and its distinctively christological aspects. Even Karl Barth, who is often criticized for emphasizing Christology in a way that requires theology to ignore the insights of nontheological perspectives entirely, got into the act.[3] Although Barth argued that it is impossible for nontheological perspectives to arrive at any knowledge of "true" humanity (i.e., humanity as it stands before God through participation in the election of Jesus), he allowed considerable room for such perspectives to analyze the "phenomena of the human," by which he meant those aspects of humanity available for study by these other disciplines (e.g., biology).[4] These examples suggest that at least some of our theologians recognized that we can make a considerable range of true statements about humanity without direct appeal to Christology by drawing on the resources provided by these other disciplines.

We could say something similar about how other theological loci contribute to our understanding of the human person. Each of our case studies clearly involved a complex interplay of multiple theological issues besides Christology, including but not limited to theology proper, soteriology, pneumatology, hamartiology, ecclesiology, and eschatology. Indeed, I suspect that we have touched on nearly all of the major doctrinal loci at some point in these various studies. Clearly, then, none of our theologians develops his or her anthropology with Christology as the exclusive doctrinal source, as though we could derive a comprehensive understanding of the human person in isolation from these broader theological concerns.

---

3. For more on this interaction, see Marc Cortez, *Embodied Souls, Ensouled Bodies: An Exercise in Christological Anthropology and Its Significance for the Mind/Body Debate* (London: T&T Clark, 2008), chapter 3.

4. See *CD* III/2, §44.2.

What, then, is the unique contribution of Christology in these *christological* anthropologies? Is Christology simply one of many voices (theological and nontheological) that can and should inform our understanding of humanity? Or is there something distinct about the role that Christology plays within this anthropological mix? For the authors in this study, at least, I think we can answer these questions in favor of the latter. Although a *complete* picture of humanity—especially the humanity that exists in the concrete particularity of this broken world—requires a range of theological and nontheological perspectives beyond that of Christology, each of our authors presents knowledge of true humanity as something that is shaped uniquely by the person and work of Jesus Christ. This provides the integrative center of their theological anthropologies, into which they incorporate additional information about the human person. Thus, for example, Julian of Norwich was certainly willing to affirm that we can derive significant knowledge about humanity from the broken humanity that we observe in the world around us, and she also recognized the importance of doctrines like the Trinity, providence, and the church for developing a comprehensive vision of humanity. Yet, in the end, she still identified the core truth of what it really meant to be human as something that we could only see in the light of the self-sacrificing love of the incarnate Lord/Servant. This then provides the integrative vision with which all other perspectives on the human person must cohere.

In their own way, each of our theologians develops a similar christological center for their theological anthropologies. We have Barth vehemently rejecting any anthropological proposal that does not cohere with the "God who is for us in Jesus Christ," Cone offering similarly harsh critiques of any anthropology that does not have liberating action at its center, Luther refusing to countenance views of humanity that do not prioritize the fact that we stand before God by faith alone, Schleiermacher dismissing anthropologies that cannot account for the actualization and mediation of Jesus' unique God-consciousness, Gregory renouncing those who think they can understand true humanity by observing humans as they currently exist, and Zizioulas presenting lengthy critiques of those who try to derive concepts of human personhood that are disconnected from the true human personhood that we only see in Jesus himself. For each of these theologians, Christology defines in some important way the fundamental truth of what it means to be human. That christological core does not say *everything* that needs to be said about humanity. Non-christological perspectives are important, maybe even essential, for developing anthropologies that are both broad and deep, adequate to the complexity of the subject matter. Nonetheless, they cannot tell us about what it means to be human at the most fundamental level. Consequently, they must be interpreted, even interrogated, by the christological center of theological anthropology.

In other words, the fact that these anthropologies are *christological* does not entail the conclusion that they are *christomonistic*. None of these figures approaches the anthropological task as though Christology was the *only* appropriate source of information about what it means to be human. That cannot be the case given the wealth of additional material they use to develop a robust view of humanity. Instead, their anthropologies build on the conviction that Jesus reveals that which is most fundamental to understanding the true nature of humanity. That is the christological center of their anthropological vision.

SOME TERMINOLOGICAL REFINEMENT

If the above summary is correct, then these case studies also suggest that we need to revise our initial definition of what constitutes a christological anthropology. In the introduction, I offered the following minimal definition: "A *minimally* christological anthropology is one in which (1) Christology warrants important claims about what it means to be human and (2) the scope of those claims goes beyond issues like the image of God and ethics." And there is an important sense in which our case studies have confirmed this as a useful starting point. Each of our theologians clearly made a number of important claims about humanity that they thought were in some way justified by their respective Christologies. (I will say more about the "in some way" part of that sentence in a moment.) Additionally, the scope of the resulting anthropological claims clearly went beyond, while still including, issues relative to the image of God and ethics. Both parts of our initial definition, then, proved sufficiently broad to encompass all of our representative case studies, while remaining sufficiently narrow to exclude at least some approaches to theological anthropology.

At the same time, though, the studies in this book suggest that a stronger definition of christological anthropology might also be justified. As I have just argued, each of these theologians presents Jesus as the revelation of true humanity in such a way that Christology informs what is *most fundamental* to being truly human. If that is the case, though, at least the first part of our definition needs strengthening. These theologians are not simply making a series of "important" claims about humanity on the basis of their Christology, as though these anthropological claims could be placed alongside other *equally important* claims derived from other sources. Instead, it seems to be the case that each of our theologians is trying to describe that which is *ultimately* important about what it means to be human. And they think these ultimate claims are in some way justified by their corresponding Christologies. Thus, while it is true that some of their anthropological claims might qualify as merely important in the weaker sense, the real focus of these christological anthropologies seems to press toward something deeper. To capture more adequately this stronger notion of what constitutes a christological anthropology, we need to revise at least the first part of our definition to include the notion that Christology warrants *ultimate* claims about true humanity.

Similarly, these case studies also raise questions about the strength of the second half of our minimal definition. As I argued in the previous section, these ultimate claims about humanity provide the christological core of their anthropologies that consequently function as the hermeneutical lens through which other anthropological data needs to be filtered and the overall framework into which such data must be integrated. However, if this is the case, it would seem that the scope of such a christological anthropology is necessarily comprehensive. *All* data about the human person should be interpreted in light of this christological vision of the human person. That does not render impotent the insights of the nontheological disciplines, as though their function is merely to repeat what has already been established on christological grounds. Other disciplines will certainly offer information and insight not available from any other perspective. The comprehensiveness of these christological anthropologies is not one that excludes or dominates other voices. Nonetheless, it seems inherent to these projects that anthropological data will necessarily be filtered through the christological lens. Thus, the second half of our definition needs to be strengthened to address the comprehensive scope of these christological anthropologies.

We thus end up with a distinction between stronger and weaker forms of christological anthropology. Or, because such terminology may suggest an implicitly evaluative stance, we can distinguish between *minimal* and *comprehensive* christological anthropologies.[5] The resulting definitions look like this:

---

5. I considered using "maximal" as the appropriate counterpart to "minimal" in this context. Yet "maximal" seemed to carry with it the connotation that such anthropologies are claiming to be as thoroughly christological as possible. Yet it does not seem that our representative theologians are claiming anything quite so robust.

- A *minimally* christological anthropology is one in which (1) Christology warrants important claims about what it means to be human and (2) the scope of those claims goes beyond issues like the image of God and ethics.
- A *comprehensively* christological anthropology is one in which (1) Christology warrants ultimate claims about true humanity such that (2) the scope of those claims applies to all anthropological data.

Both of these definitions would still stand in contrast to theological anthropologies in which Christology does not warrant important claims about being human or in which the scope of that christological analysis is sharply limited.

With this distinction in hand, we can see that all of the case studies as I have presented them qualify as examples of comprehensively christological anthropologies. All of these theologians made ultimate claims about what constitutes true humanity, and they used those claims to assess and integrate non-christological perspectives. The primary question not clearly addressed in these studies is whether these theologians would all have affirmed the comprehensive scope of their christological anthropologies. Since I intentionally limited each case study to a single anthropological issue, we need to extrapolate from how these theologians addressed those particular issues to draw conclusions about how they would have applied their christological frameworks to other issues. Although I do not have space to develop this argument in full, it seems likely to me that each of these theologians would agree that their christological vision of the human person provides an overarching framework for understanding all anthropological issues and data. I find it highly unlikely that any of these theologians would have countenanced the idea that some aspect of human life was beyond the reach of their christological vision such that it could be understood and addressed independently of that framework. Indeed, several of our theologians explicitly rejected any such attempt (Luther, Barth, and Cone), and the christological logic employed by most of the others suggests a similar conclusion.[6]

---

6. We would need to nuance "comprehensive" to some extent for Schleiermacher's anthropology. On the one hand, Schleiermacher clearly presents his understanding of the human person as a comprehensive reality, something that describes and addresses humanity as a whole, not merely certain aspects of humanity. At the same time, though, Schleiermacher's theological method in general allows for the validity of alternative theological constructions (see Catherine L. Kelsey, *Thinking about Christ with Schleiermacher* [Louisville:

Of course, some might still disagree with the way in which I have presented our various theologians, arguing that one or more exemplifies the more limited goals of a minimally christological anthropology. Some might even want to develop the stronger argument that one or more fails to satisfy the requirements of even a minimally christological anthropology. Thus, for example, anyone who remains unconvinced by the argument I presented for the essentially christological structure of Schleiermacher's theology will likely reject my conclusion that his anthropology qualifies as comprehensively christological in the sense defined above. Similarly, if someone concludes that Schleiermacher's Christology is itself driven by a general theology of religion generated by Schleiermacher's understanding of universal religious experience, thus entailing that his claims about humanity are not in fact warranted primarily by Christology, they will probably be inclined to argue that his anthropology fails to be even minimally christological. Although we would, in these cases, disagree about the best interpretation of Schleiermacher's anthropology, such a disagreement would not affect the basic definitions offered above. We would simply be disagreeing about whether Schleiermacher's anthropology qualifies as *minimally* christological, *comprehensively* christological, or merely theological.

WARRANTED "IN SOME WAY"

In the previous section, I argued that each of the theologians in this study made claims about humanity that were "in some way justified by their respective Christologies." It is time to explore that "in some way" a bit more. Yet as I noted in the introduction, questions of what constitutes proper "warrant" are among the thornier issues in contemporary epistemology. And it would take us far beyond the scope of this study to develop any robust sense of what qualifies as warrant in a christological anthropology. Not only that, but it may well end up doing injustice to the anthropologies under consideration. None of our representative theologians felt any need to explain what justifies or grounds their anthropological conclusions. Karl Barth came the closest with his discussion of how one moves indirectly from Christology to anthropology. Yet even in Barth's more nuanced method, there is an epistemological gap between

---

Westminster John Knox, 2003], 36–41), which would seem to apply to anthropology as well. By allowing for alternate and equally valid ways of understanding the human person, even if Schleiermacher's anthropology is comprehensive within his own system, it would not be absolutely comprehensive.

his second and third steps. How exactly do we move from christological claims (step 2) to anthropological claims (step 3) in such a way that the anthropological claims are clearly warranted by their christological ground? Despite wrestling explicitly with the relationship between Christology and anthropology, Barth never raised the question. Thus, even our most methodologically robust example of a christological anthropology never engages the question of precisely *how* Christology warrants anthropological claims. My concern, then, is that an overemphasis on epistemological or methodological precision at this point may well distract from the primary focus of these anthropologies.

Nonetheless, it seems difficult to avoid the conclusion that each of these theologians thought there was a real, logical relationship between their Christologies and their anthropological claims. When Gregory argued from the union of the divine and the human in Jesus Christ to his transformative understanding of human nature, he clearly thought that the former provided warrant in some way for the latter. In other words, his anthropological claim was only true *in virtue of* the truth of his christological claim. Granted, Gregory never offered an epistemologically deep explanation of this "in virtue of" relationship. Instead, he seemed to be operating with a theological intuition about the relationship between such claims. We could say the same about the other theologians in this study. Rather than focusing on methodological issues, they simply developed christological visions that drove their robust anthropologies.

We should also be careful about thinking that the relationship between Christology and anthropology in these case studies is such that particular anthropological proposals are directly warranted by specific christological claims. Although we might be able to point to instances in which one of our theologians argued in a straightforward way that christological claim P warrants anthropological claim X, the connections are often less clear. Instead, it seems more accurate to say that each of our theologians developed a broad christological vision that in turn served to provide warrant for anthropological proposals, though in ways that may be difficult to pin down in the precise language of modern epistemology. Thus, for example, Cone's vision of Christ as the great Liberator provides tremendous explanatory power for his anthropology, on the basis of which he makes a whole range of claims about the shape of true humanity in the world today. Yet it is difficult to find him arguing precisely that because Jesus was A we must be X, unless we restrict ourselves to highly abstract formulations like "Because Jesus sought the freedom of the oppressed we should also seek the freedom of the oppressed." When we look to his more specific proposals about what this entails, we find less precise forms of argument. Instead of tight logical connections between christological and anthropological claims, Cone operates out of an overall vision of Jesus Christ that warrants a range of specific proposals for how that christological vision sheds light on humanity in general.

Additionally, we need to recognize that none of this means that Christology *exclusively* warrants these anthropological proposals. It is entirely possible for even a comprehensively christological anthropology to make anthropological proposals in which those proposals receive additional warrant from other doctrines or from nontheological sources. Thus, for example, Cone makes claims about liberating action that receive at least some of their warrant from sources like Marxist political theory and the sociology of knowledge. One could similarly argue that Schleiermacher's emphasis on God-consciousness receives additional warrant from the philosophical and psychological traditions of his day. Indeed, I think it is difficult to escape the conclusion that all of these anthropologies receive at least some of their warrant from the sociocultural venues in which they were articulated. For the purposes of this proposal, though, the key is the nature of the warrant. As I have described these theological anthropologies, the kind of warrant provided by Christology is unique because Christology alone reveals the ultimate truth of humanity; consequently, it alone is the hermeneutical lens through which all other anthropological perspectives must be filtered.[7]

This has implications not only for understanding the nature of a christological anthropology, but also for the task of disagreeing with one. If the above description is accurate, it would be a mistake to think that the way to refute the anthropological claims of these christological anthropologies is to find and revise the precise christological claim that generated the relevant anthropological error. There may be times when the difficulty is so easily resolved. More often, though, revising these anthropological conclusions will require a more comprehensive look at the overall christological imagination in which that anthropological conclusion seemed warranted and the ways in which that Christology may have been used to interpret and integrate other relevant data. For

---

7. The picture is also complicated by the fact that each theologian's christological vision must itself be warranted in some way; i.e., there is some other basis on which they believe their christological proposals to be true. However, that is a question for another study.

example, I imagine that many will find Gregory's argument for the temporally limited nature of human sexuality somewhat unsatisfying. Yet it is difficult to pin that conclusion to any particular christological claim that one could revise as a way of retaining his overall christological vision while maintaining that we remain sexed beings in the resurrection. You could revise his conclusion by arguing for a larger dose of his own apophaticism—in other words, you could argue that given his transformative vision of human nature in the incarnation, he should have remained agnostic about the precise nature of human sexuality in the eschaton. Yet such an agnostic position would still leave you unable to make strong statements about the enduring fundamentality of sexuality. Thus, if you wanted to argue for something along these lines, it would seem to require either a more significant revision of the christological vision that led to that conclusion or an analysis of the ways in which Gregory used that christological vision to interpret relevant data, like, for example, his reading of particular biblical texts.

In sum, even if we say that both minimal and comprehensive christological anthropologies require that anthropological proposals be warranted by Christology, this does not commit us to any particular understanding of what constitutes proper warrant,[8] nor does it require that we envision the relationship in such a way that particular anthropological conclusions must be warranted by specific christological claims. Instead, a better description of the relationship between Christology and anthropology in these case studies would focus on the ways in which these theologians used their broad visions of Jesus' person and work to warrant claims about human persons in general.

SOTERIOLOGICAL UNIVERSALISM VS. ANTHROPOLOGICAL EXCLUSIVISM

One of the interesting repeated themes in these various studies is the tension between anthropological exclusivism and soteriological universalism. In other words, some of our studies defined true humanity in ways that seemed to exclude potentially large numbers of humans from being actually (or, at least fully) human. Thus, for example, Zizioulas's account of human personhood seems to entail the conclusion that not all humans are persons. Since personhood is essential to being fully human on his account, this entails the corresponding conclusion that not all humans

---

8. Or if these proposals do require a particular understanding of what constitutes proper warrant, that is also a task for another study.

are fully human. Similarly, Luther's argument that true humanity only occurs as people stand in right relationship with God seems to entail the corresponding conclusion that only Christians are truly human.

For many, though, such a restriction of terms like "full humanity" and "person" to only certain segments of the human race will come across as inherently problematic for a host of moral and ethical reasons. At the very least such language may appear to denigrate the value and significance of all humans, and similar language has been used historically to dehumanize entire groups of humans, contributing to devastating realities like slavery and the Holocaust. Thus, many shy away from any language suggesting that humanity and personhood are degreed properties, something that you can possess in greater or lesser quantities. Instead, they prefer to view such concepts as categorical realities. Either you are human or you are not. For such conceptions of humanity, the apparent anthropological exclusivism of several of our case studies raises significant questions.

Yet other case studies leaned strongly toward some kind of universalism. Although few went as far as Schleiermacher in openly embracing universalism, several developed their christological anthropologies in ways that left universalism as an open question (especially Gregory, Julian, Barth, and maybe Cone). This universalistic tendency appears to stem from how they understand the relationship between Christology and anthropology. Although each construes that relationship differently, they share certain common features. First, they all base their christological anthropologies on the conviction that Jesus somehow reveals the ultimate truth of what it really means to be human. To derive that claim, though, they need to explain how Jesus is related to the humanity of all other human persons in such a way as to warrant the universal claim that he reveals what it means to be human for *all* human persons. Their respective explanations of how Jesus is related to the humanity of all other human persons is precisely what generates the question of universalism. For example, according to Gregory, Jesus is related to all other humans because in the incarnation he assumed the nature that is common to all humans. Yet the assumption of human nature is also the means by which Jesus heals and saves human persons, thus generating the question of universalism. Similarly, Barth relates Jesus to all humans through the doctrine of election, which is also the ground of his soteriology. Julian does the same with her ontology of love, and Cone's theology raises many of the same questions with his emphasis on Jesus working for the freedom of all human persons. However, without these explanations for how Jesus is connected to all other humans, it is not clear how their systems can justify deriving general anthropological truths from the particular humanity of Jesus Christ. Rather than just being a historic coincidence, then, the prevalence of universalism among our various case studies seems to be importantly related to the project of developing certain kinds of christological anthropologies.

Consequently, from our representative case studies it seems that christological anthropology is caught between anthropological exclusivism and soteriological universalism. Those willing to deny the full humanity of at least some human beings or affirm the ultimate salvation of all human beings will not find this a difficult choice. Anyone who wants to avoid either of these alternatives, however, would seem caught in a difficult bind. How do we explain the relationship between Jesus and the humanity of all other human persons in such a way that we can ground the claim that Jesus truly reveals what it means to be human, without at the same time suggesting that all human persons will eventually be saved through that same relationship? There may well be ways of answering that question without having to choose either horn in this apparent dilemma. If so, that solution did not arise in any of our respective studies and remains a task for a future christological anthropology.

CONCLUSION TO THE CONCLUSION

This chapter opened with a quotation from Jürgen Moltmann about the fact that humans are the only creatures who wrestle with fundamental questions of identity. "A cow is always simply a cow. It does not ask, 'What is a cow? Who am I?' Only man asks such questions, and indeed clearly has to ask them about himself and his being. This is his question. His question follows him in hundreds of forms."[9] Since I have never engaged in significant conversation with a cow, I will have to take Moltmann's word that this is an accurate description of bovine mentality. Yet his anthropological point stands. The question of the human arises in countless ways: in the mirror, during worship, through the history of oppression, at the mall, in the face of the homeless. Whenever we are at our most mindful, we face the ambiguity of our own existence.

The fundamental intuition in each of these case studies, though, is that we are not a question without answer. Somehow, despite the

---

9. Moltmann, *Man: Christian Anthropology in the Conflicts of the Present*, 1.

apparent impossibility, the answer arrived in the form of one particular human. As Mary Hilkert affirms, "Christians believe that not only the mystery of the divine, but also the deepest truths about human life and destiny, have been revealed in Jesus Christ."[10] And yet, this answer arrives with its own questions: *Who* is Jesus? *How* do we derive knowledge about humanity in general from this one individual? *Where* should we focus our attention in trying to see Jesus and his anthropological significance? *What* issues does this help us understand more clearly? Each of our case studies wrestled with these questions, convinced that a christological vision is necessary for a theologically adequate understanding of the human person. That is what binds these case studies into a coherent whole. Yet each also demonstrated the continued diversity within this common conviction. As we have seen, these are questions without easy answers, and each answer shapes the resulting vision of humanity in important ways.

This diversity resulted not only from differences within their respective Christologies, but also from differences in the questions, challenges, and insights generated by their respective social locations. Since we have seen that theological anthropology can be *thoroughly* christological without being *exclusively* christological, such additional factors play an important role in the overall construction of one's vision of humanity. Thus, although these studies have emphasized the fundamental significance of Christology throughout, we do not need to downplay, for example, the significance of Greek philosophy for Gregory, the devastating plagues that shaped medieval England in Julian's day, and the civil rights movement for Cone. Each of these theologians developed his or her christological anthropology in particular cultural contexts that inevitably contributed to the resulting anthropological vision.

If we want to continue pursuing such christological anthropologies today, it seems that there are several ways in which we might proceed. We could stay within the territory mapped by these case studies by adopting the same basic approach as one of our representative theologians and apply it to issues yet unaddressed. Thus, for example, we might see how Nyssa's transformative vision of humanity relates to the issues raised by the transhumanist movement. Or we could bring Zizioulas's christologi-

---

10. Mary Catherine Hilkert, "Cry Beloved Image: Rethinking the Image of God," in *In the Embrace of God: Feminist Approaches to Theological Anthropology*, ed. Ann Elizabeth O'Hara Graff (Maryknoll, N.Y.: Orbis, 1995), 201.

cal personhood into dialogue with the conceptions of personhood that drive so much of modern legal discourse. Extending the territory somewhat, we could pursue the possibility mentioned earlier of combining elements of these christological anthropologies in new and interesting ways. Julian's ontology of love seems ripe for integration with Cone's liberating Christ, but it would also be interesting to draw on Luther's grace-based anthropology, particularly as it relates to vocation, as a way of further deepening our understanding of what it means to act for the sake of human flourishing. I am sure an entire range of interesting projects awaits in the intersections between these various dialogue partners. But of course, we are not limited to the possibilities suggested by these seven studies. Their very diversity almost demands that we continue exploring the relationship between Christology and anthropology in ways that will certainly lead to new proposals today. This is especially critical in light of the fact that each generation arrives with its own questions and issues, needing to wrestle anew with how we understand our humanity in light of Jesus. My next book will press more deeply into some of these issues, drawing on these historical dialogue partners as resources for developing christological anthropologies today.

In the end, these case studies suggest that the question of the human remains. Even if we affirm that Jesus is the ultimate answer to this question, we have not yet, and probably will not ever, arrive at a final and complete understanding of that answer. Jesus is an answer that leads to more questions—better and deeper questions, perhaps, but questions nonetheless. Even if we affirm that "the mystery of man reveals itself fully only in the light of Christ,"[11] the mystery remains.

---

11. John D. Zizioulas, "Human Capacity and Human Incapacity: A Theological Exploration of Personhood," in *Communion and Otherness: Further Studies in Personhood and the Church* (New York: T&T Clark, 2006), 237.

Select Bibliography

Abbott, Christopher. *Julian of Norwich: Autobiography and Theology.* Studies in Medieval Mysticism. Cambridge: D. S. Brewer, 1999.

Adams, Marilyn McCord. "Julian of Norwich on the Tender Loving Care of Mother Jesus." In *Our Knowledge of God,* 197–213. Dordrecht, Netherlands: Kluwer, 1992.

Althaus, Paul. *The Theology of Martin Luther.* Philadelphia: Fortress, 1966.

Anderson, Ray Sherman. *On Being Human: Essays in Theological Anthropology.* Grand Rapids: Eerdmans, 1982.

Anderson, Victor. *Beyond Ontological Blackness: An Essay on African American Religious and Cultural Criticism.* New York: Continuum, 1995.

Awad, Najeeb G. "Between Subordination and Koinonia: Toward a New Reading of the Cappadocian Theology." *Modern Theology* 23, no. 2 (2007): 181–204.

Ayres, Lewis. "On Not Three People: The Fundamental Themes of Gregory of Nyssa's Trinitarian Theology as Seen in 'To Ablabius: On Not Three Gods.'" In *Rethinking Gregory of Nyssa,* edited by Sarah Coakley, 15–44. Oxford: Blackwell, 2003.

Baker, Denise Nowakowski. *Julian of Norwich's Showings: From Vision to Book.* Princeton, N.J.: Princeton University Press, 1994.

Baker-Fletcher, Garth. "Black Theology and the Holy Spirit." In *The Cambridge Companion to Black Theology,* edited by Edward P. Antonio and Dwight N. Hopkins, 111–25. New York: Cambridge University Press, 2012.

Balthasar, Hans Urs von. *The Theology of Karl Barth.* Translated by Edward T. Oakes, S.J. San Francisco: Communio, 1992.

Barash, David P., and Judith Eve Lipton. *Gender Gap: The Biology of Male-Female Differences.* New Brunswick, N.J.: Transaction, 2002.

Barth, Karl. *Church Dogmatics*. Edited by G. W. Bromiley and T. F. Torrance. 13 vols. Edinburgh: T&T Clark, 1956–1975.

———. *Protestant Theology in the Nineteenth Century: Its Background and History*. Grand Rapids: Eerdmans, 2002.

———. *The Theology of Schleiermacher*. Edited by Dietrich Ritschl. Grand Rapids: Eerdmans, 1982.

Bauerschmidt, Frederick C. "Julian of Norwich—Incorporated." *Modern Theology* 13, no. 1 (1997): 75–100.

———. "Order, Freedom, and 'Kindness': Julian of Norwich on the Edge of Modernity." *Theology Today* 60, no. 1 (2003): 63–81.

Bayer, Oswald. "Being in the Image of God." *Lutheran Quarterly* 27, no. 1 (2013): 76–88.

———. *Living by Faith: Justification and Sanctification*. Grand Rapids: Eerdmans, 2003.

Beeley, Christopher A. "The Early Christological Controversy: Apollinarius, Diodore, and Gregory Nazianzen." *Vigiliae Christianae* 65, no. 4 (2011): 376–407.

Behr, John. "The Rational Animal: A Rereading of Gregory of Nyssa's De Hominis Opificio." *Journal of Early Christian Studies* 7, no. 2 (1999): 219–47.

Behrens, Georg. "Feeling of Absolute Dependence or Absolute Feeling of Dependence? (What Schleiermacher Really Said and Why It Matters)." *Religious Studies* 34, no. 4 (1998): 471–81.

Beiser, Frederick C. "Schleiermacher's Ethics." In *The Cambridge Companion to Friedrich Schleiermacher*, edited by Jacqueline Mariña, 53–72. New York: Cambridge University Press, 2005.

Bell, Theo. "Man Is a Microcosmos: Adam and Eve in Luther's Lectures on Genesis (1535–1545)." *Concordia Theological Quarterly* 69, no. 2 (2005): 159–84.

Boersma, Hans. *Embodiment and Virtue in Gregory of Nyssa: An Anagogical Approach*. New York: Oxford University Press, 2013.

Børresen, Kari Elisabeth. "God's Image, Man's Image? Patristic Interpretation of Gen 1,27 and I Cor 11,7." In *Image of God and Gender Models in Judaeo-Christian Tradition*, 188–207. Oslo: Solum Forlag, 1991.

Boyd, George N. "Schleiermacher: On Relating Man and Nature." *Encounter* 36, no. 1 (1975): 10–19.

Braaten, Carl E., and Robert W. Jenson, eds. *Union with Christ: The New Finnish Interpretation of Luther.* Grand Rapids: Eerdmans, 1998.

Brown, Alan. "On the Criticism of *Being as Communion* in Anglophone Orthodox Theology." In *The Theology of John Zizioulas: Personhood and the Church*, edited by Douglas H. Knight, 35–78. Aldershot: Ashgate, 2007.

Brown, Michael Joseph. "Black Theology and the Bible." In *The Cambridge Companion to Black Theology*, edited by Edward P. Antonio and Dwight N. Hopkins, 169–83. New York: Cambridge University Press, 2012.

Brown, Peter. "Marriage and Mortality: Gregory of Nyssa." In *The Body and Society: Men, Women, and Sexual Renunciation in Early Christianity*, 285–304. New York: Columbia University Press, 1988.

Burrow, Rufus. *James H. Cone and Black Liberation Theology.* Jefferson, N.C.: McFarland & Co., 1994.

Burrus, Virginia. "Queer Father: Gregory of Nyssa and the Subversion of Identity." In *Queer Theology*, 147–62. Oxford: Blackwell, 2007.

Bynum, Caroline Walker. *Jesus as Mother: Studies in the Spirituality of the High Middle Ages.* Berkeley: University of California Press, 1982.

Chike, Chigor. "Black Christology for the Twenty-First Century." *Black Theology* 8, no. 3 (2010): 357–78.

Ciraulo, Jonathan Martin. "Sacraments and Personhood: John Zizioulas's Impasse and a Way Forward." *Heythrop Journal* 53, no. 6 (2012): 993–1004.

Clark, R. Scott. "*Iustitia Imputata Christi*: Alien or Proper to Luther's Doctrine of Justification?" *Concordia Theological Quarterly* 70, no. 3–4 (2006): 269–310.

Clarke, F. Stuart. "Christocentric Developments in the Reformed Doctrine of Predestination." *Churchman* 98, no. 3 (1984): 229–45.

Cleage, Albert B. *The Black Messiah.* New York: Sheed and Ward, 1968.

Clements, K. W. *Friedrich Schleiermacher: Pioneer of Modern Theology.* The Making of Modern Theology. London: Collins, 1987.

Coakley, Sarah. "The Eschatological Body: Gender, Transformation, and God." *Modern Theology* 16, no. 1 (2000): 61–73.

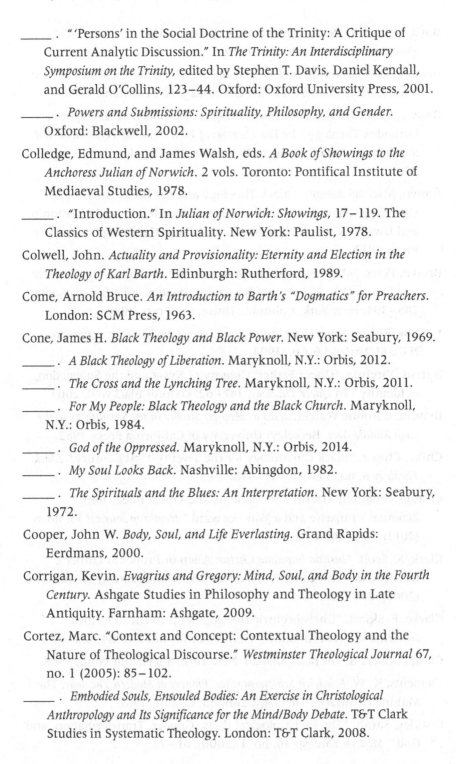

_____ . " 'Persons' in the Social Doctrine of the Trinity: A Critique of Current Analytic Discussion." In *The Trinity: An Interdisciplinary Symposium on the Trinity*, edited by Stephen T. Davis, Daniel Kendall, and Gerald O'Collins, 123–44. Oxford: Oxford University Press, 2001.

_____ . *Powers and Submissions: Spirituality, Philosophy, and Gender.* Oxford: Blackwell, 2002.

Colledge, Edmund, and James Walsh, eds. *A Book of Showings to the Anchoress Julian of Norwich.* 2 vols. Toronto: Pontifical Institute of Mediaeval Studies, 1978.

_____ . "Introduction." In *Julian of Norwich: Showings*, 17–119. The Classics of Western Spirituality. New York: Paulist, 1978.

Colwell, John. *Actuality and Provisionality: Eternity and Election in the Theology of Karl Barth.* Edinburgh: Rutherford, 1989.

Come, Arnold Bruce. *An Introduction to Barth's "Dogmatics" for Preachers.* London: SCM Press, 1963.

Cone, James H. *Black Theology and Black Power.* New York: Seabury, 1969.

_____ . *A Black Theology of Liberation.* Maryknoll, N.Y.: Orbis, 2012.

_____ . *The Cross and the Lynching Tree.* Maryknoll, N.Y.: Orbis, 2011.

_____ . *For My People: Black Theology and the Black Church.* Maryknoll, N.Y.: Orbis, 1984.

_____ . *God of the Oppressed.* Maryknoll, N.Y.: Orbis, 2014.

_____ . *My Soul Looks Back.* Nashville: Abingdon, 1982.

_____ . *The Spirituals and the Blues: An Interpretation.* New York: Seabury, 1972.

Cooper, John W. *Body, Soul, and Life Everlasting.* Grand Rapids: Eerdmans, 2000.

Corrigan, Kevin. *Evagrius and Gregory: Mind, Soul, and Body in the Fourth Century.* Ashgate Studies in Philosophy and Theology in Late Antiquity. Farnham: Ashgate, 2009.

Cortez, Marc. "Context and Concept: Contextual Theology and the Nature of Theological Discourse." *Westminster Theological Journal* 67, no. 1 (2005): 85–102.

_____ . *Embodied Souls, Ensouled Bodies: An Exercise in Christological Anthropology and Its Significance for the Mind/Body Debate.* T&T Clark Studies in Systematic Theology. London: T&T Clark, 2008.

_____. "The Madness in Our Method: Christology as the Necessary Starting Point for Theological Anthropology." In *The Ashgate Companion to Theological Anthropology*, edited by Joshua Ryan Farris and Charles Taliaferro, 15–26. Aldershot: Ashgate, 2015.

_____. "What Does It Mean to Call Karl Barth a 'Christocentric' Theologian?" *Scottish Journal of Theology* 60, no. 2 (2007): 127–43.

Crossley, John P. Jr. "Schleiermacher's Christian Ethics in Relation to His Philosophical Ethics." *Annual of the Society of Christian Ethics* 18 (1998): 93–117.

Cunningham, Mary Kathleen. *What Is Theological Exegesis? Interpretation and Use of Scripture in Barth's Doctrine of Election*. Valley Forge, Pa.: Trinity Press, 1995.

Daley, Brian E. "Divine Transcendence and Human Transformation: Gregory of Nyssa's Anti-Apollinarian Christology." In *Rethinking Gregory of Nyssa*, edited by Sarah Coakley, 67–76. Oxford: Blackwell, 2003.

_____. " 'The Human Form Divine': Christ's Risen Body and Ours according to Gregory of Nyssa." In *Studia Patristica Vol. 41*, 301–18. Leuven: Peeters, 2006.

Dearborn, Kerry. "The Crucified Christ as the Motherly God: The Theology of Julian of Norwich." *Scottish Journal of Theology* 55, no. 3 (2002): 283–302.

Del Mastro, M. L., ed. *The Revelation of Divine Love in Sixteen Showings Made to Dame Julian of Norwich*. Liguori, Mo: Triumph, 1994.

Dennis, Thomas J. "Gregory on the Resurrection of the Body." In *Easter Sermons of Gregory of Nyssa*, 55–80. Cambridge, Mass.: Philadelphia Patristic Foundation, 1981.

DeVries, Dawn, and B. A. Gerrish. "Providence and Grace: Schleiermacher on Justification and Election." In *The Cambridge Companion to Friedrich Schleiermacher*, edited by Jacqueline Mariña, 189–207. New York: Cambridge University Press, 2005.

Dinshaw, Carolyn, David Wallace, and Nicholas Watson, eds. "Julian of Norwich." In *The Cambridge Companion to Medieval Women's Writing*, 210–21. New York: Cambridge University Press, 2003.

Dragas, George D. "The Anti-Apollinarist Christology of St Gregory of Nyssa: A First Analysis." *Greek Orthodox Theological Review* 42, no. 3–4 (1997): 299–314.

Driel, Edwin Chr. van. *Incarnation Anyway: Arguments for Supralapsarian Christology*. New York: Oxford University Press, 2008.

Duffy, Stephen. *The Dynamics of Grace*. Collegeville, Minn.: Liturgical, 1993.

Duke, David Nelson. "Schleiermacher: Theology without a Fall." *Perspectives in Religious Studies* 9, no. 1 (1982): 21–37.

Eagly, Alice H., Anne E. Beall, and Robert J. Sternberg, eds. *The Psychology of Gender*. New York: Guilford, 2004.

Ebeling, Gerhard. *Luther: An Introduction to His Thought*. Philadelphia: Fortress, 1970.

––––––. "Luther's Understanding of Reality." Translated by Scott A. Celsor. *Lutheran Quarterly* 27, no. 1 (2013): 56–75.

Elgendy, Rick. "Reconsidering Resurrection, Incarnation and Nature in Schleiermacher's Glaubenslehre." *International Journal of Systematic Theology* 15, no. 3 (2013): 301–23.

Ellis, Ralph. "Consciousness, Self-Organization, and the Process-Substratum Relation: Rethinking Nonreductive Physicalism." *Philosophical Quarterly* 13, no. 2 (2000): 173–90.

Erickson, Millard J. *Christian Theology*. Grand Rapids: Baker, 1998.

Evans, Jr., James. "Black Theology and Black Feminism." *Journal of Religious Thought* 38, no. 2 (1981): 43–53.

Feinberg, John S. "Luther's Doctrine of Vocation: Some Problems of Interpretation and Application." *Fides et Historia* 12, no. 1 (1979): 50–67.

Fermer, Richard M. "The Limits of Trinitarian Theology as a Methodological Paradigm." *Neue Zeitschrift für Systematische Theologie und Religionsphilosophie* 41, no. 2 (1999): 158–86.

Finlay, Hueston E. " 'Feeling of Absolute Dependence' 'Absolute Feeling of Dependence'? A Question Revisited." *Religious Studies* 41, no. 1 (2005): 81–94.

Fiorenza, Francis Schüssler. "Schleiermacher's Understanding of God as Triune." In *The Cambridge Companion to Friedrich Schleiermacher*, edited by Jacqueline Mariña, 171–88. New York: Cambridge University Press, 2005.

Fisher, Simon. *Revelatory Positivism? Barth's Earliest Theology and the Marburg School*. New York: Oxford University Press, 1988.

Forde, Gerhard O. *Justification by Faith: A Matter of Death and Life.* Philadelphia: Fortress, 1982.

Froehlich, Karlfried. "Luther on Vocation." *Lutheran Quarterly* 13, no. 2 (1999): 195–207.

Gatta, Julia. "Julian of Norwich: Theodicy as Pastoral Art." *Anglican Theological Review* 63, no. 2 (1981): 173–81.

Gockel, Matthias. *Barth and Schleiermacher on the Doctrine of Election: A Systematic-Theological Comparison.* New York: Oxford University Press, 2006.

Greer, Rowan A. *Christian Life and Christian Hope: Raids on the Inarticulate.* New York: Crossroad, 2001.

Gregersen, Niels Henrik. "Grace in Nature and History: Luther's Doctrine of Creation Revisited." *Dialog* 44, no. 1 (2005): 19–29.

Gregory of Nyssa. *The Life of Saint Macrina.* Translated by Kevin Corrigan. Eugene, Ore.: Wipf & Stock, 2005.

_____. *On the Making of Man.* In *A Select Library of the Nicene and Post-Nicene Fathers*, edited by Philip Schaff, second series, volume 5. Grand Rapids: Eerdmans, 1978.

_____. *On the Soul and the Resurrection: St Gregory of Nyssa.* Crestwood, N.Y.: St. Vladimir's Seminary Press, 1993.

Grenz, Stanley J. *The Social God and the Relational Self: A Trinitarian Theology of the Imago Dei.* Louisville: Westminster John Knox, 2001.

Groppe, Elizabeth T. "Creation Ex Nihilo and Ex Amore: Ontological Freedom in the Theologies of John Zizioulas and Catherine Mowry LaCugna." *Modern Theology* 21, no. 3 (2005): 463–96.

Hagen, Kenneth. "A Critique of Wingren on Luther on Vocation." *Lutheran Quarterly* 16, no. 3 (2002): 249–73.

Hägglund, Bengt. *The Background of Luther's Doctrine of Justification in Late Medieval Theology.* Philadelphia: Fortress, 1971.

_____. "Luthers Anthropologie." In *Leben und Werk Martin Luthers von 1526 bis 1546: Festgabe zu seinem 500 Geburtstag*, 1:63–76. Göttingen: Vandenhoeck & Ruprecht, 1983.

Hamm, Berndt. *The Early Luther: Stages in a Reformation Reorientation.* Grand Rapids: Eerdmans, 2014.

Harris, Harriet A. "Should We Say That Personhood Is Relational?" *Scottish Journal of Theology* 51, no. 2 (1998): 214–34.

Harrison, Verna E. F. "Gender, Generation, and Virginity in Cappadocian Theology." *Journal of Theological Studies* 47 (1996): 38–68.

———. "Gregory of Nyssa on Human Unity and Diversity." In *Studia Patristica Vol. 41, Orientalia; Clement, Origen, Athanasius; the Cappadocians; Chrysostom*, 333–44. Leuven: Peeters, 2006.

———. "Receptacle Imagery in St Gregory of Nyssa's Anthropology." In *Studia Patristica Vol. 22*, 23–27. Louvain: Peeters, 1989.

Hasker, William. *The Emergent Self.* Ithaca, N.Y.: Cornell University Press, 1999.

Hector, Kevin W. "Actualism and Incarnation: The High Christology of Friedrich Schleiermacher." *International Journal of Systematic Theology* 8, no. 3 (2006): 307–22.

———. "Attunement and Explicitation: A Pragmatist Reading of Schleiermacher's 'Theology of Feeling.'" In *Schleiermacher, the Study of Religion, and the Future of Theology: A Transatlantic Dialogue*, edited by Brent W. Sockness and Wilhelm Gräb, 215–42. New York: Walter de Gruyter, 2010.

———. "The Mediation of Christ's Normative Spirit: A Constructive Reading of Schleiermacher's Pneumatology." *Modern Theology* 24, no. 1 (2008): 1–22.

Heinecken, Martin J. "Luther and the 'Orders of Creation' in Relation to a Doctrine of Work and Vocation." *Lutheran Quarterly* 4, no. 4 (1952): 393–414.

Helmer, Christine. "The Consummation of Reality: Soteriological Metaphysics in Schleiermacher's Interpretation of Colossians 1:15–20." In *Biblical Interpretation: History, Context, and Reality*, edited by Christine Helmer and Taylor G. Petrey, 113–31. Society of Biblical Literature Symposium Series, no. 26. Leiden: Brill, 2005.

———. "Schleiermacher's Exegetical Theology and the New Testament." In *The Cambridge Companion to Friedrich Schleiermacher*, edited by Jacqueline Mariña, 229–47. New York: Cambridge University Press, 2005.

Hennessey, Lawrence R. "Gregory of Nyssa's Doctrine of the Resurrected Body." In *Studia Patristica Vol. 22*, 28–34. Louvain: Peeters, 1989.

Herms, Eilert. "Schleiermacher's *Christian Ethics*." In *The Cambridge Companion to Friedrich Schleiermacher*, edited by Jacqueline Mariña, translated by Mariña, Jacqueline and Christine Helmer, 209–28. New York: Cambridge University Press, 2005.

Hieb, Nathan D. "The Precarious Status of Resurrection in Friedrich Schleiermacher's Glaubenslehre." *International Journal of Systematic Theology* 9, no. 4 (2007): 398–414.

Hilkert, Mary Catherine. "Cry Beloved Image: Rethinking the Image of God." In *In the Embrace of God: Feminist Approaches to Theological Anthropology*, edited by Ann Elizabeth O'Hara Graff, 190–205. Maryknoll, N.Y.: Orbis, 1995.

Hopkins, Dwight N. "General Introduction." In *The Cambridge Companion to Black Theology*, edited by Dwight N. Hopkins and Edward P. Antonio, 3–18. New York: Cambridge University Press, 2012.

Hunsinger, George. "*Salvator Mundi*: Three Types of Christology." In *Christology: Ancient and Modern: Explorations in Constructive Dogmatics*, edited by Oliver Crisp and Fred Sanders, 42–59. Grand Rapids: Zondervan, 2013.

Huyssteen, J. Wentzel van, and Erik P. Wiebe, eds. *In Search of Self: Interdisciplinary Perspectives on Personhood*. Grand Rapids: Eerdmans, 2011.

International Colloquium on Gregory of Nyssa. *Gregory of Nyssa: Contra Eunomium III: An English Translation with Commentary and Supporting Studies: Proceedings of the 12th International Colloquium on Gregory Of Nyssa (Leuven, 14–17 September 2010)*. Edited by Johan Leemans. Supplements to Vigiliae Christianae, volume 124. Leiden: Brill, 2014.

Jantzen, Grace. *Julian of Norwich: Mystic and Theologian*, new edition. New York: Paulist, 2000.

Jewett, Paul K., with Marguerite Shuster. *Who We Are: Our Dignity as Human*. Grand Rapids: Eerdmans, 1996.

Joest, Wilfried. *Ontologie der Person bei Luther*. Göttingen: Vandenhoeck & Ruprecht, 1967.

John-Julian, ed. *A Lesson of Love: The Revelations of Julian of Norwich*. New York: Walker, 1988.

Jones, Major J. *Christian Ethics for Black Theology*. Nashville: Abingdon, 1974.

Julian of Norwich: Showings. Translated by Edmund Colledge and James Walsh. The Classics of Western Spirituality. New York: Paulist, 1978.

Jüngel, Eberhard. *God's Being Is in Becoming*. Grand Rapids: Eerdmans, 2001.

Karras, Valerie A. "A Re-Evaluation of Marriage, Celibacy, and Irony in Gregory of Nyssa's On Virginity." *Journal of Early Christian Studies* 13, no. 1 (2005): 111–21.

_____. "Sex/gender in Gregory of Nyssa's Eschatology: Irrelevant or Non-Existent?" In *Studia Patristica Vol. 41, Orientalia; Clement, Origen, Athanasius; the Cappadocians; Chrysostom*, 363–68. Leuven: Peeters, 2006.

Kelsey, Catherine L. *Thinking about Christ with Schleiermacher*. Louisville: Westminster John Knox , 2003.

Kelsey, David H. *Eccentric Existence: A Theological Anthropology*. Louisville: Westminster John Knox, 2009.

Kerr, Fergus. "The Modern Philosophy of Self in Recent Theology." In *Neuroscience and the Person: Scientific Perspectives on Divine Action*, edited by Robert J. Russell, Nancey Murphy, Theo C. Meyering, and Michael A. Arbib, 23–44. Vatican City: Vatican Observatory, 2002.

Knight, Douglas H. "Introduction." In *The Theology of John Zizioulas: Personhood and the Church*, edited by Douglas H. Knight, 1–14. Aldershot: Ashgate, 2007.

Kolb, Robert. "Called to Milk Cows and Govern Kingdoms: Martin Luther's Teaching on the Christian's Vocations." *Concordia Journal* 39, no. 2 (2013): 133–41.

_____. "God and His Human Creatures in Luther's Sermons on Genesis: The Reformer's Early Use of His Distinction of Two Kinds of Righteousness." *Concordia Journal* 33, no. 2 (2007): 166–84.

_____. "Luther on the Two Kinds of Righteousness; Reflections on His Two-Dimensional Definition of Humanity at the Heart of His Theology." *Lutheran Quarterly* 13, no. 4 (1999): 449–66.

Kolb, Robert, and Charles P. Arand. *The Genius of Luther's Theology: A Wittenberg Way of Thinking for the Contemporary Church*. Grand Rapids: Baker Academic, 2008.

Ladner, Gerhart B. "The Philosophical Anthropology of Saint Gregory of Nyssa." *Dumbarton Oaks Papers* 12 (1958): 59–94.

Laird, Martin. "Under Solomon's Tutelage: The Education of Desire in the Homilies on the Song of Songs." In *Rethinking Gregory of Nyssa*, edited by Sarah Coakley, 77–95. Oxford: Blackwell, 2003.

Lincoln, C. Eric. "Perspective on James H. Cone's Black Theology." *Union Seminary Quarterly Review* 31, no. 1 (1975): 15–22.

Lippa, Richard A. *Gender, Nature, and Nurture*. Second edition. Mahwah, N.J.: Lawrence Erlbaum Associates, 2005.

Lohse, Bernhard. *Martin Luther's Theology: Its Historical and Systematic Development*. Minneapolis: Fortress, 1999.

Loudovikos, Nicholas. "Person Instead of Grace and Dictated Otherness: John Zizioulas's Final Theological Position." *Heythrop Journal* 52, no. 4 (2011): 684–99.

Loughlin, Gerard. *Queer Theology: Rethinking the Western Body*. Oxford: Blackwell, 2007.

Louth, Andrew. "The Body in Western Catholic Christianity." In *Religion and the Body*, edited by Sarah Coakley, 111–30. Cambridge Studies in Religion Traditions. New York: Cambridge University Press, 1997.

_____ . *The Origins of the Christian Mystical Tradition*. New York: Oxford University Press, 1981.

Lowe, E. J. "Self." In *The Oxford Companion to Philosophy*, edited by Ted Honderich. New York: Oxford University Press, 1995.

Ludlow, Morwenna. *Gregory of Nyssa, Ancient and (Post)modern*. New York: Oxford University Press, 2007.

Lumpp, David A. "Luther's 'Two Kinds of Righteousness': A Brief Historical Introduction." *Concordia Journal* 23, no. 1 (1997): 27–38.

Luther, Martin. *The Freedom of a Christian*. Minneapolis: Fortress, 2008.

_____ . "Small Catechism." In *Book of Concord*, http://bookofconcord. org/smallcatechism.php. Accessed June 20, 2015.

Magill, Kevin J. *Julian of Norwich: Mystic or Visionary?* New York: Routledge, 2006.

Mangina, Joseph L. *Karl Barth: Theologian of Christian Witness*. Aldershot: Ashgate, 2004.

Mannermaa, Tuomo. *Christ Present in Faith: Luther's View of Justification*. Minneapolis: Fortress, 2005.

Mariña, Jacqueline. "Christology and Anthropology." In *The Cambridge Companion to Friedrich Schleiermacher*, edited by Jacqueline Mariña. New York: Cambridge University Press, 2005.

_____ . *Transformation of the Self in the Thought of Friedrich Schleiermacher*. New York: Oxford University Press, 2008.

McCormack, Bruce L. "Grace and Being: The Role of God's Gracious Election in Karl Barth's Theological Ontology." In *The Cambridge Companion to Karl Barth*, edited by John B. Webster, 92–110. New York: Cambridge University Press, 2000.

_____ . "The Sum of the Gospel: The Doctrine of Election in the Theologies of Alexander Schweizer and Karl Barth." In *Toward the Future of Reformed Theology*, edited by David Willis-Watkins, Michael Welker, and Mattias Gockel, 470–93. Grand Rapids: Eerdmans, 1999.

McDonald, Suzanne. "Barth's 'Other' Doctrine of Election in the Church Dogmatics." *International Journal of Systematic Theology* 9, no. 2 (2007): 134–47.

McDowell, John C. "Learning Where to Place One's Hope: The Eschatological Significance of Election in Barth." *Scottish Journal of Theology* 53 (2003): 316–38.

McEntire, Sandra J., ed. *Julian of Norwich: A Book of Essays*. New York: Garland, 1998.

McFarland, Ian A. *Difference & Identity*. Cleveland, Ohio: Pilgrim, 2001.

McGrath, Alister E. *Iustitia Dei: A History of the Christian Doctrine of Justification*. 3rd ed. New York: Cambridge University Press, 2005.

McLean, Stuart. "Creation and Anthropology." In *Theology beyond Christendom: Essays on the Centenary of the Birth of Karl Barth*, edited by John Thompson, 111–42. Allison Park, Pa.: Pickwick, 1986.

Melnyk, Andrew. "How to Keep the 'Physical' in Physicalism." *Journal of Philosophy* 94, no. 12 (1997): 622–38.

Meredith, Anthony. *Gregory of Nyssa*. Early Church Fathers. London: Routledge, 1999.

Meyer, Eric Daryl. "Gregory of Nyssa on Language, Naming God's Creatures, and the Desire of the Discursive Animal." In *Genesis and Christian Theology*, 103–16. Grand Rapids: Eerdmans, 2012.

Miles, Margaret R. " 'The Rope Breaks When It Is Tightest': Luther on the Body, Consciousness, and the Word." *Harvard Theological Review* 77, no. 3–4 (1984): 239–58.

Moltmann, Jürgen. *Man: Christian Anthropology in the Conflicts of the Present*. London: SPCK, 1974.

Moreland, J. P., and Scott B. Rae. *Body & Soul: Human Nature and the Crisis in Ethics*. Downers Grove, Ill.: InterVarsity, 2000.

Murray, Stephen Butler. "The Dimensions of Sin and Fallenness in the Theological Anthropology of Black and Womanist Theologies." *Journal of Religion* 84, no. 1 (2004): 23–47.

Nagel, Thomas. "What Is It Like to Be a Bat?" *Philosophical Review* 83 (1974): 435–56.

Nellas, Panayiotis. *Deification in Christ: The Nature of the Human Person*. Crestwood, N.Y.: St. Vladimir's Seminary Press, 1987.

Nelson, Derek. "Schleiermacher and Ritschl on Individual and Social Sin." *Zeitschrift für Neuere Theologiegeschichte* 16, no. 2 (2009): 131–54.

Nestlehutt, Mark S. G. "Chalcedonian Christology: Modern Criticism and Contemporary Ecumenism." *Journal of Ecumenical Studies* 35, no. 2 (1998): 175–96.

Niebuhr, Richard R. *Schleiermacher on Christ and Religion: A New Introduction*. New York: Charles Scribner's Sons, 1964.

Nuth, Joan M. "Two Medieval Soteriologies: Anselm of Canterbury and Julian of Norwich." *Theological Studies* 53, no. 4 (1992): 611–45.

_____ . *Wisdom's Daughter: The Theology of Julian of Norwich*. New York: Crossroad, 1991.

Olson, Eric T. "Personal Identity." In *The Blackwell Guide to Philosophy of Mind*, edited by Stephen P. Stich and Ted A. Warfield, 352–68. Oxford: Blackwell, 2003.

O'Neill, Michael. "Karl Barth's Doctrine of Election." *Evangelical Quarterly* 76, no. 4 (2004): 311–26.

Palliser, Margaret Ann. *Christ, Our Mother of Mercy: Divine Mercy and Compassion in the Theology of the "Shewings" of Julian of Norwich*. New York: Walter de Gruyter, 1992.

Papanikolaou, Aristotle. "Divine Energies or Divine Personhood: Vladimir Lossky and John Zizioulas on Conceiving the Transcendent and Immanent God." *Modern Theology* 19, no. 3 (2003): 357–85.

_____ . "Is John Zizioulas an Existentialist in Disguise? Response to Lucian Turcescu." *Modern Theology* 20, no. 4 (2004): 601–8.

_____ . "Personhood and Its Exponents in Twentieth-Century Orthodox Theology." In *Cambridge Companion to Orthodox Christian Theology*, 232–45. Cambridge: Cambridge University Press, 2008.

Parmentier, Martien. "Greek Patristic Foundations for a Theological Anthropology of Women in Their Distinctiveness as Human Beings." *Anglican Theological Review* 84, no. 3 (2002).

Peiter, Hermann. *Christian Ethics according to Schleiermacher: Collected Essays and Reviews.* Edited by Terrence N. Tice and translated by Edwina Lawler. Eugene, Ore.: Pickwick, 2010.

Pelphrey, Brant. *Christ Our Mother: Julian of Norwich.* Way of the Christian Mystics. Wilmington, Del.: Michael Glazier, 1989.

_____ . "Leaving the Womb of Christ: Love, Doomsday, and Space/Time in Julian of Norwich and Eastern Orthodox Mysticism." In *Julian of Norwich: A Book of Essays*, edited by Sandra J. McEntire, 291–320. New York: Garland, 1998.

Pesch, Otto Hermann. "Free by Faith: Luther's Contribution to a Theological Anthropology." In *Martin Luther and the Modern Mind: Freedom, Conscience, Toleration, Rights*, edited by Manfred Hoffmann, 23–60. Lewiston, N.Y.: Mellen, 1985.

Radde-Gallwitz, Andrew. *Basil of Caesarea, Gregory of Nyssa, and the Transformation of Divine Simplicity.* New York: Oxford University Press, 2009.

Redeker, Martin. *Schleiermacher: Life and Thought.* Translated by John Wallhausser. Philadelphia: Fortress, 1973.

Rolf, Sibylle. "Luther's Understanding of *Imputatio* in the Context of His Doctrine of Justification and Its Consequences for the Preaching of the Gospel." *International Journal of Systematic Theology* 12, no. 4 (2010): 435–51.

Rolf, Veronica Mary. *Julian's Gospel: Illuminating the Life and Revelations of Julian of Norwich.* Maryknoll, N.Y.: Orbis, 2013.

Rostock, Nigel. "Two Different Gods or Two Types of Unity? A Critical Response to Zizioulas's Presentation of 'The Father as Cause' with Reference to the Cappadocian Fathers and Augustine." *New Blackfriars* 91, no. 1033 (2010): 321–34.

Ruether, Rosemary Radford. "Misogynism and Virginal Feminism in the Fathers of the Church." In *Religion and Sexism*, 150–83. New York: Simon and Schuster, 1974.

Russell, Edward. "Reconsidering Relational Anthropology: A Critical Assessment of John Zizioulas's Theological Anthropology." *International Journal of Systematic Theology* 5, no. 2 (2003): 168–86.

Russell, Norman. *The Doctrine of Deification in the Greek Patristic Tradition.* The Oxford Early Christian Studies. Oxford: Oxford University Press, 2004.

Schleiermacher, Friedrich. "On Colossians 1:15–20 (1832)." Translated by Esther D. Reed and Alan Braley. *Neues Athenaeum* 5 (1998): 48–80.

_____. *The Christian Faith.* Edited by H. R. Mackintosh and J. S. Stewart. Berkeley: Apocryphile, 2011.

_____. *Introduction to Christian Ethics.* Nashville: Abingdon, 1989.

_____. *The Life of Jesus.* Edited by Jack C. Verheyden. Translated by S. Maclean Gilmour. Philadelphia: Fortress, 1975.

_____. *Selections from Friedrich Schleiermacher's Christian Ethics.* Translated by James M. Brandt. Louisville: Westminster John Knox, 2011.

Schwanke, Johannes. "Luther on Creation." In *Harvesting Martin Luther's Reflections on Theology, Ethics, and the Church,* edited by Timothy J. Wengert, 78–98. Grand Rapids: Eerdmans, 2004.

_____. "Luther's Theology of Creation." In *The Oxford Handbook of Martin Luther's Theology,* edited by Robert Kolb, Irene Dingel, and Lubomir Batka, 201–11. New York: Oxford University Press, 2014.

Searle, John R. *Intentionality: An Essay in the Philosophy of Mind.* New York: Cambridge University Press, 1983.

Sherlock, Charles. *The Doctrine of Humanity.* Downers Grove, Ill.: InterVarsity, 1996.

Sherman, Robert. *The Shift to Modernity: Christ and the Doctrine of Creation in the Theologies of Schleiermacher and Barth.* New York: T&T Clark, 2005.

Siker, Jeffrey S. "Historicizing a Racialized Jesus: Case Studies in the 'Black Christ,' the 'Mestizo Christ,' and White Critique." *Biblical Interpretation* 15, no. 1 (2007): 26–53.

Smith, J. Warren. "The Body of Paradise and the Body of the Resurrection: Gender and the Angelic Life in Gregory of Nyssa's 'De Hominis Opificio'." *Harvard Theological Review* 99, no. 2 (2006): 207–28.

Sorabji, Richard. *Matter, Space, and Motion: Theories in Antiquity and Their Sequel.* Ithaca, N.Y.: Cornell University Press, 1988.

Spearing, Elizabeth. *Revelations of Divine Love (Short and Long Text)*. New York: Penguin, 1998.

Spitz, Lewis William. "Luther's Impact on Modern Views of Man." *Concordia Theological Quarterly* 41, no. 1 (1977): 26–43.

Stewart, Carlyle F. "The Method of Correlation in the Theology of James H. Cone." *Journal of Religious Thought* 40, no. 2 (1984): 27–38.

Swinburne, Richard. *Mind, Brain, and Free Will*. New York: Oxford University Press, 2013.

Tanner, Kathryn. *Jesus, Humanity and the Trinity: A Brief Systematic Theology*. Minneapolis: Fortress, 2001.

Taylor, Charles. *Sources of the Self*. New York: Cambridge University Press, 1989.

Thompson, John. "The Humanity of God in the Theology of Karl Barth." *Scottish Journal of Theology* 29 (1976): 249–69.

_____. *Theology beyond Christendom: Essays on the Centenary of the Birth of Karl Barth*. Allison Park, Pa.: Pickwick, 1986.

Torrance, Alan J. *Persons in Communion: An Essay on Trinitarian Description and Human Participation*. Edinburgh: T&T Clark, 1996.

Torrance, Alexis. "Personhood and Patristics in Orthodox Theology: Reassessing the Debate." *Heythrop Journal* 52, no. 4 (2011): 700–707.

Torrance, Thomas F. *Karl Barth, Biblical and Evangelical Theologian*. Edinburgh: T&T Clark, 1990.

Trueman, Carl. "*Simul Peccator et Justus*: Martin Luther and Justification." In *Justification in Perspective: Historical Developments and Contemporary Challenges*, edited by Bruce L. McCormack, 73–98. Grand Rapids: Baker Academic, 2006.

Turcescu, Lucian. " 'Person' versus 'Individual,' and Other Modern Misreadings of Gregory of Nyssa." *Modern Theology* 18, no. 4 (2002): 527–39.

Turner, Denys. *The Darkness of God: Negativity in Christian Mysticism*. New York: Cambridge University Press, 1998.

_____. *Julian of Norwich, Theologian*. New Haven, Conn.: Yale University Press, 2011.

_____. " 'Sin Is Behovely' in Julian of Norwich's *Revelations of Divine Love*." *Modern Theology* 20, no. 3 (2004): 407–22.

Turner, Robert. "Eschatology and Truth." In *The Theology of John Zizioulas: Personhood and the Church*, edited by Douglas H. Knight, 15–34. Aldershot: Ashgate, 2007.

Vainio, Olli-Pekka, ed. *Engaging Luther: A (New) Theological Assessment*. Eugene, Ore.: Cascade, 2010.

_____ . *Justification and Participation in Christ: The Development of the Lutheran Doctrine of Justification from Luther to the Formula of Concord (1580)*. Studies in Medieval and Reformation Traditions. Leiden: Brill, 2008.

Van Engen, Abram. "Shifting Perspectives: Sin and Salvation in Julian's *A Revelation of Love*." *Literature and Theology* 23, no. 1 (2009): 1–17.

Volf, Miroslav. *Exclusion and Embrace: A Theological Exploration of Identity, Otherness, and Reconciliation*. Nashville: Abingdon, 1996.

Wannenwetsch, Bernd. "Luther's Moral Theology." In *The Cambridge Companion to Martin Luther*, edited by Donald K. McKim, 120–35. Cambridge: Cambridge University Press, 2003.

Watkins, Reneé Neu. "Two Women Visionaries and Death: Catherine of Siena and Julian of Norwich." *Numen* 30, no. 2 (1983): 174–98.

Watson, Nicholas. "The Composition of Julian of Norwich's *Revelation of Love*." *Speculum* 68, no. 3 (1993): 637–83.

_____ . "The Trinitarian Hermeneutic of Julian of Norwich's *Revelation of Love*." In *Julian of Norwich: A Book of Essays*, edited by Sandra J. McEntire, 61–90. New York: Garland, 1998.

Watson, Nicholas, and Jacqueline Jenkins, eds. *The Writings of Julian of Norwich: A Vision Showed to a Devout Woman* and *A Revelation of Love*. University Park, Pa.: Penn State University Press, 2006.

Watson, Philip S. "Luther's Doctrine of Vocation." *Scottish Journal of Theology* 2, no. 4 (1949): 364–77.

Webster, John. "Rescuing the Subject: Barth and Postmodern Anthropology." In *Karl Barth: A Future for Postmodern Theology?* edited by Geoff Thompson and Christiaan Mostert, 49–69. Hindmarsh: Australian Theological Forum, 2001.

Webster, John B. *Barth's Ethics of Reconciliation*. Cambridge: Cambridge University Press, 1995.

_____ . *Barth's Moral Theology: Human Action in Barth's Thought*. Edinburgh: T&T Clark, 1998.

Wengert, Timothy J. "Introduction." In *Harvesting Martin Luther's*

Reflections on Theology, Ethics, and the Church, edited by Timothy J. Wengert, 1–19. Grand Rapids: Eerdmans, 2004.

Wicks, Jared. "Justification and Faith in Luther's Theology." *Theological Studies* 44, no. 1 (1983): 3–29.

Wilks, John. "The Trinitarian Ontology of John Zizioulas." *Vox Evangelica* 25 (1995): 63–88.

Williams, Delores. *Sisters in the Wilderness: The Challenge of Womanist God-Talk*. Maryknoll, N.Y.: Orbis, 1993.

Wilmore, Gayraud S. *Black Religion and Black Radicalism*. Garden City, N.Y.: Doubleday, 1972.

Windeatt, Barry. "Julian's Second Thoughts: The Long Text Tradition." In *A Companion to Julian of Norwich*, edited by Liz Herbert McAvoy, 101–15. Cambridge: D. S. Brewer, 2008.

Winden, J. C. M. van. "In Defence of the Resurrection." In *Easter Sermons of Gregory of Nyssa*, 101–21. Cambridge, Mass.: Philadelphia Patristic Foundation, 1981.

Wingren, Gustaf. *Luther on Vocation*. Translated by Carl C. Rasmussen. Philadelphia: Muhlenberg, 1957. Reprint, Eugene, Ore.: Wipf & Stock, 2004.

Wolters, Clifton. "Introduction." In *Revelations of Divine Love*. London: Penguin, 1966.

World Council of Churches. *Christian Perspectives on Theological Anthropology: A Faith and Order Study Document*. Faith and Order Paper, no. 199. Geneva: World Council of Churches, 2005.

Wyman, Walter E. "Sin and Redemption." In *The Cambridge Companion to Friedrich Schleiermacher*, edited by Jacqueline Mariña. New York: Cambridge University Press, 2005.

Zimmerman, Dean W. "Christians Should Affirm Mind-Body Dualism." In *Contemporary Debates in Philosophy of Religion*, edited by Michael L. Peterson and Raymond J. VanArragon, 315–26. Oxford: Blackwell, 2004.

Zizioulas, John D. *Being as Communion: Studies in Personhood and the Church*. Crestwood, N.Y.: St. Vladimir's Seminary Press, 1985.

_____ . *Communion and Otherness: Further Studies in Personhood and the Church*. New York: T&T Clark, 2006.

_____ . *The Eucharistic Communion and the World*. London: T&T Clark, 2011.

_____ . *Lectures in Christian Dogmatics*. New York: T&T Clark, 2008.

Subject Index

253

Author Index